PUBLISHING ADDICTION SCIENCE: A GUIDE FOR THE PERPLEXED

SECOND EDITION

EDITED BY THOMAS F. BABOR, KERSTIN STENIUS, SUSAN SAVVA, AND JEAN O'REILLY

A publication by the International Society of Addiction Journal Editors
First edition published 2004, © World Health Organization and International Society of Addiction Journal Editors
Second edition published 2008

ISBN 978-0-906522-97-4

Library Cataloguing-in-Publication Data

Publishing addiction science: a guide for the perplexed / Thomas F. Babor, Kerstin Stenius, Susan Savva, and Jean O'Reilly (eds.)

1.Substance abuse 2.Substance-related disorders 3.Psychotropic drugs 4.Publishing 5.Scientific misconduct 6.Manuals
I.Babor, Thomas F. II.Stenius, Kerstin. III.Savva, Susan. IV.O'Reilly, Jean.

NLM classification: WM 270

Designed by Matthew West: enquiries@vascographics.co.uk

Index compiled by Indexing Specialists (UK) Ltd.

Printed and distributed by Multi-Science Publishing Company, Ltd., 5 Wates Way, Brentwood, Essex CM15 9TB, United Kingdom
Telephone: 01277 224632; international: +44(0)1277 224632
Fax: 01277 223453; international: +44(0)1277 223453
Web catalog: http://www.multi-science.co.uk
Email enquiries: info@multi-science.co.uk

Price: £18/€27/$36US, plus shipping and handling charges
Bulk orders (20 books or more) are £12.50/€18.75/$25US each, plus shipping and handling charges

For more information about the International Society of Addiction Journal Editors see http://www.isaje.net or write to Executive Officer, International Society of Addiction Journal Editors, National Addiction Centre, 4 Windsor Walk, London SE5 8AF, United Kingdom.

Printed in Great Britain

TABLE OF CONTENTS
PUBLISHING ADDICTION SCIENCE: A GUIDE FOR THE PERPLEXED
SECOND EDITION

FOREWORD TO THE SECOND EDITION

The momentum for strengthening research around the globe is growing. The need to build research capacities in low and middle income countries and to place health research within the wider context of research for development is being discussed at different levels, including the Global Ministerial Forum on Research for Health, organized by the World Health Organization and other intergovernmental organizations. Building up research capacity and the evidence base in the area of substance abuse in low and middle income countries is one of prerequisites for developing adequate and evidence-based approaches to public health problems caused by harmful use of alcohol. *Publishing Addiction Science: A Guide for the Perplexed* is an important element to this venture as it promotes the much needed research and effective dissemination of research findings to inform policy and programme development and enhance international collaboration in the area of substance abuse.

This book was initiated by the International Society of Addiction Journal Editors (ISAJE). ISAJE was founded "to promote excellence in the communication and dissemination of information on addiction and related sciences within the scientific community and to those who have responsibility for the prevention, treatment, cure, professional training and policy formation in the field." Because this objective coincides with the knowledge function of the WHO, also in the area of substance abuse, the WHO Department of Mental Health and Substance Abuse is pleased to collaborate with ISAJE on contributing to worldwide dissemination of research findings, particularly from low and middle income countries.

Psychoactive substance use and dependence are serious and growing problems and contribute to a significantly high proportion of disease burden worldwide. According to the World Health Organization, alcohol and tobacco were responsible for 4.0% and 4.1% respectively of the global disease burden in 2000, measured in terms of disability-adjusted life years. In many parts of the world injecting drug use contributes significantly to new HIV cases and the transmission of other blood-borne infections. Of particular relevance to this publication is the growing prevalence of alcohol and other substance use disorders in low and middle income countries. However, much more needs to be learnt and understood in this part of the world, as lack of information hinders the public health community from seeing the full scale of the arising problem and developing appropriate interventions. It is there where the tradition of dissemination of research findings also often needs improvement, and where a book of this nature will be a useful tool, especially to young researchers, enabling higher research efficiency and successful contributions to the field.

Helping to build local capacity for research in the field of substance abuse and wide dissemination of accumulated knowledge by researchers in low and middle income countries is an important objective for WHO and the public health community: it will operate for a common goal to reduce the global burden of disease attributable to psychoactive substance use. The publication of this book will go a long way in contributing to the achievement of this objective.

Dr Benedetto Saraceno
Director
Department of Mental Health and Substance Abuse
World Health Organization

August, 2008

AN IDEA WHOSE TIME HAS COME

The development of this book had many complex motives but a single purpose. The motives include improving scientific integrity in the field of addiction studies, sharing information with junior investigators, and strengthening addiction specialty journals. The single purpose of this volume, however, is to provide a practical guide to scientific publishing in the addiction field that is used often enough to affect personal decisions, individual careers, institutional policies, and the progress of science. The time is ripe for such an ambitious undertaking: the field of addiction research has grown tremendously in recent years and has spread to new parts of the world. With that growth has come a concomitant increase in competition among researchers, new bureaucratic regulations, and a growing interest in research by health agencies, policy-makers, treatment and prevention specialists, and the alcohol industry. New professional societies, research centres, and university programs have taken root; and regulatory responsibilities such as conflict of interest declarations, human and animal subjects assurances, and the monitoring of scientific misconduct are now common.

The journal-publishing enterprise, the main organ of scientific communication in the field, has an important role to play in all of these developments, and a guide such as the present one will contribute to the further development of addiction science. The inspiration for the first edition of this volume came from the International Society of Addiction Journal Editors (ISAJE), which also provided financial and moral support at all stages of the project. ISAJE is not only the first society for addiction journal editors, it is also the first international organization specifically devoted to the improvement of scientific publishing in the addiction field.

From its inception, ISAJE has recognized a need for ethical guidelines for member journals. There are several reasons why ethical issues are particularly important in the addiction science field. Strong industries, such as pharmaceutical manufacturers, tobacco companies and alcohol producers, have important financial interests to protect, and they pay special attention to the work of addiction scientists. Further, many addiction-related issues are politically loaded, a situation that could affect the objectivity of researchers. Many of the individuals who are the object of addiction research are vulnerable and in need of special protections. Finally, the field of science has become much more ethically challenging because of its growing importance and complexity. Although ISAJE offers a set of ethical guidelines, abstract policy statements and moral pronouncements are rarely read carefully or applied to the day to day business of conducting research and communicating ideas to the scientific community.

This book aims to improve transparency in addiction publishing, and in the process show how young investigators can negotiate the complex and sometimes bewildering ethical challenges to a successful career in the field.

RATIONALE FOR SECOND EDITION

There are several reasons why a second edition of *Publishing Addiction Science* is necessary. First, rapid developments in the field of addiction publishing necessitate revisions of parts of this book. At least thirteen new journals have been identified since the book went to press in 2004. These resources have been added to the information provided in Chapter 2.

Second, many journals have revised their mission statements and journal policies since the book's publication, so that information, too, needed to be updated. Rather than update that information in hard-copy form in an appendix to the book, we have placed all of these changeable details on the ISAJE website http://www.isaje.net so that they can be updated more rapidly.

Another reason for the second edition is related to experience from our *Publishing Addiction Science* workshops, which have been conducted during the past few years in the United Kingdom, the Czech Republic, Finland, Nigeria, the United States and Brazil. The workshops identified new areas of interest that needed attention. The second edition has accordingly added new chapters on how to write a publishable article, how to publish qualitative research, how to deal with conflicts of interest, the unique challenges faced by graduate students and postdoctoral fellows, and participation in the peer review process.

SPONSORSHIP AND ACKNOWLEDGEMENTS

In addition to ISAJE, the Society for the Study of Addiction (SSA) provided critical financial support for both editions. As with ISAJE, the SSA's founding principles -- to "support the communication of scientific knowledge about dependence on alcohol, nicotine and other drugs" and "encourage the systematic study of dependence and to promote policy analysis" -- reveal why this learned society chose to support *Publishing Addiction Science.*

Financial support from the US National Institute on Drug Abuse has made it possible for the editors to develop an on-line tutorial that closely follows the content of the book's chapters. This tutorial is now available at http://www.parint.org and additional funding from the US National Institute on Alcohol Abuse and Alcoholism have made it possible to expand the tutorial to include the five new chapters in the second edition.

There are many other people and organizations that deserve credit for making this volume possible. We are grateful to the academic institutions that enabled the authors and editors to work on this collaborative effort, including The University of Connecticut Alcohol Research Center, Farmington, USA; Centre for Social Research on Alcohol and Drugs, Stockholm University, Sweden; the National Research and Development Centre for Welfare and Health, Helsinki, Finland; and the Institute of Psychiatry, University of London, and University College, London, UK. A number of individuals provided key contributions to the second edition. In particular, we thank

Betsy Thom, Griffith Edwards, Vladimir Poznyak, Hem Raj Pal, Jie Shi, Andreas Plüddemann, Evgeny Kruptisky, Andrea Mitchell, John Noble, Gillian Tober, and Holger Weiss. Finally, we also acknowledge the contribution of the editors and staff members who supplied information about their journals for Tables 2.1 and 2.2.

CLOSING REMARKS

We hope that the second edition of this book will aid the training of young researchers and the continuing education of seasoned addiction scientists around the world. Given the rapidly changing nature of the field, it is our intention to learn from the feedback we receive from colleagues in order to continue improving the efficiency, integrity and ethicality of addiction science.

The Editors

Thomas F. Babor is Professor and Chair, Department of Community Medicine and Health Care, University of Connecticut School of Medicine, USA. He is Associate Editor-in-Chief of the journal *Addiction.*

Robert L. Balster is Director of the Institute for Drug and Alcohol Studies, Luther A. Butler Professor of Pharmacology and Toxicology, and Research Professor of Psychology and Psychiatry at Virginia Commonwealth University, USA. He is Editor-in-Chief of the journal *Drug and Alcohol Dependence.*

Gerhard Bühringer is Professor for Addiction Research in the Department of Clinical Psychology and Psychotherapy at the Technische Universitaet in Dresden, Germany, and Director of the IFT Institut fuer Therapieforschung in Munich, Germany. He is Editor-in-Chief of the journal *Sucht* (Addiction).

Erikson F. Furtado is an Associate Professor in the Department of Neurology, Psychiatry and Medical Psychology in the Faculty of Medicine at Ribeirão Preto, University of São Paulo, Brazil.

Roman Gabrhelík is a postdoctoral research fellow at the Centre for Addictology, Psychiatric Clinic, First Medical Faculty and General Teaching Hospital, Charles University in Prague, Czech Republic.

Florence Kerr-Corrêa is Professor of Psychiatry, Department of Neurology, Psychology and Psychiatry, Botucatu Medical School, São Paulo State University (UNESP), Brazil.

Phil Lange has retired. He was Editor of the *Journal of Gambling Issues*.

Klaus Mäkelä, now retired, was Research Director of the Finnish Foundation for Alcohol Studies and Professor of Sociology, Helsinki University, Finland.

Thomas McGovern is Professor of Psychiatry and Director of the Ethics-Humanities Programme for the School of Medicine at Texas Tech University Health Sciences Centre, Lubbock, Texas, USA. He is Editor of the journal *Alcoholism Treatment Quarterly.*

Peter Miller is NHMRC Howard Florey Fellow at the School of Psychology, Deakin University, Geelong, Australia. He is Commissioning Editor of the journal *Addiction.*

Michal Miovsky is Head of the Center for Addictology, Psychiatric Clinic at Charles University in Prague, Czech Republic, and a research fellow at the National Focal Point for Drugs and Drug Addictions. He is Editor-in-Chief of the Czech journal *Adiktologie* (Addiction).

Dominique Morisano is a Postdoctoral Fellow in Addiction and Mental Health Research at the Centre for Addiction and Mental Health (CAMH) and the University of Toronto Faculty of Medicine, Canada.

Neo Morojele is Deputy Director of the Alcohol & Drug Abuse Research Unit for the South African Medical Research Council. She is an Associate Editor of the *African Journal of Drug and Alcohol Studies*.

Jean O'Reilly is a consulting book editor for the Department of Community Medicine and Health Care, University of Connecticut School of Medicine, USA. She lectured in Connecticut's Department of English for eight years.

Isidore Obot is Professor and Chair, Department of Behavioral Health Sciences, Morgan State University School of Community Health and Policy, USA. He is Editor-in-Chief of the *African Journal of Drug and Alcohol Studies*.

Susan Savva is Managing Editor of the journal *Addiction*. She helped to set up the International Society of Addiction Journal Editors (ISAJE) and serves as its executive officer.

Kerstin Stenius is a Senior Lecturer in Social Work at the University of Helsinki, Finland, and a guest professor at the Centre for Social Research on Alcohol and Drugs (SoRAD) at Stockholm University, Sweden. She is Editor-in-Chief of the journal *Nordisk alkohol- & narkotikatidskrift* (Nordic Studies on Alcohol and Drugs).

Ian Stolerman is Professor of Behavioural Pharmacology at the Institute of Psychiatry, King's College London, UK. He served as President of ISAJE and as co-editor of the journal *Drug and Alcohol Dependence*.

Robert West is Professor of Health Psychology and Director of Tobacco Studies, Cancer Research UK Health Behaviour Research Centre, Department of Epidemiology and Public Health, University College London, UK. He is Editor-in-Chief of the journal *Addiction*.

Erin L. Winstanley is a Postdoctoral Research Fellow at Johns Hopkins University School of Medicine, USA. She is a consultant with the U.S. National Institute on Drug Abuse International Program.

CHAPTER 1
A GUIDE FOR THE PERPLEXED
THOMAS F. BABOR AND KERSTIN STENIUS

The task of the improver of mankind is not to preach morality, but to alter the inner self of mankind by transforming the external conditions for its moral health.

Edith Södergran (1984)

To be perplexed is to be puzzled or even confused by the intricacy of a situation. One way to deal with perplexing situations is to find a guide who can provide advice, information, and direction. Many such guides have risen to the occasion throughout the ages, providing useful knowledge for the perplexed students of literature, religion, philosophy and science. One of the most influential philosophical treatises, for example, was Maimonides' *Guide for the Perplexed*. In a time of religious, moral, and political change, Maimonides (1135-1204) sought to harmonize Greco-Roman, Christian, Jewish, and Arabic thought into a philosophical guide for those who seek meaning in life. In a sense, *Publishing Addiction Science* is intended to be a similar (albeit less ambitious!) guide for those of us who from time to time are perplexed about how to find our way through the complex world of addiction science. The chapters in this book constitute a journey to the practical, scientific, moral, and even philosophical destinations with which we must become acquainted if we are to succeed, either as temporary visitors to the field or as career scientists dedicating our lives to the study of addiction.

It is our contention, and a guiding theme of the book, that the key to successful publishing in addiction science is to understand not only how to write a scientific article and where to publish it, but also how to do these things honestly and ethically. So in addition to the practical business of publishing scientific papers in both disciplinary and addiction specialty journals, the ultimate goal of this book is to enhance scientific integrity in the publication process, giving special consideration to the main organ of scientific communication, the scholarly journal.

WHAT IS A JOURNAL?

According to Lafollette (1992, p. 69), "a journal is a periodical that an identifiable intellectual community regards as a primary channel of communication of knowledge in its field and as one of the arbitrators of the authenticity or legitimacy of that knowledge." Journals establish intellectual standards, provide a forum of communication among scientists, bring valuable information to the public, set the agenda for a field of study, provide an historical record of a particular area of knowledge, and confer implicit certification on authors for the authenticity and originality of their work (Lafollette 1992). In addition, they have the potential to serve the interests of career advancement and personal reward for scholarly achievement.

Journals are joint enterprises typically managed through a division of labour among owners, publishers, editors, reviewers, and authors. How this cast of characters is organized into an integrated set of players varies from one journal to another. The owners of a journal can be non-profit organizations (such as learned societies, universities or professional organizations), government agencies, or private publishers. The publishers of a journal range from small printers to large-scale multinational organizations that distribute and often own hundreds of journals. Journal editors tend to be appointed by the owners, society officers, or publishers. Editors of some of the larger scientific and medical journals are paid for their services and have full-time staff at their disposal. Editors of smaller journals are generally unpaid, and have a small editorial staff with some volunteer assistant editors. Reviewers are usually established investigators who have specialized knowledge of the subject matter. They provide critical and typically anonymous evaluations of manuscripts written by their peers without remuneration as a service to the field.

Without journals, addiction science would have a limited audience and a short half-life; therefore, if an addiction scientist wishes to search for truth and benefit humankind, he or she must understand the inner workings and current complexities of the journal publication process.

PURPOSE OF THE GUIDE

The addiction field has grown tremendously in the past twenty-five years, and addiction publishing has been no exception. Currently there are eighty-eight journals publishing in eighteen languages that are devoted primarily to the dissemination of scholarly information about addiction and related health problems, and many more journals that publish addiction science as part of their broader mission. Despite the growing amount of published material and the increasing opportunities for publication, there exists no guide designed to inform prospective authors about the opportunities, requirements, and challenges of publishing addiction science. Moreover, the addiction field has become perhaps one of the first areas of science where interdisciplinary collaboration between biomedical and psychosocial researchers is essential to progress (see Edwards 2002). As investigators begin to identify as much with addiction studies as they do with their own professional disciplines, it is important to have a publishing guide that looks at the field as an inter-related whole rather than as a collection of separate disciplines.

The primary purpose of *Publishing Addiction Science* is therefore to advise potential authors of articles in the addiction field of the opportunities for publishing their work in scholarly journals, with emphasis on addiction specialty journals. Although all prospective authors will find such a guide useful, it should be particularly helpful to students, younger investigators, clinicians, and professional researchers. The book's broader purpose is to improve the quality of scientific publishing in the addiction field by educating authors about the kinds of ethical and professional issues with which the International Society of Addiction Journal Editors (ISAJE) has long been concerned: scientific misconduct, ethical decision-making, the publication process, and the difficulties experienced by authors whose first language is not English.

GUIDE TO THE GUIDE

Publishing Addiction Science is organized into three sections. The first section covers general issues of how and where to publish. The initial overview chapter (Chapter 2) deals with how to choose a journal, a very important decision in the publication process. The chapter describes the range of journals that publish articles related to addiction and psychoactive substances, summarizes the growth in addiction journals, including the move into open-access journals and on-line subscriptions, and explains eight steps to choosing a journal. Related to this chapter, the ISAJE-sponsored PARINT Web site (Publishing Addiction Research Internationally, located at http://www.parint.org) contains a database of practical information about nearly ninety addiction specialty journals (e.g., mission statement, website, editor, publisher, submission procedures, etc.). It is designed to assist authors with the selection of an appropriate journal. The next chapter in this section ("Beyond the Anglo-American World: Advice for Researchers from Developing or Non-English-Speaking Countries") describes the practical and professional issues addiction scientists face in countries that are less resourced or where English is not the main language, how authors who come from these countries can improve their chances of publishing in English-language journals, the possibilities for authors to publish in both English and an additional language so they can communicate to different audiences, and how to decide whether an article may better serve the public by being published in the author's mother tongue. Finally, Chapter 4 ("Getting Started: Publication Issues for Graduate Students, Postdoctoral Fellows, and other Novice Addiction Scientists") describes the challenges and rewards of publishing early in one's professional career, including authorship issues, timetables, ethical dilemmas, and the pressure to publish.

The second section provides a detailed guide to the practical side of addiction publishing. Chapter 5 ("How to Write a Scientific Research Paper for a Peer-reviewed Journal") describes the development of a typical data-based research article from the planning stage to the completion of the final draft, emphasizing scientific writing techniques, the structure of a scientific article, and effective methods of scientific communication. The following chapter ("How to Write Publishable Qualitative Research") explores the differences and commonalities between qualitative and quantitative research, identifies the hallmarks of exemplary qualitative research, and offers practical advice not only for writing a qualitative article but also for getting it published. Chapter 7 ("Use and Abuse of Citations") describes appropriate and less appropriate citation practices with recommendations for good behaviour, and gives a critical appraisal of citation indexes, particularly the Journal Impact Factor, which is used to evaluate the importance attributed to different journals. Chapter 8 ("Coin of the Realm: Practical Procedures for Determining Authorship") deals with the often vexing question of how to assign authorship credits in multi-authored articles. We offer practical recommendations to provide collaborating authors with a process that is open, fair, and ethical. Chapter 9 ("Preparing Manuscripts and Responding to Reviewers' Reports: Inside the Editorial Black Box") focuses on how to negotiate the peer review process. It describes how the process works and how journal editors make decisions about publishing an article.

It also considers editors' criteria for selecting papers, and explains how to revise a paper when an editor asks for a response to the reviewers' comments. The final chapter in this section ("Reviewing Manuscripts for Addiction Journals: An Application of the Golden Rule") covers the peer review process, what journal editors expect from reviewers, and how to prepare a constructive critical review.

The third section of *Publishing Addiction Science* is devoted to ethical issues. The first article in this section (Chapter 11, "Dante's Inferno: Seven Deadly Sins in Scientific Publishing and How to Avoid Them") reviews seven types of scientific misconduct in the context of a broader definition of scientific integrity. The seven 'sins' are carelessness in citing and reviewing the literature, redundant publication, failure to declare a conflict of interest, unfair authorship, failure to conform to minimal standards of protection for animal or human subjects, plagiarism, and scientific fraud. We discuss each of these ethical improprieties in terms of its relative importance and possible consequences, and suggest procedures for avoiding them. Chapter 12 ("The Road to Paradise: Moral Reasoning in Addiction Publishing") discusses the same issues in the context of a framework for making ethical decisions. We use case studies to illustrate the seven ethical topics, with a commentary on each case that demonstrates a practical approach to making sound decisions. Chapter 13 ("Relationships with the Alcoholic Beverage Industry, Pharmaceutical Companies, and Other Funding Agencies: Holy Grail or Poisoned Chalice?") reviews recent trends in the funding of addiction research and the ethical risks involved in accepting funding from industry as well as non-industry sources.

In the book's concluding chapter (Chapter 14: "Addiction Publishing and the Meaning of (Scientific) Life"), the editors describe the pursuit of scientific integrity as a journey worth taking, as much for the joy of honest discovery as for the achievement of fame and fortune.

HOW TO USE THIS GUIDE EFFECTIVELY

Chapters 2 through 10 have been written to stand alone and can be read independently of each other. Chapter 11 is closely linked to Chapter 12, the former presenting the most common ethical problems in addiction publishing and the latter giving fictitious examples modeled on real cases with instructions on how to analyze and resolve important ethical dilemmas. Both are relevant to the issues discussed in Chapter 13 on the potential influence of funding sources.

The authors have collectively striven to present practical advice as well as 'best practices'. In most cases, such as resolving authorship disputes or ethical problems, the solutions are not always simple or obvious, but rather depend on the situation and on an open dialogue among colleagues in the research milieu. For these cases, we offer advice on how to use effective problem-solving techniques that will allow the reader to develop skills that can be applied to a variety of situations. The authors would like to emphasize that no addiction researcher, however experienced in the game of science, can argue that she or he has all the right answers. This book is best seen as providing a basis for discussions about concrete problems in various research environments.

The chapters are also meant for use as background readings for lectures and workshops and a new on-line tutorial (available at http://www.parint.org). The authors of this book developed the tutorial with the support of the US National Institute on Drug Abuse. It has been expanded with support from the US National Institute on Alcohol Abuse and Alcoholism.

Recognizing that there are important institutional responsibilities in the ethical conduct of addiction research, we hope that this book will also inspire research institutions to develop guidelines and policies that support the ethical practices considered in these chapters. Although we have sub-titled the book as a *Guide for the Perplexed*, we would point out that its chapters will be helpful as well to those who believe they have all the answers, including professional organizations and scientific institutions.

REFERENCES

Edwards, G. ed. (2002). Addiction: evolution of a specialist field. Oxford, UK: Blackwell Publishing.

Lafollette, M.C. (1992). Stealing into print: fraud, plagiarism and misconduct in scientific publishing. Berkeley CA: University of California Press.

Södergran, E. (1984). Complete poems (Trans. David McDuff). Newcastle upon Tyne, UK: Bloodaxe Books.

CHAPTER 2
HOW TO CHOOSE A JOURNAL: SCIENTIFIC AND PRACTICAL CONSIDERATIONS

THOMAS F. BABOR, DOMINIQUE MORISANO, KERSTIN STENIUS, ERIN L. WINSTANLEY, AND JEAN O'REILLY

INTRODUCTION

One of the most important and least understood decisions made in the course of publishing a scientific article is the choice of a journal. The decision determines the audience reached, the context in which scholarly work is presented, and the time it takes to achieve formal publication. At best, the right choice of a journal results in the rapid publication of an article that achieves the exposure it deserves. At worst, the wrong choice results in rejection, delay, and even loss of an author's motivation to persist in seeking publication for a potentially valuable scientific contribution.

Journal choice is little understood even by those who have spent decades in the field of addiction research. One reason for this state of affairs is that the field is rapidly changing, with new publication opportunities constantly arising (e.g., electronic journals) and more traditional outlets of communication (e.g., print journals) adapting to new technology. Another reason for the difficulty in choosing a publication outlet is that until recently there was little communication between journal editors and their potential authors. As indicated in Chapter 9, the process by which a journal decides to accept or reject a given article is often mysterious; most journals have carefully preserved the mystery within the 'black box' of editorial decision-making. With virtually no formal training programs on how to write for and publish in scholarly journals, the learning process for novices has been left to chance or the luck of finding an experienced mentor.

This chapter provides guidance on how to choose a journal for a scholarly publication on the subject of addiction, broadly defined as any topic dealing with psychoactive substances as well as compulsive behaviours such as gambling. We begin with the basic assumption that the primary purpose of publishing is to communicate findings and ideas to a broader audience than one's immediate circle. Our focus is on scholarly journals, which have become the primary organ (in addition to conference presentations, posters, books, and abstracts) of the scientific communication system that has evolved over the past century. Although we will provide some information about publishing in disciplinary journals that serve the scholarly interests of professional groups such as biologists, neuroscientists, physicians, sociologists, psychologists, and social workers, our primary interest is in the addiction specialty journals, which limit their subject matter primarily to psychoactive substances and related addictive behaviours.

GROWTH OF ADDICTION SPECIALTY JOURNALS AND OTHER PUBLICATION SOURCES

As noted in Chapter 1, a scientific journal has multiple functions. Journals provide a forum for scientific communication and certify the scientific value of an individual author's work. They provide access to reliable knowledge, and at the same time confer scholarly prestige that facilitates career advancement (see Lafollette 1992). Figure 2.1 provides a striking illustration of the increase of scientific publishing in the addiction field, which parallels the growth in most other areas of science during the past century (Babor 1993a). The figure shows the cumulative record of addiction specialty journals, plotted according to the number of journals publishing articles since the late nineteenth century, when addiction publishing first began. The 1970s and 1980s showed dramatic growth in the development of new addiction journals, an exponential trend that shows no signs of reaching asymptote. By 2008, there were 88 addiction specialty journals operating throughout the world, which can be interpreted as an indication of the remarkable growth in addiction science during the past 50 years.

FIGURE 2.1 CUMULATIVE NUMBER OF ADDICTION JOURNALS PUBLISHED SINCE 1884, DISAGGREGATED ACCORDING TO LANGUAGE OF PUBLICATION (ENGLISH AND NON-ENGLISH)

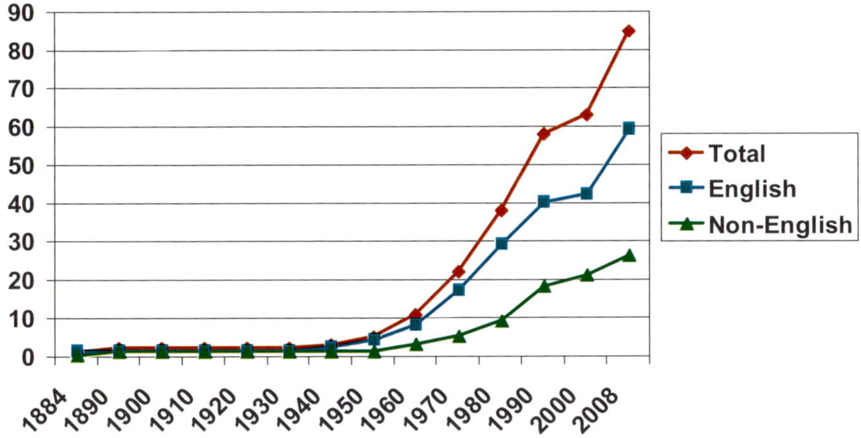

In addition to the total number of journals published each decade, Figure 2.1 also subclassifies the journals according to language of publication. Approximately two-thirds of these journals are published in the English language, which has emerged as the main language for international scientific communication (Babor 1993b). Details about the journals plotted in Figure 2.1 are provided in Tables 2.1 and 2.2. The data in these tables were compiled from a survey conducted by the International Society of Addiction Journal Editors (ISAJE). The survey results were supplemented by a review of public information sources, such as the journal's Web page (if available), print copies of the journal, and its instructions to authors.

Additional information about these journals, including their mission statements, submission details, and contact information, is available on the ISAJE-sponsored PARINT Web site (http://www.parint.org).

Table 2.1 lists the titles of the English-language journals along with information about the substances or addictive behaviours with which they are concerned (e.g., alcohol, tobacco, licit and illicit drugs, pathological gambling); general topical areas (e.g., treatment, prevention, biological mechanisms, including information about whether the journal publishes qualitative research); and details about the journals' frequency of publication, print circulation, acceptance rate, Impact Factor score (a measure of how often articles in the journal are cited), and abstracting or indexing services. Table 2.2 provides the same information for journals published in languages other than English, with the exception of Impact Factor (at this writing none of the non-English language journals have reported an Impact Factor). Almost all of the journals listed in the tables are peer-reviewed.

Growth in the number of specialized addiction journals tells only part of the story of how the addiction field has grown in size and complexity. A significant portion of the addiction literature is published in scholarly journals that have a more general scientific, professional, or disciplinary orientation such as medicine, psychology, biology, sociology, economics, and public health. Figure 2.2 shows the results of a content analysis that describes the kinds of journals currently publishing articles on alcohol-related research. We chose alcohol research for this analysis because this literature was catalogued relatively well on an international level. We counted and classified a sample of 344 journal articles published in 2001 that were abstracted in ETOH, a comprehensive index of the world scientific literature on alcohol and alcohol problems. The results showed that 58% of the alcohol-related articles were published in general or disciplinary journals and 42% were published in addiction specialty journals. When we subclassified the articles as either 'biomedical' (i.e., dealing with biological or medical topics) or 'psychosocial' (i.e., dealing with topics such as treatment, prevention, epidemiology, psychology, or social policy), we found that the addiction journals published a higher percentage of articles on psychosocial topics, whereas more general disciplinary journals published a greater share of the biomedical articles. Our review also indicated that authors of articles on alcohol-related topics publish in a tremendous variety of journals. In 2001, ETOH abstracted articles from over 50 addiction journals and 125 disciplinary and general scientific journals.

Table 2.1 COMPENDIUM OF ADDICTION JOURNALS PUBLISHED IN THE ENGLISH LANGUAGE

Journal Name	Substances[a]	Areas of Interest[b]	Issues per Year[c]	Print Circulation/Online Subscriptions[d]	Acceptance Rate[e]	Impact Factor[f]	Abstracting/ Indexing Services[g]
Addiction*	A,D,T,O	P,T,H,E,Q	12	1600/-------	19%	4.09	51
Addiction Biology*	A,D,T,O	T,B	4	500-1500/-------	45%	1.75	33
Addiction Research and Theory	A,D	P,T,Q	6	250/-------	60%	0.66	13
Addictive Behaviors*	A,D,T	T,P,B,E,Q	12	-------/5268	35%	1.85	20
Addictive Disorders and Their Treatment	A,D,T,O	T,P,E,B,H,R	4	-------/-------	90%	N/A	4
African Journal of Drug and Alcohol Studies*	A,T,D,O	T,P,E,B,H,R,Q	2	600/0	65%	-------	1
Alcohol: An International Biomedical Journal	A	B,T,P,E	8	100/2000	57%	2.02	14
Alcohol and Alcoholism	A	T,P,E,B,H,Q	6	850/~275	55%	2.06	8
Alcohol Research and Health	A	T,B,E,P,Q	4	1500/-------	N/A	0.46	7
Alcoholism: Clinical and Experimental Research*	A,T,O	T,P,B,E,H,R	12 + 2-3S	2000/~400	60%	2.93	42
Alcoholism: Journal on Alcoholism and Related Addictions*	A,D,T,O	T,B,P,E,H,R	2	1000/-------	75%	-------	11
Alcoholism Treatment Quarterly*	A	T,P,E,B,H,R,Q	4	340/-------	65%	pending	33
American Journal of Drug and Alcohol Abuse	D,A	T,P,Q	6	300/-------	60%	1.15	26
American Journal on Addictions	A,D,T,O	T,P,E,B	6	1200/-------	60-70%	1.40	15
Contemporary Drug Problems	A,T,D,O	E,P,H,Q	4	1800/-------	50%	N/A	10
Drug and Alcohol Dependence*	A,T,D	T,P,E,B,H,R,Q	18+ 3S	837/-------	33%	3.21	19
Drug and Alcohol Review*	A,T,D	T,P,B,E,H,Q	6	461/-------	67%	1.42	17
Drugs and Alcohol Today	A,T,D,O	T,P,E,H,R	4	350/-------	-------	N/A	7
Drugs: Education, Prevention and Policy*	A,T,D	P,T,H,Q	6	200/-------	60%	0.52	27
European Addiction Research*	A,T,D,O	T,P,B,E,H,Q	4	800/-------	25%	1.67	5+
Experimental and Clinical Psychopharmacology*	A,T,D,O	T,P,E,B,H,Q	6	858/858	40%	1.62	8
Harm Reduction Journal	D,A,T	T.P.E.B.H,Q	continuous online	open access: 80,000 downlds/yr.	85%	N/A	4

Journal Name	Substances[a]	Areas of Interest[b]	Issues per Year[c]	Print Circulation/Online Subscriptions[d]	Acceptance Rate[e]	Impact Factor[f]	Abstracting/ Indexing Services[g]
International Gambling Studies	O	T,P,E,B,H,R,Q	3	-------/-------	55%	-------	7
International Journal of Drug Policy*	A,T,D	T,P,E,H,R,Q	6+1-2S	500/3500	50%	-------	10
International Journal of Drug Testing	A,T,D,O	T,P,B,E,H	1	-------/-------	75%	N/A	0
International Journal of Mental Health and Addiction*	A,D,T,O	T,P,E,B,H,R,Q	4	N/A / N/A	55-60%	N/A	4
Journal of Addiction Medicine	A,T,D,O	T,P B,E,H	4	-------/-------	-------	-------	-------
Journal of Addiction Science & Clinical Practice [formerly Science and Practice Perspectives]*	A,D,T	T,P,B	2	25,000/-------	N/A	N/A	0
Journal of Addictions Nursing*	A,O	T, P,Q	4	900+/-------	45%	N/A	2
Journal of Addictive Diseases*	A,D	T,P,E,B	4	4000/-------	50%	1.42	47
Journal of Alcohol and Drug Education	A,T,D	P,Q	3	1,100/-------	35%	0.08	15
Journal of Child and Adolescent Substance Abuse	A,D	E,P,T,Q	4	500/-------	50%	0.39	45
Journal of Drug Addiction, Education, and Eradication	D,A,T	T,E,P,B,H,R	4	-------/-------	-------	-------	-------
Journal of Drug Education	A,D,T	P,E,Q	4	-------/-------	60%	0.42	36
Journal of Drug Issues*	A,D,T	T,P,E,B,H,R,Q	4	700/700+	30%	0.76	7+
Journal of Dual Diagnosis: Research and Practice in Substance Abuse Comorbidity	A,D,T,O	T,P,B,E,Q	4	218/218	75%	N/A	2
Journal of Ethnicity in Substance Abuse	A,D,T	T,P,E,H,R,Q	4	-------/-------	50%	N/A	49
Journal of Gambling Issues*	O	T,P,E,B,H,R,Q	3	N/A / 6000	44%	-------	1
Journal of Gambling Studies	O	T,P,E,B,H	4	-------/-------	15%	N/A	8
Journal of Maintenance in the Addictions	D	T	4	225/-------	75%	-------	18
Journal of Opioid Management	D	T,P	6	-------/-------	-------	-------	-------
Journal of Psychoactive Drugs*	A,D,T,O	T,P,E,B,H,R,Q	4	800/ N/A	60%	0.83	21
Journal of Smoking Cessation	T	T,Q	2	N/A / 75	-------	-------	-------
Journal of Social Work Practice in the Addictions*	A,D,T,O	T,P,H,Q	4	240/-------	39%	-------	22

Journal Name	Substances[a]	Areas of Interest[b]	Issues per Year[c]	Print Circulation/Online Subscriptions[d]	Acceptance Rate[e]	Impact Factor[f]	Abstracting/ Indexing Services[g]
Journal of Studies on Alcohol and Drugs*	A,D,T	T,P,E,B,H,R,Q	6	1733 / N/A	33%	1.88	28
Journal of Substance Abuse Treatment*	A,D,T,O	T,Q	8 + occasional supplements	475-500/2000+	30%	2.01	14
Journal of Substance Use*	A,D,T,O	T,P,B,E,Q	6	200/-------	60%	N/A	12
Journal of Teaching in the Addictions*	A,O,D	T,P,E,H,Q	2	-------/-------	38%	-------	-------
Nicotine and Tobacco Research	T	T,E,P	12	1000+/-------	35%	2.30	8
Psychology of Addictive Behaviors	A,D,T,O	T,P,E	4	2030/-------	15 %	2.17	12
Psychopharmacology*	A,D,T,O	T,P,E,B	24	575/-------	50%	3.63	3+
The Social History of Alcohol and Drugs: An Interdisciplinary Journal	A,D,T,O	P, H	2	75/-------	50%	-------	2
Substance Abuse	A,D,T	T,P,B,E,H,R	4	600/-------	40%	N/A	19
Substance Abuse Treatment, Prevention, and Policy	A,D,T	P,E,T,B,H,Q	continuous online	open access	84%	N/A	3+
Substance Use and Misuse	A,D,O	T,P,H,Q	14	-------/-------	-------	1.38	29
Tobacco Control	T	P,E,H,Q	6	1200/-------	12%	2.80	~20

[a] Main substances and other addictive behaviors addressed by the journal. A=alcohol, D=licit and illicit psychoactive drugs other than alcohol; T=tobacco and other nicotine products; O=other substances and addictive behaviors including gambling and eating disorders

[b] Primary and secondary areas of interest to the journal. T=treatment; P=prevention and policy, E=epidemiology; B=biological mechanisms or effects; H=history; R=religion and spirituality; Q = qualitative research

[c] The first number reflects the number of regular issues per year. The second number, if included, refers to the number of supplements (S) published per year

[d] Taken from most recent issue published in 2007; includes library subscriptions and copies distributed to professional society members

[e] Proportion of peer reviewed research reports accepted for publication, based on the total number of research reports submitted for review

[f] Figures cited refer to 2006, except for the *Journal of Alcohol and Drug Education*, which is based on 2001 data

[g] Number of abstracting and indexing services that include this journal

*Member journal, The International Society of Addiction Journal Editors (ISAJE)

N/A means not applicable; ------- means information not available

Titles in italics are new since 2004

Additional information about many of these journals (e.g., mission statement, web address, submission information, etc.) can be found at www.parint.org

Information about the following recently established journals was not available when this table was being compiled: *Current Drug Abuse Reviews*, *International Journal of Addiction Researchers*, *Mental Health and Substance Use: Dual Diagnosis*, and *The Open Addiction Journal*

Table 2.2 COMPENDIUM OF ADDICTION JOURNALS PUBLISHED IN LANGUAGES OTHER THAN ENGLISH

Journal Name (*English Translation*)	Language	Sub-stances[a]	Areas of Interest[b]	Issues per Year[c]	Print Circulation/Online Subscriptions[d]	Acceptance Rate[e]	Abstracting/ Indexing Services[f]
Abhängigkeiten (*Addictions*)	German (English/French abstracts)	A,D,T,O	T,P,E,B,H,Q	3	600/-------	90%	1
Addiktológia – Addictologia Hungarica (*Addiction*)*	Hungarian (English abstracts)	A,D,T,O	T,P,E,B,H,R,Q	4	1000/-------	70%	4
Adiktologie (*Addiction*)*	Czech (+ English articles & abstracts)	A,D,T,O	T,P,E,B,H,R,Q	4 + 1-2S	1000/-------	85%	1
Adicciones (*Addiction*)*	Spanish (English abstracts)	A,D,T,O	T,P,E,B,H,R,Q	4 + 1S	1500/-------	70%	9
Alcoologie et Addictologie (*Alcohol and Addiction Studies*)	French (English abstracts)	A,D,T,O	T,P,E,B,H,R,Q	4 +1-2S	2200/0	67 %	4
Alkoholizm i Narkomania (*Alcohol and Drug Abuse*)*	Polish (English abstracts, table of contents, tables and graphs)	A,D,T	T,P,E,B,H,Q	4	1700/1700	77 %	1
Alkoholizmus a Drogové Závislosti (*Alcoholism and Drug Addictions*) [formerly Protialkoholický obzor (*Antialcoholic Review*)]	Slovak, Czech, some English (English abstracts)	A,D,T,O	T,P,E,B,H,Q	5 + 1-2S	1000/0	60-70%	0
BlutAlkohol: Wissenschaftliche Zeitschrift für die Medizinische und Juristische Praxis (*Blood Alcohol: Scientific Journal for Medical and Legal Practice*)	German (some English articles)	A	P,B	6	3200/-------	25%	0
Chinese Journal of Drug Abuse, Prevention, and Treatment	Chinese (English abstracts)	A,D,T,O	T,P,E,B,H,Q	6	2000/-------	80%	12
Chinese Journal of Drug Dependence	Chinese (English abstracts)	A,D,T	T,P,E,B,H,Q	6	1700/-------	80%	12
Drogues, Santé et Société (*Drugs, Health and Society*)	French (English and Spanish abstracts)	A,D,T	T,P,E,H,Q	2	150/open access	65%	4
Eradicciones	Spanish	A,D,T,O	T,P,E,B,H	2	2,000/-------	75%	0
Exartisis (*Addictions*)*	Greek (English abstracts)	A,D,T,O	T,P,E,H	2	1,000/-------	100%	0

Journal Name (*English Translation*)	Language	Sub-stances[a]	Areas of Interest[b]	Issues per Year[c]	Print Circulation/Online Subscriptions[d]	Acceptance Rate[e]	Abstracting/ Indexing Services[f]
Japanese Journal of Alcohol Studies & Drug Dependence	Japanese	A,D,T	T,P,E,B,H	6	1200/-------	100%	0
Narcologia (*Addiction Studies*)*	Russian (English abstracts)	A,D,T,O	T,P,E,B,H,R,Q	12	500/0	-------	0
Nordisk alkohol- & narkotikatidskrift (*Nordic Studies on Alcohol and Drugs (NAT)*)*	Swedish, Danish, Norwegian, English	A,D,T,O	T,P,E,H,Q	3-4 Scandanavian languages; 2-3 English	1200 / -------	80%	8
Personalità/Dipendenze * (*Personality/Dependencies*)	Italian (English & sometimes French abstracts)	A,D,T,O	T,P,E,R,Q	3	1000/-------	90%	0
Psychotropes (*Review: Psychotropic*)	French	D,T,A,O	T,P,E,B,H,R	4	-------/-------	-------	-------
Revista Española de Drogodependencias (*Spanish Drug Dependency Review*)	Spanish (English and French abstracts)	D,A	T,P,B,H	4	-------/-------	-------	1
Salud y Drogas (*Health and Addictions*)*	Spanish (articles also accepted in English, French, and Portuguese; English and original language abstracts)	A,D,T,O	T,P,E,H,Q	2	300/1100	-------	7
SMAD Revista Eletrônica Saúde Mental Álcool e Drogas (*SMAD Electronic Journal of Mental Health, Alcohol, and Drugs*)	Portuguese (articles also accepted in Spanish and English)	A.D.T.O	T,P,E,B,R,Q	2	N/A / -------	70%	5
Sucht: Zeitschrift für Wissenschaft und Praxis (*German Journal of Addiction Research and Practice*)*	German (English titles, key words, abstracts; 10% English articles per year)	A,D,T,O	T,P,E,B,H	6 + 1-2S	3500/-------	58%	9
Suchtmedizin in Forschung und Praxis (SuchtMed) (*Addiction Medicine in Research and Practice*)*	German (English abstracts & some English articles)	A,D,T,O	T,P,E,B	4	500-1000 / 50	90%	4

Journal Name (*English Translation*)	Language	Sub-stances[a]	Areas of Interest[b]	Issues per Year[c]	Print Circulation/Online Subscriptions[d]	Acceptance Rate[e]	Abstracting/ Indexing Services[f]
Suchttherapie (*Addiction Treatment*)	German (English abstracts)	A,D,T,O	T,P,E,B	4 + 2-3S	2000/-------	60-70%	2
Toxicodependências (*Drug Addiction*)*	Portuguese (articles in French, Spanish; English/ French/ Portuguese abstracts)	A	P,E,B,H,Q	3	2500/0	70%	0
Trastornos Adictivos* (*Addictive Disorders*)	Spanish (English abstracts & some English articles)	A,D,T,O	T,P,E,B,	4	2000/ ~3000 downloads per issue	80%	3
Voprosy Narkologii (*Addiction Problems*)	Russian (English abstracts)	A,D,T	T,P,E,B,H	6	1500/-------	62%	0

[a] Main substances and other addictive behaviors addressed by the journal. A=alcohol; D=licit and illicit psychoactive drugs other than alcohol; T=tobacco and other nicotine products; O=other substances and addictive behaviors including gambling and eating disorders

[b] Primary and secondary topical areas of interest to the journal. T=treatment; P=prevention and policy, E=epidemiology; B=biological mechanisms or effects; H=history; R=religion and spirituality; Q=qualitative research

[c] The first number reflects the number of regular issues per year. The second number, if included, refers to the number of supplements (S) published per year

[d] Taken from most recent issue published in 2007; includes library subscriptions and copies distributed to professional society members

[e] Proportion of peer reviewed research reports accepted for publication, based on the total number of research reports submitted for review

[f] Number of abstracting and indexing services that include this journal

* Member journal, The International Society of Addiction Journal Editors (ISAJE)

N/A means not applicable; ------- means information not available

Additional information about many of these journals (e.g., mission statement, web address, submission information, etc.) can be found at www.parint.org

FIGURE 2.2 PERCENTAGE OF 2001 JOURNAL ARTICLES ON ALCOHOL PUBLISHED IN ADDICTION SPECIALTY JOURNALS AND DISCIPLINARY JOURNALS, CLASSIFIED AS EITHER BIOMEDICAL OR PSYCHOSOCIAL SUBJECT MATTER

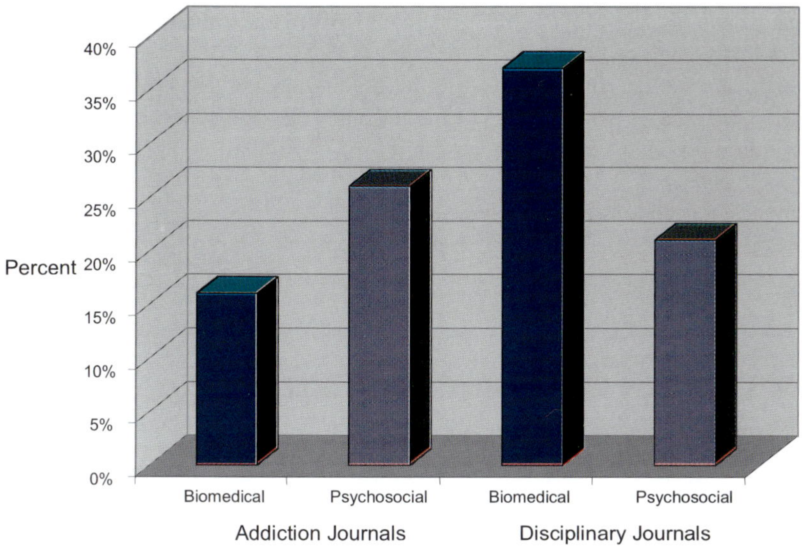

In addition to the expanding array of journals from which addiction authors may choose, many publishers have increased the standard number of issues released per year, added supplements or 'special issues', and created new electronic formats for browsing and submitting articles. With the increase in the number, frequency, and breadth of scholarly journals covering addiction-related research, there has never been a greater opportunity to publish on the subject of addiction. Nevertheless, the plethora of journals has created new challenges and questions for prospective authors. What are the relative merits of publishing in disciplinary versus addiction specialty journals? How does an author find the most appropriate journal for a particular article? What are the chances that an article will be accepted by a given journal? Which journals have the greatest impact on the field? How does an author know whether a journal will reach an article's intended audience? The answers to these and related questions are the subject of the remainder of this chapter.

To assist prospective authors in the choice of the most appropriate journal, Box 2.1 describes the kinds of decisions that authors must make during the selection process. The following sections expand upon this outline, discussing each step in the process. Although our review focuses primarily on how to publish a standard article based on original research involving the collection of empirical data, the publication of other types of articles (e.g., review papers, theoretical articles, case reports) can also be informed by following these steps.

BOX 2.1 MAJOR STEPS IN CHOOSING A JOURNAL

1. Decide whether the article is primarily of interest to a national or international audience
2. Consider the language of publication
3. Consider whether to publish in a general scientific, disciplinary or addiction specialty journal
4. Determine whether your article's general content areas (e.g., type of drug, clinical/basic science, etc) fit the journal's mission statement
5. Gauge your exposure by reviewing the journal's circulation, abstracting services, and open access
6. Evaluate your chances of acceptance
7. Consider, but don't be fooled by, impact factors
8. Take into account time to publication and other practical matters

MAJOR STEPS IN CHOOSING A JOURNAL

1. DECIDE WHETHER THE ARTICLE IS PRIMARILY OF INTEREST TO A NATIONAL OR INTERNATIONAL AUDIENCE

This is partly a matter of the article's information content, and partly a matter of presentation or appeal. If the topic is primarily of local or national interest (e.g., prevalence of substance abuse among Brazilian secondary school students, or an evaluation of a local treatment program) and the presentation is oriented toward professionals in a particular country, then the article should be submitted to a journal capable of reaching that audience, such as one sponsored by a national professional society. If the topic is likely to appeal to scientists or professionals in many countries, and the presentation speaks to this broader audience, then consider sending your article to an international journal.

However, the distinction between domestic and international journals can become unclear. Many of the addiction specialty journals that are published in English are international in scope. Approximately 37% of authors published in two English-language addiction specialty journals live in countries outside of the United States, according to a citation analysis (Gust and Winstanley, 2007) of articles published in two international journals, *Drug and Alcohol Dependence* and *Addiction*, over a seven-year period. The authors represented 60 different countries, and 10% (n=177) of the articles had authors from more than one country. The greatest number of authors came from three English-speaking countries: the United States, the United Kingdom, and Australia.

In general, the best way to determine the scope and audience of a journal is to read the journal's mission statement, usually to be found in each hard-copy issue of the journal, on the journal's Web site, or at www.parint.org.

2. CONSIDER THE LANGUAGE OF PUBLICATION

Increasingly, as noted above, English has become the main language of scientific communication throughout the world. Nevertheless, significant numbers of scientific articles are published in German, Russian, Japanese, French, Spanish, Portuguese, Italian, Chinese, and the Nordic languages, as indicated by the journals listed in Table 2.2. For most researchers, choosing a language in which to publish depends largely on the author's native tongue, the country in which the study was conducted, the potential audience, and the availability of an addiction journal that publishes in that language and accepts papers on the author's topic.

If one is writing for an international audience, it is wise to choose an English-language journal that can be read by scholars in most countries. In many circumstances, an article in English will have greater exposure, especially when included in major abstracting and indexing services (e.g., MEDLINE, PsycINFO), most of which operate in the English language. English-language authors can choose between national, specialized journals, or the bigger international journals, depending on the quality of the paper, the importance of the findings, and the audience one wishes to reach (see Step 1). If the article is likely to be of interest to an international audience, but it is not written in English, the author can consider publishing it in English, in addition to his or her native language. Multiple publication in different languages, however, requires permission from both of the journal editors involved. Alternatively, researchers writing in languages other than English should consider publishing in journals that provide English-language abstracts (see Table 2.2), thereby gaining entry into some of the world's major abstracting services (listed in the journal section of www.parint.org).

In general, journals published in languages other than English provide a valuable service to national and regional audiences that have a special interest in addiction studies. For example, if an article has special relevance to French-speaking populations, the journal *Alcoologie et Addictologie* (*Alcohol and Addiction Studies*) provides immediate access to that audience not only because of the language in which it is written, but also because of the network through which the journal is distributed (i.e., the French Society on Alcoholism and Addiction). In addition, many non-English language journals demonstrate an intentional internationalism that is expressed in a readiness to publish articles submitted from many different countries. *Nordisk alkohol- & narkotikatidskrift* (*Nordic Studies on Alcohol and Drugs*), for example, defines its scientific role as going beyond the borders of one country to include the analysis of alcohol policy in the Nordic countries as well as the international arena.

Overall, non-English language journals serve as an important medium for communication among clinicians, scientists, and policymakers within major linguistic areas of the world. They increase the range of cultural and scientific diversity in the addiction field, and in this way, provide new opportunities for authors and readers. Authors whose first language is English should not ignore the advantages of publishing in these journals, which often have a higher acceptance rate and, in some cases, are open to submissions written in English. Depending on the topic and scope of the article, some journals are willing either to translate into the language of publication or to publish the article in English.

3. CONSIDER WHETHER TO PUBLISH IN A GENERIC, DISCIPLINARY OR ADDICTION SPECIALTY JOURNAL

The third step involves examining whether the results of a study are mainly of interest to other addiction researchers or to a more general readership, as in a general scientific journal or disciplinary journal. It is probably easier to get an addiction article accepted in an addiction specialty journal. Publishing in a non-addiction journal may require authors to write the article in a way that is comprehensible to those who do not speak the 'addiction dialect'. Some general scientific journals, such as *Nature* and *Science*, are multidisciplinary and oriented toward the larger scientific community. Other journals, like *Lancet* and the *Bulletin of the World Health Organization*, publish articles dealing with a specific discipline, such as medicine or public health, respectively. In countries without addiction specialty journals, a journal in psychiatry can, for instance, be an important channel for addiction research.

Although this chapter deals primarily with addiction specialty journals, there are several reasons to consider submitting an article to one of the more broadly oriented journals, in part because they publish more than half of the scientific literature on alcohol-related research. These journals are generally published by and oriented towards professional groups associated with the major disciplines contributing to addiction studies, i.e., biology, psychology, medicine, psychiatry, public health, sociology, and anthropology. Addiction researchers sometimes favour disciplinary journals because they are thought to have greater prestige value within a given discipline than an addiction specialty journal would offer. Professional advancement for academic researchers is often based on such subtle considerations. Moreover, some of the most popular disciplinary journals (e.g., *Lancet, New England Journal of Medicine*) have higher circulation numbers and Impact Factors (discussed below) than addiction specialty journals, which adds to their prestige value.

One way to identify potential target journals outside of the addiction field is to use a Web-based search engine to query your area of specialized research. There are several Web-based search engines, such as PubMed, Web of Science, PsycINFO, ETOH, and SCOPUS. Some of these Web sites are not publicly available because they must be accessed through a university library or another organization that has a subscription to the service. Also, an individual search engine may not provide an exhaustive list of publications. As an example, we searched the Web of Science for several terms related to alcohol, tobacco, and illicit drug use to identify articles published in 2006. We identified over 9,000 research articles across 1,728 different journals. We then ranked the top 50 journals by the number of research articles, finding that 44% of these were classified as addiction-specialty journals. The top 25 general scientific and disciplinary journals are presented in Table 2.3, along with their 2007 Impact Factors. Given the limitations in using any one search engine, it is possible that there are other journals that are not indexed in the Web of Science that were not included in this analysis. The number of general scientific and disciplinary journals publishing addiction-science research articles suggests a larger opportunity to publish than one might anticipate. Nevertheless, the average Impact Factor score of these journals (3.6) is almost twice as high as the average for the addiction-specialty journals (1.8) listed in Table 2.1, suggesting that it may be more difficult to publish in these journals.

TABLE 2.3 TOP 25 GENERALIST AND DISCIPLINARY JOURNALS THAT PUBLISHED THE HIGHEST NUMBER OF ADDICTION RESEARCH ARTICLES IN 2006 ALONG WITH CURRENT JOURNAL IMPACT FACTOR

	Journal Title	**2007 JIF**
1	Psychopharmacology*	3.6
2	Neuropsychopharmacology	5.9
3	Pharmacology Biochemistry and Behavior	2.1
4	Brain Research	2.3
5	Journal of Neuroscience	7.5
6	Journal of Adolescent Health	2.7
7	Neuroscience	3.4
8	European Journal of Pharmacology	2.5
9	Neuroscience Letters	2.1
10	Behavioural Brain Research	2.6
11	Journal of Pharmacology and Experimental Therapeutics	4.0
12	Experimental and Clinical Psychopharmacology*	1.6
13	American Journal of Public Health	3.7
14	Psychiatric Services	2.4
15	European Journal of Neuroscience	3.7
16	Journal of Clinical Psychiatry	5.5
17	Pediatrics	5.0
18	American Journal of Psychiatry	8.3
19	Anesthesia and Analgesia	2.1
20	Preventive Medicine	2.4
21	Social Science & Medicine	2.8
22	BMC Public Health	1.6
23	Synapse	2.9
24	Journal of Neurochemistry	4.3
25	Neuropharmacology	3.9

*=Also listed as an addiction specialty journal in Table 2.1

Furthermore, the chances of publishing an article on an addiction-related subject are sometimes reduced if a journal does not have reviewers or editors who are familiar with the topic. If a particular disciplinary journal rarely publishes articles on addiction, it is advisable to contact the editor before submitting a paper. In addition, if a disciplinary journal has a large circulation and a high Impact Factor, authors should make sure that the article is likely to be seen as important before submitting it for review. In the remainder of this chapter, we discuss the relative merits of publishing in addiction specialty journals, as those journals offer a range of opportunities to prospective authors comparable to those available in the disciplinary journals.

4. REVIEW THE JOURNAL'S CONTENT RANGE AND GENERAL CULTURE

Every journal has a culture of its own, sometimes developed over many years of serving a particular professional society, or through the influence of editors who have placed their own particular imprint on the journal. The best way to understand that culture is to review several issues of the journal in their entirety, including editorials, letters to the editor, and scientific papers. A visit to the journal's homepage, if available, will accomplish the same purpose. Prospective contributors should also read the journal's mission statement (most of the mission statements for the journals listed in Tables 2.1 and 2.2 are summarized at www.parint.org), which often describes the focus, goals, preferences, and audience of the journal. Although these statements are sometimes dated and often written in general terms, they should provide a broad outline of the journal's traditions, image, priorities, and aspirations. Tables 2.1 and 2.2, provide information about the major substances and areas of interest that each journal considers to be part of its purview. Some journals (e.g., *Nicotine and Tobacco Research*) are interested in one particular substance, while others are quite generic (e.g., *Drug and Alcohol Dependence*). The topical areas covered by a journal are also an important consideration. Some specialize in treatment research, others in biological effects or mechanisms, and still others in prevention or policy. The less a particular article meets a journal's priority substance and content areas, the more likely it is to be rejected. Even when the editors consider an article to be scientifically sound and relevant to the addiction field, they may reject it because it does not meet the journal's current priorities and stated mission. It is therefore important for authors to narrow their choice of journals to those whose history and current contents demonstrate an interest in (or at least an openness to) the article's topic and scope. Another point to consider is the type of article you have written. For example, very few journals will accept unsolicited literature reviews, and many do not accept case reports or historical studies. When in doubt, it is always a good idea to talk with colleagues and communicate with journal editors. By asking someone with experience in publishing for advice, younger or less experienced authors can obtain up-to-date information about the priorities and preferences of particular journals and their editors.

5. EVALUATE THE JOURNAL'S EXPOSURE

One of the most important goals of scientific publication is to reach one or more specific audiences, such as the scientific community, clinical practitioners, or policymakers. A journal's ability to provide exposure to these audiences is determined by its circulation (print and electronic) and its dissemination capabilities, as determined by access to abstracting and indexing services. Tables 2.1 and 2.2 summarize information relevant to these two aspects of exposure for addiction specialty journals.

Print circulation refers to the number of copies printed for the journal's subscribers as well as those who receive free copies. Scholarly journals have two major types of subscribers: libraries and members of professional organizations. In addition, there are smaller numbers of personal and institutional subscribers. Before the Internet, the number of journal copies in circulation provided a good indicator of a journal's exposure.

Given the increasing availability of articles on the World Wide Web, it is likely that the number of times articles are downloaded from a journal will be as important a consideration as the journal's Impact Factor. Some journals now report their average monthly downloads on their websites. As you can see from Tables 2.1 and 2.2, some journals have many more online subscriptions than they do print subscriptions, while other journals deal strictly in print copies.

It is worth taking a moment here to address the topic of open-access (OA) journals. While many journals offer online as well as print subscriptions, some journals do not bother with subscriptions at all, allowing free online access to their articles, reports, reviews, letters, etc. (Box 2.2). Rather than selling print or online subscriptions, OA journals generate revenue through dissemination fees charged to authors as well as the sale of auxiliary products and services. Some researchers are reluctant to submit articles to OA journals, preferring print journals that offer rigorous peer review, copyright protection, greater prestige, and the knowledge that one's article is preserved on paper in libraries around the world. In fact, OA journals can offer the same prestige, peer review, and protection as print journals, with the added incentive of a much wider potential readership (Suber 2002). The Budapest Open Access Initiative (2002) stresses the importance of peer review in scientific journals, an emphasis reiterated in later OA statements such as the Bethesda Statement and the Berlin Declaration. Researchers should assess OA journals just as they would print journals, paying particular attention to the journal's mission statement, archiving strategies, alignment with relevant OA initiatives, and commitment to peer review.

Some print journals, recognizing the power of open access, have now developed hybrid approaches to publishing, allowing open access to some or all of their articles once a prescribed period of time has passed or allowing authors to self-archive their articles (deposit digital versions of their articles in a publicly accessible website) either pre- or post-printing. Such approaches can significantly boost an article's potential exposure to the scientific community -- for example, *Drug and Alcohol Dependence* averages over 26,000 downloads per month.

One issue currently under scrutiny regarding OA journals is whether open access -- and researchers' reliance on a small number of easy-to-use databases -- encourages convenience citation, which is citation of the easiest material to find rather than the most relevant material (De Groote and Dorsch 2003; Antelman 2004; Harnad and Brody 2004; Eysenbach 2006). Convenience citation is discussed at greater length in Chapter 7.

BOX 2.2 DEFINITION OF AN OPEN ACCESS PUBLICATION

An Open Access Publication[1] is one that meets the following two conditions:

A. The author(s) and copyright holder(s) grant(s) to all users a free, irrevocable, worldwide, perpetual right of access to, and a license to copy,use, distribute, transmit and display the work publicly and to make and distribute derivative works, in any digital medium for any responsible purpose, subject to proper attribution of authorship[2], as well as the right to make small numbers of printed copies for their personal use.

B. A complete version of the work and all supplemental materials, including a copy of the permission as stated above, in a suitable standard electronic format is deposited immediately upon initial publication in at least one online repository that is supported by an academic institution, scholarly society, government agency, or other well-established organization that seeks to enable open access, unrestricted distribution, interoperability, and long-term archiving (for the biomedical sciences, PubMed Central is such a repository).

Notes:
1. Open access is a property of individual works, not necessarily journals or publishers.
2. Community standards, rather than copyright law, will continue to provide the mechanism for enforcement of proper attribution and responsible use of the published work, as they do now.

Excerpted from the Bethesda Statement on Open Access Publishing, 2003

Putting aside the question of open access, if an article is relevant to the members of a particular learned society (e.g., the British Society for the Study of Addiction to Alcohol or Other Drugs), professional group (e.g., the Canadian Medical Association), and scientific organization (e.g., the Research Society on Alcoholism), then it might make sense to submit the manuscript to a journal sponsored by that organization. Many of the journals listed in Tables 2.1 and 2.2 are sponsored by professional organizations or learned societies that provide free subscriptions or reduced rates to their members. For example, *Alcoologie et Addictologie* (*Alcohol and Addiction Studies*) is sponsored by the French Society of Alcohol and Addiction Studies, which distributes free copies of the journal to its 1,400 members. *Psychology of Addictive Behaviors* is published by the American Psychological Association, which makes the journal available to its members at a reduced subscription rate.

The number of library subscriptions also affects a journal's range of exposure. Libraries, especially university libraries, guarantee exposure to students and scholars, thereby providing direct access to perhaps the most important audience for any scientific communication.

Library subscriptions are the main conduit by which a publication reaches a broader audience than the members of a particular learned society. The world of library science and informatics is rapidly changing, with electronic subscriptions supplementing or replacing print copies available on the library shelf. University libraries and other large information sources have begun to pool resources to increase the electronic availability of full-text journals. Moreover, OA journals are available to any library or individual with Internet access, free of charge.

Beyond the journal's print circulation and subscriber base, an article's exposure is now determined to a far greater extent than before by the electronic databases that index the published literature by author, topic, and bibliographic reference, and that provide abstracts of articles for potential readers in search of particular types of information. Appendix 2.1 lists some of the main abstracting and indexing services used by the addiction specialty journals listed in Tables 2.1 and 2.2. These secondary information sources provide a variety of important services that dramatically increase an article's potential exposure. In general, these databases are available in both print and electronic versions. Electronic databases have become the information source of choice for those who search for topical information via the Internet. They are comprehensive, rapid, and often inexpensive or free. They permit searches of the current and past literature according to author, title, and keywords, often providing the author's abstract for review.

A journal's ability to provide a listing of its articles and abstracts to these secondary information sources greatly increases an article's exposure to scholars and students throughout the world. The greater the number of indexing and abstracting services a journal belongs to (as indicated in Tables 2.1 and 2.2), the more likely it is that an article will reach its intended audience. Although many of the non-English language journals indicate minimal coverage in abstracting and indexing databases, this situation is changing rapidly, and most of these journals now provide English abstracts, an important first step in reaching an international audience.

6. EVALUATE YOUR PROBABILITY OF ACCEPTANCE

A major consideration in the choice of a journal is the likelihood of acceptance of your article. Journals vary tremendously in the criteria they use to select articles for publication, and in the competition that a given article will encounter in relation to other authors seeking to claim the same journal space. Some journals have high acceptance rates and are often looking for articles to publish. Other journals have a surfeit of submissions, making it necessary to reject articles that would nevertheless be worthy of publication in less competitive journals. A journal's acceptance rate provides a rough estimate of an author's chances of eventual acceptance, but the rates listed in Tables 2.1 and 2.2 are subject to a number of limitations. First, some journals do not know or choose not to reveal their acceptance rate. Second, several journals (e.g., *Alcohol Research and Health, Journal of Addiction Science and Clinical Practice*) operate primarily by commissioning authors to write papers on a topic or theme, which accounts for their high acceptance rates.

Beyond a journal's acceptance rate, an author's chances of acceptance depend on many other considerations, some of them scientific, some stylistic, others administrative. As discussed in Chapter 5, scientific considerations include the importance of the findings, the originality of the ideas, the sophistication of the research methods, the appropriateness of the data analyses, and the implications of the results. Stylistic factors include the quality of the writing and the way in which the data are presented. If the article is poorly written or organized, reviewers might see this as a limitation and not recommend the article for acceptance; similarly, editors might be reluctant to take the time to work with authors to bring the article up to the journal's standards. Some journals have more resources for editorial assistance than others. Administrative factors include the length of the article, the amount of revision required, and the appropriateness of the topic to the journal's mission. If an article is too long, it may lose out to a more concise article on the same topic. If the article is not appropriate to the journal's current priorities or mission statement, it might be rejected even before it is sent out for peer review. Finally, the number of articles published by a journal could affect the chances of acceptance. Journals that are published monthly or weekly accept more articles than journals that publish less frequently. But journals that publish more frequently also tend to be more competitive.

7. CONSIDER, BUT DON'T BE FOOLED BY, IMPACT FACTORS

The so-called Impact Factor attempts to provide an objective measure of the extent to which a scientific author's work is cited by other authors. Such a measure can also be used to determine how often the articles from a specific journal are cited. Thus, the impact of a journal on a field of study is assumed to be a function of the extent to which a journal's articles are cited by authors publishing in that and other indexed journals. In 1962, the Institute for Scientific Information (ISI) began publishing the Science Citation Index (SCI). By the early 1990s, 3,200 journals belonged to the "core" or citation journals of SCI (Seglen 1998). Since 1972, ISI has also published the Journal Citation Reports. These reports give information about different journal impact factors, of which the standard Journal Impact Factor (JIF) is the one most followed. It is presented as a figure that indicates the average citation frequency of the articles in the journal. It is based on the average number of times in a given year that the articles appearing in the two preceding years received citation in other SCI-indexed journals (Rydholm 1998).

The JIF was originally developed to compare the quality of journals. Increasingly, however, the data used to calculate impact factors have been used as a shortcut to compare and rank individual articles, researchers, and research groups. The JIF has been criticised almost from its inception (Seglen 1998; Stenius 2003) for a number of reasons. The ISI's databank covers only a small share of the world's scientific journals. Different research fields have different coverage in the database. The database has a clear preference for English-language journals (particularly those based in the USA). National or regional journals in other languages are not well represented (Seglen 1998), as indicated by the fact that none of the journals listed in Table 2.2 has an Impact Factor.

All journals from a field that is under-represented will receive low JIFs. In addition, the use of citations varies among different research fields. Thus, it is not acceptable to compare JIFs for journals from different fields. A journal representing a field that typically favours large numbers of references will automatically receive a higher Impact Factor, especially if the field is growing. Research fields that get references from related disciplines earn higher JIFs. This explains why basic science journals have higher values. The humanities are in a particularly unfavourable position. Disciplines where national or regional research is important, as well as publications in local languages, tend to get lower JIFs as well (Rousseau 2002).

As a measure of impact, the JIF, with its two-year time frame, is more appropriate for quickly developing research fields, such as molecular medicine. Applied, clinical, and social sciences do not fare as well with the two-year window (Mäkelä 2000; Andersen 1998; Luukkonen 1994). Non-English language journals or bilingual journals (for instance Japanese-English), even if included in SCI, will on average receive a lower JIF.

Finally, it is important to note that a citation is not necessarily an indication of research quality. Every researcher knows that there are numerous reasons (apart from quality) for citing a scientific publication. Authors may cite or quote for polemical reasons, to flatter their readers, or to promote their own research (or that of their friends, colleagues or patrons). West and McIlwaine (2002) studied 79 articles published in *Addiction* between 1995 and 1998 and found no correlation between citation frequency (up to the year 2000) and an independent quality rating. Interestingly, they also found that articles from the developing world received fewer citations than the quality ranking would have led them to expect. (See Chapter 7 for further discussion of citation procedures)

In conclusion, Impact Factors should be treated with caution. Until the deficiencies in the system have been corrected and its limitations better understood, the JIF remains a relatively crude index of the value of a particular journal. According to Jones (1999), authors should not overemphasize the Impact Factor of a journal. Rather, they should give more consideration to the speed and efficiency of the editorial handling of their manuscripts, and to the quality and timeliness of the peer review (as covered below in Step 8). In a time when electronic publishing has become more common, the quick (and often free) availability of research results on the Internet might, in many cases, compete with measures of impact such as the Impact Factor.

8. OTHER PRACTICAL CONSIDERATIONS

There are several other factors authors should take into account when selecting a journal. One is the lag time to publication. Some journals take longer than others to process their manuscripts. Most journals do not reveal how long it takes to arrive at a decision, however, and even when this information is available, the average time is affected by the number of manuscripts that are rejected before being sent out for peer review. Another factor is the time between the acceptance of a revised manuscript and its final publication. This will depend in part on the number of issues published by the journal per year, the number of accepted manuscripts, and the efficiency of the publisher. In general, journals that publish more frequently are likely to have a shorter lag time to publication. The best way to obtain information about the review process is to consult the journal's instructions to authors or the journal's Web site. It is best not to rely on hearsay, anecdote, or the journal's reputation.

SUMMARY

Journals differ in the quality of articles they publish, the exposure they provide to an author's work, and their subject matter. Once an author has a clear idea of the results of a particular study or project, he or she should conduct a preliminary review of the journals most likely to publish an article on that subject. As indicated in Tables 2.1 and 2.2, there are many peer-reviewed addiction specialty journals to choose from, and possibly over 1,000 disciplinary and multidisciplinary journals. The careful selection of a journal, taking into account both scientific and practical considerations, is clearly worth the effort. Not only is the process likely to save valuable time for authors, peer reviewers, and journal editors, but it will also increase the likelihood that an article will contribute as much to science as it does to the author's curriculum vitae.

REFERENCES

Andersen, H. (1998) Acta Sociologica på den internationale arena: hvad kan SSCI fortelle? [Acta Sociologica on the international arena: what can SSCI tell us?] *Dansk Sociologi,* VII, 72-78.

Antelman, K. (2004) Do open-access articles have a greater research impact? College and Research Libraries, 65(5), 372-382. Website: http://www.ala.org/ala/acrl/acrlpubs/crljournal/crl2004/crlseptember/antelman.pdf. Last accessed 20 December 2007.

Babor, T. F. (1993a) Beyond the invisible college: a science policy analysis of alcohol and drug research. In: Edwards, G., Strang, J., and Jaffe, J. H., eds. *Drugs, Alcohol and Tobacco: making the science and policy connections*, pp. 48-69. Oxford: Oxford University Press.

Babor, T. F. (1993b) Megatrends and dead ends: alcohol research in global perspective. *Alcohol Health and Research World*, 17, 177-186.

Bethesda statement on open access publishing (2003) Website: http://www.earlham.edu/~peters/fos/bethesda.htm. Last accessed 20 December 2007.

Budapest open access initiative (2002) Website: http://www.soros.org/openaccess/index.shtml. Last accessed 20 December 2007.

De Groote, S. and Dorsch, J. (2003) Measuring use patterns of online journals and databases. *Journal of the Medical Library Association*, 91(2), 231-241. Website: http://www.pubmedcentral.nih.gov/articlerender.fcgi?artid=153164. Last accessed 20 December 2007.

Eysenbach, G. (2006) Citation advantage of open access articles. *PLoS Biology*, 4(5), e157, 0692-0698. Website: http://biology.plosjournals.org/perlserv/?request=get-document&doi=10%2E1371%2Fjournal%2Epbio%2E0040157&ct=1. Last accessed 20 December 2007.

Gust, S. and Winstanley E.L. (2007) A bibliometric study of two drug addiction research specialty journals. Poster Presentation at the College on the Problems of Drug Dependence (CPDD), Board #172.

Harnad, S. and Brody T. (2004) Comparing the impact of open access (OA) vs. non-OA articles in the same journals. *D-Lib Magazine*, 10(6). Website: http://webdoc.sub.gwdg.de/edoc/aw/d-lib/dlib/june04/harnad/06harnad.html. Last accessed 20 December 2007.

Jones, A. W. (1999) The impact of Alcohol and Alcoholism among substance abuse journals. *Alcohol and Alcoholism*, 34, 25-34.

Lafollette, M. C. (1992) *Stealing into Print. Fraud, Plagiarism, and Misconduct in Scientific Publishing*. Berkeley, CA: University of California Press.

Luukkonen, T. (1994) Viiteanalyysi ja tutkimuksen arviointi. [Reference analysis and evaluation of research.] *Signum*, 27, 130-132.

Mäkelä, K. (2000) personal communication. Helsinki, Finland.

Rousseau, R. (2002) Journal evaluation: technical and practical issues. *Library Trends*, 50, 418-439.

Rydholm, A. (1998) Impact factors. *Acta Orthopaedica Scandinavica*, 69, 221.

Seglen, P. (1998) Citation rates and journal impact factors are not suitable for evaluation of research. *Acta Orthopaedica Scandinavica*, 69, 224-229.

Stenius, K. (2003) Journal impact factor - mittari joka vahvistaa tutkimusmaailman hierarkiaa. [The journal impact factor - an indicator that strengthens the hierarchy of the research world.] *Tieteessä Tapahtuu*, 7, 35-39.

Suber, Peter (2002) Open access to the scientific journal literature. *Journal of Biology*, 1, 3f.

West, R. and Mcllwaine, A. (2002) What do citation counts count for in the field of addiction? An empirical evaluation of citation counts and their link with peer ratings of quality. *Addiction*, 97, 501-504.

APPENDIX 2.1 A SELECTION OF ABSTRACTING AND INDEXING SERVICES USED BY ADDICTION SPECIALTY JOURNALS

Addiction Abstracts is a quarterly journal published simultaneously in print and online editions. This international abstracting service covers all addictive substances as well as other compulsive behaviours. It reviews approximately one hundred journals from such areas as psychology, psychiatry, public health, medicine, health behaviour, treatment, and prevention.

AGORA (Access to Global Online Research in Agriculture) provides free or low cost online access to over 1,100 journals in agriculture and related biological, environmental and social sciences to public institutions in eligible developing countries. Users can search for articles by subject area or publisher. Major subject areas include biology, biotechnology/applied microbiology, chemistry/biochemistry/physics, economics/social science, food science/nutrition, and multidisciplinary subjects. The URL for AGORA is http://www.aginternetwork.org/en.

CSA Sociological Abstracts provides an index and abstracts of journal articles from the international literature in sociology and related disciplines in the social and behavioural sciences. Its database is drawn from over 1,700 serial publications. Major subject areas include evaluation research, family and social welfare, health law, substance abuse, and addiction.

Current Contents provides access to bibliographic research information from articles, editorials, meeting abstracts, and other sources gathered from more than 8,000 scholarly journals, with separate editions for clinical medicine, life sciences, and social and behavioural sciences. Current Contents Connect provides Internet access.

DrugScope is a British-based independent centre of expertise on drugs. DrugScope Information Service allows access to a multi-disciplinary library of over 80,000 documents from around the world (see http://www.drugscope.org.uk/about/home.asp).

EMBASE is a comprehensive index of the world's literature on human medicine and related disciplines. EMBASE classifies and indexes each record using terms and synonyms that assist the process of searching for specific subjects. Subject coverage includes AIDS, drug dependence, psychiatry, and public health. EMBASE provides access to articles from more than 2,900 journals from 110 countries.

ETOH refers to the Alcohol and Alcohol Problems Science Database, a comprehensive online resource covering all aspects of alcohol abuse and alcoholism. It was produced and supported by the US National Institute on Alcohol Abuse and Alcoholism until 2004. ETOH contains both abstracts and bibliographic references to journal articles and other information sources that cover medicine, biochemistry, psychology, psychiatry, epidemiology, sociology, anthropology, treatment, prevention, education, accidents and safety, legislation, criminal justice, public policy, and health services research.

Each ETOH reference is assigned one broad subject heading (i.e., genetics and biological behavioural determinants, incidence and prevalence, medical consequences, metabolism, neuroscience, occupational and workplace issues, pregnancy, prevention, psychological and developmental determinants, public policy, socioeconomic aspects, social consequences, special populations, and treatment). These 'keywords' are designed to facilitate the search for particular types of information by means of the ETOH Web site (http://etoh.niaaa.nih.gov/).

HINARI (Health InterNetwork Access to Research Initiative) is a WHO initiative that provides free or low cost online access to over 3,000 journals in the biomedical and related social sciences to local, not-for-profit institutions in developing countries. Eligible institutions include national universities, research institutes, professional schools (e.g., medicine, nursing, pharmacy, public health, dentistry), teaching hospitals, government offices and national medical libraries. Users can search for articles by journal title, publisher, subject area, or language. Access this site via http://www.who.int/hinari/en.

MEDLINE (Medical Literature, Analysis, and Retrieval System Online) is the US National Library of Medicine's bibliographic database. It contains over 12 million references to journal articles in the life sciences with a concentration on biomedicine, including nursing, allied health, and pre-clinical sciences such as biology and chemistry. It can be searched free of charge in most libraries through the Internet via PubMed or the home page of the National Library of Medicine (http://www.nlm.nih.gov). Currently, MEDLINE documents citations from over 4,600 journals published in 30 languages, although nearly 89% of the cited articles are published in English. Approximately 76% of English abstracts are printed verbatim from published articles. For over 3,000 journals, there is a link from a MEDLINE reference to the publisher's Web site to access the full article.

PsycINFO is the electronic version of Psychological Abstracts. It contains summaries (abstracts, bibliographic information, and indexing) of English-language articles from journals originating in more than fifty countries. It is available through libraries and to members of the American Psychological Association. It covers more than 1,800 journal titles, with articles selected for their psychological relevance.

SCOPUS is a large abstract and citation database of research literature and web sources. Updated daily, it covers 15,000 peer-reviewed journals (including open access journals, trade publications, and conference proceedings), 33 million abstracts, 386 million scientific Web pages, and 21 million patent records. SCOPUS differentiates itself from other indexing services by emphasizing the size of its database and its easy-to-use interface. Access SCOPUS through http://info.scopus.com.

TOXIBASE is a French language database designed to provide access to scientific information and documentation dealing with psychoactive drugs and addiction. It is part of the French Reseau National d'Information et de Documentation, a national network of information and documentation centres with partners in France and other countries. It is available at http://www.toxibase.org.

CHAPTER 3
BEYOND THE ANGLO-AMERICAN WORLD: ADVICE FOR RESEARCHERS FROM DEVELOPING OR NON-ENGLISH-SPEAKING COUNTRIES

KERSTIN STENIUS, ISIDORE OBOT, FLORENCE KERR-CORRÊA, ERIKSON F. FURTADO, AND THOMAS F. BABOR

INTRODUCTION

Today, 85 % of the world's population lives in countries categorised as low and middle income (LAMI) (World Bank 2003). Relatively few addiction journals are published in these countries (see Table 2.2, Chapter 2), despite the growing need for specialized knowledge in countries like China, India, South Africa, Mexico and Brazil, where addiction problems are prevalent. Presently, between 5% and 9% of the world's population grows up with English as their first language. The dominance of English within scientific communication is, however, overwhelming. It is estimated that 80% of the world's scientific articles are in published in English language journals (Montgomery 2004) whereas about two-thirds of the known addiction journals communicate in English.

This chapter deals with the challenges encountered by addiction scientists who work in countries with few resources as well as those whose first language is not English. The aims of the chapter are to discuss: a) the practical and professional issues that are faced by these scientists; b) how authors who come from these countries can improve their chances of publishing in English language journals; c) the possibilities for authors to publish in both English and an additional language so they can communicate to different audiences; and d) how to decide whether an article serves the public best by being published in the author's mother tongue and/or a local or regional journal.

THE STRUCTURAL BARRIERS

THE SKEWED DISTRIBUTION OF SCHOLARLY COMMUNICATIONS

There is a fundamental imbalance between available resources and resource needs in the addiction field. On the one hand, there is as noted above a disproportionate concentration of addiction science and addiction publishing in the richer and English speaking countries (North America, Europe and Australia). On the other hand, the majority of the world's population and an increasing share of the addiction problems can be found in low and middle income countries and countries where the native language is not English (Room et al. 2002). This presents a serious challenge to those interested in the most effective and efficient use of current resources in the interests of public health on an international level.

In November 2003, the World Health Organization (WHO) arranged a meeting on 'Mental Health Research in Developing Countries: Role of Scientific Journals'. The joint statement by participating journal editors and WHO (2004) describes the barriers to scientific publishing experienced by researchers from low and middle income countries in the mental health research field.

The document states that the accumulation of scientific knowledge is dependent on free and accessible communication across the world. The promotion of good research increasingly requires not only the ability to access research from other parts of the world, but also the opportunity to communicate research results. Researchers from LAMI countries often have difficulties in publishing their findings in scientific journals. The reasons include limited access to information, lack of advice on research design and statistics, the difficulty of writing in a foreign language, as well as material, financial, policy and infrastructural constraints. Limited appreciation of the research needs of LAMI countries and the comparative anonymity of their researchers may constitute additional barriers. According to the WHO (2004, p. 226) report, many researchers from LAMI countries 'are daunted by the seemingly insurmountable chasm between their research effort and its publication in international journals'.

Most of these problems could be applied to the addiction field. Many countries with few resources are striving to develop scientific research capabilities. These efforts do not always have sufficient political support. Politicians and decision makers in these countries -- as in many others -- are not necessarily interested in whether certain measures are evidence-based or not. Also, research can be difficult to translate into policy. For these reasons, research and scientific publishing may not be high on the list of political priorities. Career scientists and professionally trained clinicians are needed, but except for government-sponsored university programmes, there is little support for clinical, epidemiological and policy research. Very few countries have specialist addiction societies where locally relevant and topical problems can be discussed and solutions developed. Training opportunities are lacking. In some countries the number of masters and doctoral students has grown, as well as specialization courses at the universities. But many addiction professionals entering the work force are clinicians in private practice who may do academic work voluntarily or for a small salary. Under the circumstances, the development of addiction research will be slow.

Communication with researchers in other countries is often restricted by lack of resources. Many libraries have run out of journal subscription funds and addiction journals are seldom a priority. In some countries, influential research-funding agencies are now supporting programmes that give most universities free access to online periodicals. These programmes have improved the availability of international research, but the situation is still not adequate.

The formal communication of locally relevant addiction research is encountering other challenges. Local journals are necessary to deal with sociocultural peculiarities and the priorities of different societies. Presently there is a strong movement in several countries to publish good quality articles, preferably in English, in local journals. Because competition in the scientific field is intensifying, publication in indexed journals is a priority for researchers who need scientific credit for their work. Alcohol and drug science is, however, a young and relatively small field. Local addiction journals have difficulties meeting the criteria for inclusion in the US and international indexing systems, such as the Institute of Scientific Information (ISI) and MEDLINE. A sign of how problematic the situation can be is that no addiction journal from the Latin American region has yet been included in the register for Latin American and Caribbean health sciences, LILACS (see http://www.bireme.br/abd/E/ehomepage.htm, accessed 23 August 2004). As a consequence, many addiction scientists publish in indexed public health or mental health journals when writing for the local or regional audience in this part of the world. Only a small number of these articles are published in English. Publishing in these journals is, of course, in itself not a bad thing. But for the development of the addiction field in a particular country or region, a specialized journal can play an important role. In India, the situation is no less problematic. There is no local language or English language addiction journal, and the only psychiatric journal which publishes addiction articles is not indexed. Indian researchers working in institutes that demand publications in indexed journals therefore have no option other than to publish in English language journals from outside India.

However important national or local journals are, it sometimes can be hard for a researcher from a country with few resources to rely on them. These journals often have limited funds, may be published irregularly, or have long delays between submission and publication of an article. Not infrequently these journals will find themselves in a vicious circle: they are not regarded as prestigious enough, which means that they will not get enough good articles, which in turn means that they will not get enough resources and not enough good articles.

The International Society of Addiction Journal Editors (ISAJE) has acknowledged the importance of getting journals from all parts of the world, and published in different languages, indexed and included in the important databases. A work group with the aim of improving this situation has been established within the organisation.

MARGINALISATION OF LAMI RESEARCH IN THE INTERNATIONAL DISCOURSE

In academia nowadays, faculty are often evaluated by the number of their publications and the impact of the journals in which their papers are published. Publishing in high impact journals has become the principal aim for many, owing to the fact that grants, positions and funding go to scientists, faculty and departments that succeed in this respect (see for instance Linardi et al. 1996). When research funds are in short supply, resources are concentrated in the hands of a few investigators, and the dominance of impact factors contributes to this concentration.

The Institute of Scientific Information, which publishes the most commonly-used impact factors, has a less than complete coverage of the world's scientific journals. English language journals and especially US journals are better represented. This means that, in general, research conducted in LAMI countries and reported in languages other than English is under-represented. Of Brazil's 4,580 nationally indexed scientific journals, for example, only 117 are indexed in the ISI database (Targino and Garcia 2000). See Chapters 2 and 4 for a full discussion of this topic.

The problems for LAMI researchers who seek to publish internationally may be compounded by structural factors associated with the management of the English language scientific journals. A survey of the editorial and advisory boards of leading international journals in the field of mental health (e.g., *Archives of General Psychiatry, American Journal of Psychiatry, Schizophrenia Bulletin, British Journal of Psychiatry, Adolescent Psychiatry*) found only four representatives from the LAMI countries out of a total of 530 board members (Saxena et al. 2003). The absence of LAMI representation on the editorial boards of the major journals may explain why authors from developing countries often feel that their articles do not receive sympathetic treatment.

Thus, research from LAMI countries is likely to be regarded as less relevant in the international discourse. This is supported by a study of articles published in *Addiction* (West and McIlwaine 2002), which found that papers from LAMI countries were cited significantly less often than papers ranked by independent peer reviewers to be of the same quality as those from the developed world. Other studies have shown that an increase in the number of articles published from LAMI countries is not paralleled by a similar increase in citation of these articles (Volpato and Freitas 2003; Holmgren and Schnitzer 2004).

Other factors which may account for the relatively limited number of publications from these countries include poor research methods, inadequate sample sizes, less sophisticated statistical analyses, lack of national or regional journals and limited English-language competence. In a survey of 116 international journals on physics, chemistry and biology (Gosden 1992, p.130), about one-third of the responding editors reported that bias existed against papers submitted by writers who did not have English as their native language. Some stated specific bias against certain parts of the world or certain countries, based on how their science culture was perceived. If it appeared that multiple publications were non-controversial in a particular country, or that the citation tradition was ethnocentric, this tended to lead to negative bias towards all papers from that country.

THE LANGUAGE AND CULTURE TRAP

English is the lingua franca of scientific research today and will be in the foreseeable future. However, as Montgomery (2004) points out, to call it 'the universal language of science' is ahistorical and possibly inattentive to the complex linguistic developments taking place in the world. In the future, more and more people will be bilingual and languages other than English will grow in importance. For the present, however, the English language has a dominant position in addiction science. For instance, all addiction journals with an ISI Impact Factor (see Chapters 2 and 4) are published in English, and none of the addiction journals published in other languages has an Impact Factor.

The scientific world today is dominated by a small group of rich countries. The USA is in the lead, followed by UK, Canada, Australia, and the European nations which are oriented towards a similar scientific tradition and where English language training is well developed. The disproportionate influence of US research extends to basic science, prevention, epidemiology, and treatment research. American researchers tend to cite American researchers (see further discussion in Chapter 4 and in Babor 1993). The same applies (perhaps to a lesser degree) to other countries, but with the dominance of journals from the USA and other English language or English-language oriented countries there is a bias across the research field as a whole. Research that is performed in the USA may represent a priori for many Anglo-American readers - and other uncritical readers as well - a more universal truth than results from a study conducted in a country such as India. Researchers in some Western nations (for instance the Nordic countries) have adapted to the dominant research paradigms and seem to manage quite well, in terms of citation measurement (Ingwersen 2002). The under-representation of non-English speaking nations in indexed journals and in cited research extends to several developed countries, such as Spain, Germany and France (Maisonneuve et al. 2003), suggesting that general linguistic and cultural influences may be at work. The US dominance of science on an international level may imply a serious bias in the selection of research topics, questions asked, methods used, and types of research conducted. One should remember that US research is primarily (and legitimately) oriented towards that country's own social and economic priorities, which do not necessarily apply to cultures for instance in the developing world. The problem of the US dominance is thus not only one of maldistribution of opportunity.

There are other problems inherent in this hierarchy within addiction research. Addiction science has at least two subdivisions - basic and applied research. The former is more or less universal in its nature, and scientific knowledge from basic research can be applied everywhere in the world. The latter is contextual. Public health research, for instance, belongs to this category. Today, public health research in LAMI countries suffers from a double disadvantage: the difficulty in getting published and quoted in the influential journals; and unfair competition at the national and international level with the much better funded neurobiological research (cf. Midanik 2004). In short, this means that the world literature on substance misuse is rarely determined by the research priorities of the developing countries.

Commerce plays a role as well and may not favour the public health interests of the poorer parts of the world. Randomized clinical trials of new medicines have a greater probability of being published than brief interventions to treat alcohol and drug users. Not all policymakers realize that alcohol and tobacco are more important issues than heroin and cocaine in the developing countries (Ezzati et al. 2002).

For researchers from LAMI countries, some of the problems in getting published come from not being familiar with the codes of international scientific communication. In the above-mentioned survey of physics, chemistry and biology journals (Gosden 1992), the editors summarized the problems encountered by researchers who were not native English speakers. The most often mentioned problem was that research results and discussion were not well written: that is, an inability to communicate the importance and relevance of the research. Another important problem was the fact that authors did not know the written and unwritten 'rules of the publishing game'.

For instance, they failed to cite sufficient references to earlier research, and were not familiar with the argumentation style or scientific level of the journal (ibid, pp 132-133). Writing a good scientific article for an international audience demands not only technical skill, such as being able to carefully follow the instructions to authors, but also an acquired competence in social communication. The best way to gain this is by reading some of the journals mentioned in Chapter 2 and getting feedback on your writing from more experienced researchers. This is not always easy in a LAMI country.

WHAT DO WE KNOW ABOUT ADDICTION JOURNALS' LANGUAGE AND CULTURAL POLICIES?

Unfortunately, we have almost no research to show how addiction journals in general deal with articles from LAMI countries, and only a small amount of information about their language policies. However, in two surveys conducted by ISAJE, Edwards and Savva (2002a; 2002b) mapped the language policies of 14 English language journals and nine non-English language journals.

Half the editors of the English language journals who responded had not mastered any language besides English. This is a handicap in a multilingual scientific world. Based on the ISAJE questionnaire, it seems that the English language addiction journals outside the USA have greater international representation on their editorial boards. Fifteen percent of the editorial board members of the US journals represented other nationalities, while the figure for other English language journals was 79%. The composition of an editorial board can give an indication of the internationalism of a journal. We have no exact knowledge of how the LAMI countries are represented on the editorial boards, but they are likely to be few.

Among the responding English language journals, the share of research articles from non-English language countries varied from 0% to 57%. There was large variation in the rejection rates of articles by non-English language authors: from less than average to three times higher. In this, perhaps biased, sample about one-third had a policy to give special support to authors with other mother tongues. Only three journals declared that they could not give any language editing support. Of the non-English language journals responding to the questionnaire, the majority published only in the language of the country of publication. Several published articles that had already been published in English. Only one journal had resources to finance translations. Several had regional or international ambitions. All the editors knew English, and several were competent in more than one foreign language. All journals had English summaries. The editorial boards often had representatives from other countries.

WHAT CAN AN AUTHOR DO?

In this section we turn to some practical suggestions that may help to correct the imbalance, level the playing field, and improve the diversity of addiction science.

CROSSING THE CULTURAL BORDER TO THE ENGLISH LANGUAGE PUBLICATIONS

As noted above, it may be particularly difficult for authors from LAMI countries and non-English speaking countries to get an article accepted in an English language journal. It is thus especially important for a LAMI country author to show that he or she has mastered the rules of the game: to carefully follow the instructions to authors, checking that the structure, the language and the presentation of the study and its results are clear and logical and that the references are correct. If the formalities are not followed, even a study containing strong and original findings might immediately be turned down. Cultural bias may put higher demands on the substance of research from countries where resources are few. The famous Chilean pharmacologist Jorge Mardones concluded in an interview (Edwards 1991, p.392) after a long career:

> I do not know why there is a generalized attitude of doubt concerning results reported in papers coming from Latin American laboratories. In order to overcome this situation, we need to be extremely certain about the accuracy and high significance of our results, before submitting a paper for publication. I feel that this is an advantage, because the worst thing a scientist can do is to pollute the scientific environment with data of poor value.

Before submitting a manuscript, an author should find a mentor or an experienced investigator who could read through the article and give advice on the presentation of the results. This may however be difficult in many countries where the addiction research milieu is very small. A survey of Nigerian papers published in a psychology journal showed that more than 75% of the articles were published by single authors, a figure that was much higher than that found in American journals at the time (Obot, personal communication, 2004). One suggestion is to try to work in a team that includes people with expertise in different areas, such as statisticians and social scientists. This may help to improve the quality of the study, and enhance its appeal to a greater number of readers. Another possibility is to work within a joint project with researchers from non-LAMI countries, or within a large, international network. This is in most cases only possible if you have already published in an international English language journal, or work with other researchers who have international contacts and reputation. International conferences can provide possibilities for networking, but to attend them you need financial resources.

Technical requirements are relatively easy to identify and follow. A more difficult challenge is that conventions about how to write an article differ among countries. Burrough-Boenisch (2003, p.2), in a text on editing problems, gives some examples that show how culturally embedded our scientific writing endeavours are. For an Anglo-American, the author states, the German tradition of writing may seem both pretentious and less well organized. The four-unit pattern of writing, which is traditional in some Asian cultures, such as China, Japan, Korea and Thailand, may give an incoherent impression. And when French scientists transfer the French convention of reporting science in the present tense to their English writing, they seem to be stating general truths, rather than describing their own procedures and findings.

In most cases it is not possible for an author to communicate with the readers of a journal if she or he cannot talk to them in the 'scientific dialect' of that particular publication. (This is of course also true when you choose a publication channel within one linguistic area.) This requires that the author is fairly well acquainted with the specific journal, knows what types of article are published and in what format.

Some English language journals are more sympathetic than others to articles from other countries and cultures. This is possible to find out by:

- looking at the journal's mission statement to see if they have any policy regarding articles submitted from different countries or cultures;

- checking whether the journal has previously published articles by non-English language authors;

- checking to what extent the editorial board is international, which may imply a greater understanding of cultural diversity and a more multicultural peer reviewer pool; and

- contacting the editor to find out if the journal may be interested in your work - pointing out its particular importance and the possible mitigating circumstances of being from a LAMI or non-English speaking country.

CROSSING THE LANGUAGE BORDER

Montgomery (2004) points out that the linguistic future of the world will be one of diversity, bilingualism or even multilingualism. An important goal in this world will therefore be 'to increase tolerance towards variation in scientific English - to avoid the imperial attitude that one standard must be obeyed' (p. 1335). Until this tolerance is developed, however, authors of scientific articles have to take the language issue seriously.

As noted above, the way in which authors present their results is often crucial to how the editor and reviewers will view the research report. The importance of good English language usage cannot be over-emphasised. The presentation of the study and the results is particularly important when the topic or setting may seem new and exotic to the editor and reviewers. It is not just a matter of using the right terminology. Many English-speaking editors and reviewers (in the same way as many French, German or Swedish speaking editors) will have a rather strict idea of what constitutes good language. Gosden (1992), in his survey of editors of physics, chemistry and biology journals, identified features that English language journal editors found most important when judging texts by non-English language authors: sentences should be linked logically and clearly; they should be grammatically correct; the language used when making your claims should be skilful; and the author should use language in a way that reflects awareness of his or her status.

Should one do a full language check before sending in an article? Although it is expensive and time consuming, the answer is YES. If a researcher is certain that she or he has a good case, a more experienced person has read the article and found it good, and the author wants to publish it in a journal with no resources to help with language editing, it will definitely increase the chances of acceptance. There is also the risk that if the paper is considered to be a 'borderline case', it will be rejected if there are language problems. However, in rare cases, if the author knows that the journal and the editor have a policy of accepting articles by non-English language authors and has the resources to do a language check, it may not be necessary to have perfect English at the time of the first submission. But this is a case where contacting the editor beforehand is definitely worthwhile.

KILLING TWO BIRDS WITH ONE STONE: DUAL LANGUAGE PUBLICATION

Where the topic of the article is such that it would be important to publish both at the national level and in an international journal, the author could consider trying to publish the same text in more than one language. In fact, if an author feels that his or her results should be considered in the development of local policy, publication of the results in an international journal may very well give the findings more prestige among the politicians of his or her country. Some addiction journals will agree to publish an article that has already been published in another language, or to simultaneously publish the article in several languages. A few addiction journals have officially established networks with this aim (*Addiction* and *Exartisis*; *Addiction* and *Sucht; Drugs: Education, Prevention and Policy* and *Nordisk alkohol- & narkotikatidskrift*). Others may be sympathetic to this idea.

These practices do not violate ethical codes regarding duplicate publication (see Chapter 12) as long as the editors agree, and the simultaneous publication is mentioned along with the source of the original. The general rule for the author is to find out the policy of the journal(s), if there is an interest in presenting the article to several audiences.

IMPORTANCE OF NATIONAL AND LOCAL PUBLICATIONS

As a researcher one should not be blinded by the prestige of internationalism, but instead try to protect the diversity and applicability of research. The diffusion of relevant research to a national audience fulfils important democratic, social and health policy aims. The development of culturally specific research is also important for the global development of addiction research. Nevertheless, some research may lack universal relevance.

Research on specific treatment systems, special treatment modalities or on effects of nationally implemented policy measures in LAMI countries may sometimes be irrelevant outside their national or regional audience. In parallel, some of the research published in the big international journals, based on findings in North America or Europe, may not be relevant in other cultural circumstances or in developing countries.

As long as most of the important databases and indexing systems favour English language journals and journals from the affluent countries, journals published in LAMI countries and non-English journals may be regarded as less prestigious publication channels. However, in some countries, such as Nigeria, there has been a growing acceptance of locally published papers as part of a person's academic curriculum vitae. This situation may be helped by the recently established *African Journal of Drug and Alcohol Studies*. The journal was set up in response to the fact that the number of addiction researchers in Africa has grown and that some of the issues of national importance would not be of interest to international journals, the only channels for African researchers in earlier times. The wider acceptance of local publications also recognizes the reality that it is difficult for many researchers to get published in international journals. The number of scientists has increased, but not the resources and support, such as libraries and translation services, which are needed to conduct the kind of research and produce the kind of article that would be interesting for an international journal. This does not mean that the research is not valuable.

For an African researcher or researchers from other LAMI regions, pragmatism in the choice of a publication channel seems essential. As noted above, it can sometimes be problematic to rely only on national or local journals, especially those with few resources, but the situation may be improving.

CONCLUSIONS

Addiction problems and their solutions have strong local, national and cultural characteristics. Addiction research needs to communicate within these milieus. It is important to preserve linguistic and cultural diversity in the communication of scientific findings. Addiction problems are an unfortunate fact of life in many countries, and are growing in Latin America, Africa and Asia. International communication is clearly necessary for the spread of information and can be personally rewarding, as indicated in Box 3.1. The research communities in LAMI countries need support and encouragement. In a world of increasing globalization, the English-speaking developed world can easily become isolated, not recognizing that it has much to learn from experience in other parts of the world.

Many international and English language journals are sympathetic towards publishing research from other countries and linguistic areas, as a recent survey of journal editors has shown (Edwards and Savva 2002a and b). The activities within international organizations such as ISAJE will hopefully increase the awareness of resource, language and cultural issues among journal editors and the research community in general, through fostering networks and striving to change the discriminative practices of the databases and indexing systems. This is the good news for researchers from less resourced countries and non-English language cultures.

The bad news is that the competition within research is hardening, strengthening existing hierarchies in the world of science and putting increasing demands on researchers from LAMI countries. Researchers from these countries face special challenges. General advice and rules of conduct are of limited value.

Hard work and a good dose of pragmatism are needed if you want to communicate your research to the appropriate audience and get scientific credit for it.

In this chapter we have pictured the unique challenges faced by addiction scientists who work outside the cultural and linguistic mainstream. It will take a great deal of skill, persistence and courage to get to the top of your field. But the rewards awaiting you at the summit may be that much greater, because you will have acquired the skill to read the map and orient yourself both in your country of origin and in the world that lies beyond.

BOX 3.1 PROFESSOR MUSTAPHA SOUEIF ON 'BILINGUALISM' IN ADDICTION PUBLISHING

The following quotation from an interview with Professor Mustapha Soueif, an Egyptian psychologist, cannabis researcher and internationally recognized addiction expert, shows how exciting it can be to confront the challenges of publishing in multiple languages and different cultures:

I have to be 'bilingual' if I care for international readership and acknowledgement. And bilingualism is not an easy job. You cannot reduce it to a pendular movement from Arabic to English and vice versa. Rather, you switch off a whole way of thinking, feeling and mode of expression; and tune yourself to a totally different wave length. At the start of your career you find that this exercise is really tough, and overloaded with frustrating moments. But you accept it the way it is, because you chose to have it this way. Gradually, you attain higher levels of relevant skills; your troubles decrease, yet they never disappear.

Another implication is that you have to accept a double load of responsibilities most of the time; I mean your local duties (the university, the private clinic, sharing in national meetings and writing in periodicals) and international requests (usually meetings and writings). Sometimes you have to turn down a request from one side or the other. But you have to be very careful if you intend to play the two roles with optimum smoothness. It takes creative effort to find points of convergence between both, and it is, therefore, highly rewarding.

A third implication is that gradually your role is redefined for you. You are no more just a local scientist with international resonance. You are transformed into a culture-transmitter or a bridging factor. You are expected to behave as a medium for communication between two cultures. Whenever you cross the fence you should do something useful and interesting to the people on the other side. Of course what you carry with you should always be relevant to scientific endeavour. But it is sometimes peripheral. Yet it proves to be quite instrumental in promoting mutual understanding between investigators trying to transcend national and/or cultural barriers. This is all the more important when it comes to an area like research in drug abuse.

Soueif, M. from Edwards ed. (1991, p.438-439)

REFERENCES

Babor, T.F. (1993) Megatrends and dead ends: alcohol research in global perspective. Alcohol Health and Research World 17(3), 177-186.

Burrough-Boenisch, J. (2003) Editing texts by non-native speakers of English. In: Science Editors Handbook. Surrey, UK: European Association of Science Editors.

Edwards, G., ed. (1991) Addictions: personal influences and scientific movements. New Brunswick and London: Transaction Publishers.

Edwards, G. and Savva, S. (2002a) Hur icke-engelskspråkiga tidskrifter på beroendeområdet arbetar med språkliga frågor: en enkät av ISAJE. [How non-English language journals in the addiction work with language questions: an ISAJE questionnaire.] Nordisk alkohol- & narkotikatidskrift 19(3), 207-210.

Edwards, G. and Savva, S. (2002b) Hur engelskspråkiga tidskrifter på beroendeområdet arbetar med språkliga frågor: en enkät av ISAJE. [How English language journals work with language questions: an ISAJE questionnaire.] Nordisk alkohol- & narkotikatidskrift 19(3), 211-215.

Ezzati, M., Lopez, A.D., Rodgers, A., Vander Horn, S. and Murray, C.J.L. (2002) The comparative risk assessment collaborating group (2002). Selected major risk factors and global and regional burden of disease. Lancet 360, 1347- 1360.

Gosden, H. (1992) Research Writing and NNSs: from the Editors. Journal of Second Language Writing 1(2), 123-139.

Holmgren, M. and Schnitzer, S.A. (2004) Science on the rise in developing countries. PLOS Biology, January 2(1):e1-. http://www.pubmedcentral.nih.gov/articlerender.fcgi?artid=314462

Ingwersen, P. (2002) Visibility and impact of research in psychiatry for north European countries in EU, US and world context. Scientometrics 54(1), 131-144.

Linardi, P.M., Coelho, P.M.Z. and Costa, H.M.A. (1996) The 'impact factor' as a criteria for the quality of scientific production is a relative, not absolute, measure. Brazilian Journal of Medical and Biological Research 29, 555-561.

Maisonneuve, H., Berard, A. and Bertrand, D. (2003) International submissions to journals. Lancet, 361, 1388-1389.

Midanik, L. T. (2004) Biomedicalization and alcohol studies: implications for policy. Journal of Public Health Policy 25(2), 211-228.

Montgomery, S. (2004) Of towers, walls, and fields: perspectives on language in science. Science 303, 27 February, 1333-1335.

Obot, I. Personal communication, February 2004.

Room, R., Jernigan, D., Carlini-Marlatt, B., Gureje, O., Mäkelä, K., Marshall, M., Medina-Mora, M.E., Monteiro, M., Parry, C., Partanen, J., Riley, L. and Saxena, S. (2002) Alcohol in developing societies: a public health approach. Helsinki: Finnish Foundation for Alcohol Studies, in collaboration with World Health Organization, vol. 46.

Saxena, S., Levaw, I., Maulik, P. and Saraceno, B. (2003) How international are the editorial boards of leading psychiatric journals? Lancet 361, 6090.

Targino, M.G. and Garcia, J.C.R. (2000) Ciencia Brasiliera na base de dados do Institute for Scientific Information [Brazilian periodicals in the Institute for Scientific Information]. Ciencia da Informacao - Brasilia 29, 103-117

Volpato, G.L. and Freitas, E.G. (2003) Desafios na publicação cientifíca [Challenges in scientific publication]. Pesquisa Odontologica Brasileira 17 (suppl. 1), 49-56.

West, R. and McIlwaine, A. (2002) What do citation counts count for in the field of addiction? An empirical evaluation of citation counts and their link with peer ratings of quality. Addiction 97, 501-504.

World Bank (2003) World Development Indicators 2003. Washington DC: The World Bank.

World Health Organization (2004) Galvanizing mental health research in low- and middle-income countries: role of scientific journals. A joint statement issued by editors of scientific journals publishing mental health research. Department of Mental Health and Substance Abuse, WHO, Geneva, January 2004. Bulletin of the World Health Organization 82(3), 226-228.

CHAPTER 4
GETTING STARTED: PUBLICATION ISSUES FOR GRADUATE STUDENTS, POSTDOCTORAL FELLOWS, AND OTHER NOVICE ADDICTION SCIENTISTS

DOMINIQUE MORISANO, THOMAS F. BABOR, ERIN L. WINSTANLEY, AND NEO MOROJELE

INTRODUCTION

In recent years, there has been increasing pressure on graduate students[1], postdoctoral fellows, masters degree students, and even research assistants and lab technicians to write or co-author scientific publications. In some countries, the number of publication credits is now a key criterion for students' acceptance to advanced study, postdoctoral opportunities, and internship placements, as well as for the receipt of scholarships, fellowships, grants, and employment. More competitive universities sometimes urge students to compose theoretical papers and review articles, and to write up unpublished data from their research labs. In some countries, students are advised to publish articles while writing the monograph dissertation; in others, they are expected to focus solely on the production of a dissertation that will lead to (eventual) publication(s); in still others, dissertations are based on published articles. In any case, authorship is now at the forefront of issues faced in doctoral and post-graduate education in many countries.

This chapter presents issues that are particularly relevant to publishing as a graduate student or postdoctoral fellow, but anyone early in his or her publishing career might benefit from reading through the topics covered. The chapter begins with a discussion of general issues related to authorship, and then addresses the more specific topic of publishing graduate-level theses. The latter section focuses on the entire process of thesis publication, ranging from issues that might come up prior to writing one's thesis all the way to eventual post-publication submission to an appropriate journal. Our main sources of information on this topic come from North American universities, but the issues and solutions discussed below should be relevant to students at universities in other regions. In addition, special attention is given to the challenges encountered by students or novice investigators in less resourced countries.

GENERAL ISSUES

The challenges and rewards of publishing as a graduate student, postdoctoral fellow, or research assistant often include making authorship decisions, determining timetables, encountering ethical dilemmas, dealing with pressures to publish, opening doors for career advancement, and potentially gaining financial remuneration.

---

[1] Throughout the chapter, the term *graduate student* (interchangeable with the term *postgraduate student*) refers primarily to doctoral students, but might also apply to masters students and medical students who are incorporating research and/or theses into their studies.

AUTHORSHIP

As noted in Chapter 8, authorship of peer-reviewed journal articles is the "coin of the realm" in academic settings, although the ability to write even unpublished reports is a valuable asset in any work situation. For the great majority of graduate students, early-career authorship will only come from collaboration with faculty members[2], senior researchers, and supervisors. As such, both mentors and mentees should consider a number of ethical and practical issues that can arise (also see Chapters 11 and 12 for a discussion of ethical issues involved in authorship). At the heart of such faculty-student (or even supervisor-employee) collaborations lies an inherent power imbalance (Fine and Kurdek 1993; Murray 1998). Often, the faculty members with whom students have the most interactions (and thus the greatest chance to do research) are responsible for preparing letters of recommendation for those students, in addition to assigning their grades, providing them with critical feedback, and evaluating their work. Furthermore, many students start out with minimal experience and competence in publishing, and must rely on faculty support and guidance. Even if students and post-doctoral trainees are consulted during the process of assigning authorship, faculty members generally make the ultimate decisions on where (or whether) students are placed on the author list. Students who disagree with or misunderstand such decisions often fail to voice their opinions for fear of negatively influencing the ways in which those faculty members will evaluate them.

In addition, the academic level of the collaborating faculty member or supervisor can influence the authorship decision-making process. Senior faculty with established research grants might be more likely to give students on co-authored publications the opportunity for first authorship. With potentially bigger labs or projects and greater numbers of volunteers and research assistants, senior faculty might even provide their students with more chances to publish in general, handing over projects, ideas, and datasets to their mentees. In contrast, junior faculty members are often still under pressure to get their own names on publications in order to earn research grants and advance to higher faculty positions. As a result, they might be more concerned about sustaining and advancing their own careers than about taking time to help their students publish.

Box 4.1 provides a satirical view of authorship situations sometimes encountered by students who work on publications with more experienced or higher-ranked investigators. Although the cartoon might seem cynical, many students would agree that it is not very far from the truth in some research labs, centres, and departments. However, the procedures determining faculty-student co-authorship are likely to vary by discipline, institution, and even culture, and should ideally reflect a dynamic process that evolves as the authors revise and resubmit their article.

---

[2] For the general purposes of streamlining and efficiency, the term faculty member or faculty (as an adjective) is used throughout this chapter to represent any kind of higher education advisor, supervisor, teacher, or researcher who might otherwise be called a researcher, a lecturer (junior or senior), a professor, etc. It should be noted that, depending on the country and/or institution, different terminology is often used.

Box 4.1 "PILED HIGHER AND DEEPER" AUTHORSHIP CREDIT COMIC BY JORGE CHAM (2005)

Graduate students, postdoctoral fellows, and young professionals working in basic and applied research settings are often uninformed about acceptable procedures for deciding authorship within a given field or discipline. In addition, procedures seem to vary so greatly even within departments that it can be difficult to stay abreast of what constitutes acceptable practice. The availability of specific guidelines is indispensable to establish equal opportunities for student authorship and consistent procedures for student-faculty collaborations. As in the case of the more general issue of authorship (discussed above), there are specific guidelines available that can facilitate this process at some universities, and that can help to prevent problems from arising in the first place. Some examples of these guidelines are discussed below. If they are not readily available, however, it is often possible to adopt guidelines from another institution or professional society (see Chapter 8 for an example), especially when several students work with a sympathetic faculty member.

As a rule, graduate students should be the first authors of journal articles based on their thesis or dissertation manuscripts. Many disciplines and institutions enforce this broad principle. For example, the American Psychological Association's Ethical Principles of Psychologists and Code of Conduct (American Psychological Association, 2002) explicitly states, "Except under exceptional circumstances, a student is listed as principal author on any multiple-authored article that is substantially based on the student's doctoral dissertation" (Section 8.12). Further, the American Psychological Association indicates that faculty advisors should discuss publication credit with students as early as feasible and throughout the research and publication process. However, the "exceptional circumstances" mentioned highlight a universal grey area, and it is often the case that other factors might complicate seemingly straightforward authorship assignment, for instance when the graduate student's dissertation is based on part of their advisor's grant.

In line with changing times, several higher learning institutions have posted general authorship guidelines on their websites. In 1998, the University of Pennsylvania's Graduate Council of the Faculties (1998) put forth a policy (http://www.upenn.edu/grad/authorpolicy_alpha.html) requiring individual departments to develop and post guidelines regarding faculty student co-authorship in a way that reflects prevailing standards in each discipline, because different traditions of joint authorship exist in different disciplines and departments. Mandating such procedures within each graduate group clarifies expectations concerning authorship for both students and faculty members. Specific departmental guidelines cover such topics as authorship criteria (specific and general principles regarding the kind of work that warranted a publication credit), whom to consult in order to resolve disputes, and the issues that faculty should discuss with students when beginning joint projects. Examples of such issues include a) whether the graduate student would share authorship credit, b) the order of authorship expected, c) the division of labour on the project, and d) when to revisit or review work that is being completed by each collaborating member of the pair or group. As of 2007, the website of the University of Alberta (Canada) included a similar set of guidelines, originally developed in 1996 (http://www.uofaweb.ualberta.ca/vpres_policies/nav02.cfm?nav02=11203&nav01=11159)

In general, with the expansion of the Internet as the primary tool of communication in most circles of higher education, website-posted policies appear to be an efficient and user-friendly way of spreading authorship guidelines to young investigators, although those from low and middle income (LAMI) countries might not have adequate access to the Internet (as discussed in a later section of this chapter). Harvard Medical School (1999; http://www.hms.harvard.edu/integrity/authorship.html), McGill University (1995; http://www.mcgill.ca/researchoffice/policies/sponsored/policies/ethics/), Washington University in St. Louis (2002; http://www.wustl.edu/policies/authorship.html), and the University of Cambridge (2002; http://www.rsd.cam.ac.uk/about/policies/practice/), among some others, also provide statements on authorship for members of their institutions, though they are rather brief in nature. The University of Pennsylvania and University of Alberta guidelines provide the best models for the development of similar policies in higher learning institutes across the world. Such university-wide policies are an excellent way to keep students, postdoctoral fellows, and faculty members informed about the most fair and equitable procedures to follow in joint authorship situations.

In what has become a US benchmark article for writings on student-faculty co-authorship, Fine and Kurdek (1993) produced a set of authorship guidelines based on the idea that both faculty and students should meaningfully participate in the authorship decision-making process. Fine and Kurdek recommended that supervisors and faculty collaborators should provide new students and post-docs with information about how authorship decisions are made at the very initiation of joint projects. They also put forth a series of specific and potentially controversial recommendations about student authorship, arguing, for example, that supervisors cannot and should not expect as much from students as from experienced professional colleagues.

Instead, the authors suggested that there should be a different standard for the level of professional contribution required by students to attain a given level of authorship credit within a student-faculty collaboration. At the same time, however, they maintained that student contributions must be professional in nature: that is, creative, intellectual, and integral to completion of the paper. Examples of such contributions might include developing the research design, writing sections of the manuscript, integrating diverse theoretical perspectives, developing new conceptual models, designing assessments, contributing to data-analysis decisions, and interpreting results. Other tasks such as entering data, carrying out statistical analyses specified by the supervisor, and typing a manuscript might warrant footnoted acknowledgement, but they would not, according to the authors, deserve authorship credit. Fine and Kurdek suggested that supervisors and students decide early in the publication process what combinations of professional activities would merit a given level of authorship credit for both parties.

Fine and Kurdek (1993) raised a variety of issues and case scenarios surrounding authorship in faculty-student collaborations that are still relevant in the fifteen years since their article was first published. Chapter 8 of this edition of *Publishing Addiction Science* is a direct response to articles like this, as well as to the diverse but brief and scattered array of individual university guidelines mentioned above. Students, postdoctoral fellows, and other early investigators in the process of article publication should refer often to the general set of very practical authorship guidelines provided in this chapter. These guidelines span the planning, drafting, and finalization stages of authorship. Indeed, Chapter 8 is an ideal place for beginning researchers to refer as they try to determine where (or if) they should appear on the papers of projects on which they have worked. The chapter touches on potentially controversial issues, such as what constitutes a substantive authorship contribution? For example, if a graduate student has developed, coordinated, and carried out a research project for a mentor or supervisor, but did not come up with the original idea, analyze or interpret the resulting data, or participate in the writing of the ensuing manuscript, does he or she deserve to be listed as an author on publications arising from the project? According to the recommendations in Chapter 8, the answer is no, as there is no involvement in the writing process (and to be an author, one must write!). However, one might argue that this student should at least be given the option of contributing in a more substantive way to the publication process in order to earn authorship. Students might also want to explicitly express their interest in being involved in future publications.

In summary, it is clear that there is a great amount of room for improvement in the authorship game for students, postdoctoral fellows, and early investigators. Furthermore, the opportunities to learn about this area are unlimited. The mentorship of a seasoned investigator can provide his or her students, postdoctoral fellows, or other trainees with a golden opportunity to learn how the publication process works. Unfortunately, the learning process has not been clearly documented in terms of student and young investigator rights, responsibilities, and roles. While progress has been made in clarifying the issues and formalizing some long overdue policies, much remains to be done at both the level of the academic institution and the level of the individual faculty and student. At the very least, the sharing of articles and chapters such as this one might help to raise awareness of the issues and how to deal with them.

PUBLISHING ONE'S THESIS OR DISSERTATION

For most addiction researchers and clinicians, graduate school represents the first opportunity to publish, whether the material is from a research project, a master's thesis, or part of the doctoral dissertation. As noted above, there are many incentives to begin publishing early, particularly for those who are interested in pursuing academic careers. Given the amount of work that is invested in the preparation of a thesis or dissertation, this is often the ideal place to begin one's publication career. The following section describes the publication process.

BEFORE WRITING ONE'S DISSERTATION: FORMAT CONSIDERATIONS

There are several different doctoral dissertation formats, which vary in acceptability depending on the country and the university in which they are written. Two of the more popular formats are the monograph style and the separate manuscript style. Many graduate programs increasingly favour dissertations that depart from the traditional monograph style and instead facilitate the translation of the dissertation into publishable manuscripts. The manuscript style of dissertation, while it might have different names, generally requires that chapters be written in article format. For example, at the Johns Hopkins Bloomberg School of Public Health, a student can write either a traditional monograph style dissertation or a "three-paper option." The latter format requires that three of the dissertation chapters take the shape of publishable manuscripts, with one chapter usually serving as a literature review, and two chapters comprising empirical analyses. Some universities require that the resulting "papers" be submitted for publication as part of degree requirements; others require that they already be published (and perhaps supplemented with a synthesis or independent introduction).

The extent to which manuscripts need to be inter-related and reflect a single focus of research, as in a monograph-style dissertation, varies across different institutions, departments, and advisors. It is contingent, in part, on the clarity of the institutional guidelines provided. Anecdotal evidence suggests that the rules are not concrete. Furthermore, if one is writing a literature review chapter, it is helpful to keep in mind that the majority of addiction journals do not accept unsolicited review papers, and that getting this type of manuscript published can be a special challenge.

If one has the opportunity to choose which dissertation format to take, it is important to consider the benefits and particular challenges of a style that is meant to facilitate the publication process[3]. For example, even if one chooses to write one's thesis in the manuscript style, resulting chapters might still require significant revision if they need to be shortened and formatted later for a particular journal, and written with a broader audience in mind than one's dissertation committee (Chamberlin 1999).

---

[3]In the Nordic countries (Norway, Sweden, Finland, Denmark), dissertation articles must be published before the dissertation can be passed.

IN THE TRENCHES: WRITING ONE'S DISSERTATION WITH PUBLICATION IN MIND

While writing the thesis or dissertation, it might be helpful to think about whether or not it will eventually be suitable for journal publication. If the answer is yes, then several issues arise that should be addressed sooner rather than later. For instance, if one hopes to publish one's data in a particular journal when the thesis requirement has been completed, it might be useful to consider the intended audience of that journal early on (See Chapter 2 for issues related to choosing a journal). One might also tailor the writing and formatting style of the dissertation towards specific journal requirements (Luey 2004). Even if a journal has not yet been identified, the audience can be narrowed down (e.g., to clinicians or policy makers) in a way that can help refine the scope of the manuscript.

Furthermore, it is likely that a significant amount of time will lapse between creating initial drafts of one's dissertation and preparing to publish the content in a journal. Accordingly, it will be important to maintain adequate documentation of analyses and datasets. The lengthy combined process of writing one's dissertation and preparing a future manuscript could result in the situation where, anywhere from months to years later, a journal reviewer (or even committee member) requests that data analyses be revised or substantially expanded. While this issue should be relevant to all authors, the significant time that it takes to complete the dissertation amplifies the importance of keeping an adequate record of completed work.

In sum, the wise student will balance dissertation requirements with potential journal submission requirements. This is not always easy. Dissertations typically require a much higher level of detail than most journal manuscripts. This means that significant portions of the dissertation will need to be reduced, edited, and streamlined for publication. Writing style might also need to be altered depending on the intended audience (e.g., dissertation committee vs. journal editors and reviewers vs. the scientific community-at-large). There are benefits to this process, however. Chamberlin (1999) notes that the process of converting dissertations to publishable articles teaches graduate students not only to summarize research findings in a succinct manner, but also how to communicate to a broader audience than faculty and committee members.

As one works during those final dark hours to make last-minute edits and cross-check references, keep in mind that in addition to fulfilling degree requirements and contributing to scientific advancement, all of one's hard work can be directly applied to making progress on the career front. Writing the dissertation with publication in mind makes these connections all the more salient.

PREPARING FOR PUBLICATION

Once the dissertation has been approved, and the appropriate celebrations have commenced, the time for publication is nigh[4]. Frequently, suggestions made during the final dissertation defence will be relevant to the initial stages of preparing for publication. During this phase, several issues will inevitably come to the surface.

[4]For students at some institutions, the dissertation articles must be published before the dissertation can be approved, and publication must therefore be prepared at an earlier stage.

The first is authorship. As discussed above, the student should be the first author the majority of the time. In the case of multiple authors, institutional and disciplinary guidelines, or even the authorship chapter in this book (See Chapter 8), can help to determine authorship order. If committee members are to be invited as potential co-authors, it should be made clear that all authors are required to have made substantial contributions to the journal manuscript itself, as opposed to simply "being a part" of the dissertation development conversation. Given the fact that many journals now require written statements that specify authorship contribution, this is no longer just a traditional courtesy.

Assignment of authorship is a dynamic process that will depend on the amount of time that has lapsed since graduation, the extent of revisions required for publication, and the context in which those revisions are being made. For example, revisions are sometimes required at the final stage of the dissertation approval process, and it might not be feasible to anticipate the target journal until after graduation. If substantial revisions are requested, the opportunity might arise to seek expertise outside of the dissertation committee. The recruitment of new co-authors can offer several advantages. First, fresh insight might facilitate the process of tailoring a manuscript for a particular target audience. Alternatively, external experts might be able to address weaknesses in a manuscript that fall outside the new graduate's field knowledge.

One should also consider the publication of the dissertation itself, with or without an accompanying short-form article. This is a requirement at many European institutions. Some graduate programs might recommend and provide structured guidance regarding the process of indexing the dissertation, copyrighting dissertation materials, and publishing the dissertation as a complete document. Alternatively, there are an increasing number of low-cost opportunities to publish one's full work on the Internet. A sampling of websites offering this possibility is presented in Box 4.2. For example, Dissertation Abstracts Online indexes dissertation abstracts and disseminates the data across a wide range of literature search engines. ProQuest Dissertations and Theses allows new graduates the option to purchase a permanent URL for dissertation abstracts; this can be useful for citation purposes. Other sites offer interested readers the choice to either download or receive a paper-copy of a dissertation for a nominal fee.

In general, however, if one is looking to reach the widest audience, writing the dissertation in manuscript style can facilitate the process of actually achieving one or more timely first-author publications. Finding the time for even one paper can be difficult after graduation, when important life changes (e.g., finding or starting a new job, starting a family, catching up on things that might have been on hold during graduate school) are often inevitably competing for one's time. This is why a post-doctoral position, when available, offers an ideal solution: the very nature of the job often includes the development of publications as a primary goal. Further, depending on the area of research covered, post-doctoral research positions that are limited to 1 to 3 years might not allow a sufficient amount of time to be a part of a new project from inception to publication. Therefore, entering the position with one's own dissertation to publish provides an immediate publishing goal.

Box 4.2 ONLINE DISSERTATION INDEXING AND PUBLISHING RESOURCES

1. UMI Dissertation Publishing (http://il.proquest.com)
   a. ProQuest Dissertations & Theses (PODT) database
   b. American Doctoral Dissertations (ADD)
   c. Masters Abstracts International (MAI)
   d. Dissertations & Theses @
2. Dissertation Abstracts International (DAI)/Comprehensive Dissertation Index
3. Networked Library of Digital Dissertations and Theses (www.ndltd.org)
4. Theses Canada Portal (http://www.collectionscanada.gc.ca/thesescanada/index-e.html)
5. DissOnline (http://www.dissonline.de/index.htm)
6. Die Deutsche Bibliothek
7. Database of African Theses and Dissertations
8. Networked European Deposit Library (http://nedlib.kb.nl)
9. Google Scholar (http://scholar.google.com/)

PUBLICATION TIMELINES

Some supervisors and faculty members feel that it is important to set limits on the time that a student has to publish his or her thesis or project data in a scholarly journal. When this time limit is expired, it is thought that the right to publish these data should be forfeited to the faculty supervisor or members of the dissertation committee. It is a common belief that if work is not published in a timely manner, it is unlikely to be published at all (Rudestam and Newton 1992). In most cases, the student should have the right to publish his or her results, even with considerable delays. However, if the timely dissemination of important scientific findings is at the root of such policies, then these procedures are probably warranted. Graduate students sometimes lose interest in publishing thesis and project data after their projects have been defended (or even before!), and important or interesting scientific results are often buried under more salient tasks at hand (e.g., seeking full-time employment). Regarding specific policies, this is an issue that supervisors and dissertation-committee members should discuss with their students early in the process of collaboration. Perhaps the most reasonable solution for the various parties in these cases is to designate a mutually agreeable time period together, and then sign a written agreement that would bind them to it.

One example of an individual professor's policy that was put together and published on the Internet is that of Karl Wuensch, PhD (2006, East Carolina University, http://core.ecu.edu/psyc/wuenschk/thauth.htm). On his website, Professor Wuensch clearly states his policy regarding timeliness of publication for student theses. For example, if the thesis is the student's idea, the student does most of the work (i.e., collects and analyzes the data, writes the manuscript), and the manuscript is prepared within 18 months from the date of the initiation of the research or one year from the date of the defence of the thesis, then the student is the first author. If warranted by their contributions, the thesis director and other committee members might also be listed as authors. However, if the student does not complete the research, including defending and depositing the thesis and preparing the manuscript for submission for publication within the time limits mentioned above, then all rights to use of the data from that thesis revert to the director of the thesis committee. On his website, Professor Wuensch also indicates procedures for other situations that might arise, for example, if the student-submitted manuscript is not accepted upon initial submission to a journal.

Professor Bruce M. Shore, an educational psychologist at McGill University (Montreal, Canada), took this process a step further, and created a formal contract (Shore, 2007) covering various supervision matters such as authorship order, publication credit, and general responsibilities of both the advisor and the student within the supervisor-supervisee relationship. He requires that all of his students read, discuss, and sign the contract prior to agreeing to work with him, and he often raises the issues involved with authorship before projects even germinate. He agreed to share his contract as an example of an advisor-advisee agreement for the purposes of this chapter (see Appendix 4.3). The process outlined in the box might even be described as refreshing, for regardless of whether a student agrees with the various conditions of the contract, at least the issues are discussable and out in the open from the very onset of the mentor-mentee relationship.

Moreover, in the discussion of publication timelines, it is important to remember that there are always exceptions. If one fails to publish one's article within the agreed-upon period, despair is not the only alternative. As long as steady progress is shown, the pressure that might come from thesis advisor(s), co-authors, and committee members can be reduced. Sometimes the issue lies not even with one's own progress, but with getting co-authors to respond in a reasonable amount of time. While all authors might struggle with the multiple-author publication process, novice writers in particular must learn to develop effective strategies, ideally from their advisors. A basic word of advice is to set specific time frames for co-authors with concrete deadlines and frequent email reminders. If response time becomes highly unreasonable, a direct conversation with these authors about their place on the manuscript might become necessary.

FINANCIAL REMUNERATION

Conversations about financial remuneration can arise in the creation of a manuscript. Some faculty and supervisors feel that students who are paid as research or graduate assistants should not be given authorship because credit for performed work is being given in the form of a salary. These same faculty members often feel that publication credit replaces the need for financial remuneration, as the students will ultimately benefit from having their name listed on a paper. Fine and Kurdek (1993) are firm in their position that paying a research assistant or graduate student should not substitute for authorship credit, where credit for professional and intellectual contributions is due. The controversy surrounding financial remuneration clearly indicates that this topic should be covered when creating institutional and departmental guidelines surrounding authorship procedures. In light of the authorship criteria discussed elsewhere in this chapter and in Chapter 8, it is clear that neither financial reimbursement nor its absence should be considered in the determination of authorship credits.

THE NITTY GRITTY: SUBMITTING A MANUSCRIPT AND THE FIRST REJECTION

After carefully choosing a target journal (see Chapter 2 for advice), one should normally write a cover letter to the journal's editor and a brief description of the manuscript. Some journal editors might have sympathy for novice writers when sending back written feedback (e.g., by providing more detail), so one's inexperience could potentially be worth noting in the cover letter. One should be mindful that some journals require specific content in the cover letter (e.g., word count or a statement of conflict of interest), so author guidelines should be consulted ahead of time. These are most often found either in the paper copy of the journal itself, or in "instructions for authors" on journal websites.

Even for the most fastidious researchers and stellar writers, the dreaded day will likely arrive when a rejection letter arrives in the mail. If the rejected work is based on one's dissertation data, the decision can be particularly devastating, given the time and energy invested (and all of issues considered above). It is therefore important to realise that rejection is simply a part of the writing and publication process, and to know that even senior researchers have manuscripts rejected from time to time. It is surprisingly easy to forget that if one is reaching for the stars and submitting to a competitive journal, acceptance rates are low. The most productive step to take upon rejection is to read the reviewer feedback, incorporate it as much as possible into a new draft, and try, try again (at another journal, unless resubmission is specifically invited). Box 4.3 provides a first-person account of how one of the authors reacted to her first rejection letter, and what she would have done differently in retrospect.

Box 4.3 DEALING WITH REJECTION (BY NEO MOROJELE)

Shortly after the defence of my doctoral thesis, I prepared and submitted an article that was based on my PhD studies to a journal for publication. I was extremely dejected upon receiving the rejection letter from the journal's editor. This rejection led me, unreasonably, to question the quality and validity of my doctoral work, to which I had devoted hard work, many years, and much energy. My feelings were compounded by the fact that I had already been involved in the publication process--as a minor co-author of work from previous research assistantships, and as a primary author of papers based on earlier stages of the doctoral research. I could not understand why the final product (my doctoral dissertation) was not as worthy of publication as pieces of work that I considered to be less complete. At the time, I was not at all familiar with the range of possible reasons why articles might not be accepted for publication on first submission, or at all (see Chapter 9 for a discussion of this topic). If faced with the same situation today, I would welcome the feedback (often both valuable and valid), revise the paper accordingly, and submit it to another (perhaps more appropriate) journal. Knowing about the process of rejection ahead of time can simultaneously temper hurt feelings and facilitate a productive response.

SPECIAL ISSUES OF RELEVANCE TO STUDENTS AND YOUNG INVESTIGATORS FROM LOW AND MIDDLE INCOME COUNTRIES

Thus far, this chapter has focused on publication issues that are likely to be most relevant to those from resourced countries with an established scientific community in the addiction field. Students and junior investigators in less resourced countries face a number of different issues related to conducting and disseminating research data. The following section addresses the special challenges encountered by students and novice addiction researchers from low- and middle-income (LAMI) countries, as well as those from LAMI countries who have received their degrees from universities in developed countries and have then returned to a developing country. There is an important need at both the national and international levels to publish research on addiction issues that is relevant to countries outside of Europe, Australia, and North America. High-quality dissertation research can have a major influence on addiction science. Those from LAMI countries have a particularly strong obligation to conduct research and publish the results, given the importance of research for shaping the policy agenda and influencing programmes in these countries.

Indeed, much of the existing knowledge about which policies and treatments "work" for addressing addiction-related problems is based on studies conducted in North America, Europe, and Australia. Research conducted in LAMI countries can help to determine whether those policies and treatments popular in the developed countries have the same impact in other parts of the world.

GENERAL CAPACITY CHALLENGES

Publishing in countries with minimal research infrastructure is particularly challenging because publishing often takes a back seat to the tasks directly related to conducting the research. The final product is more often a report for a local or national agency than a formal journal article. Reports are an important mechanism to communicate research findings. However, redrafting some of these reports as journal articles would allow the data to reach a broader scientific audience.

Finding the opportunity to redraft reports under such work constraints can be a significant, albeit surmountable, challenge. If the immediate work environment does not provide novice researchers with sufficient opportunities to learn how to write for journal publication, external resources can help to fill that gap. For example, the International Society of Addiction Journal Editors (ISAJE) has developed a writing mentorship program that provides novice writers with the opportunity to be mentored by senior researchers (see www.isaje.net for more information).

In South Africa, as in many other LAMI countries, the capacity of individuals to conduct and publish research varies considerably across institutions. In many academic environments, pay is low, teaching loads are high, and faculty members have competing demands on their time that prevent them from writing up their work. For example, personal financial constraints might compel academics to undertake other activities, such as seeing private patients, to supplement their incomes. Further, academics in LAMI countries often have minimal staff support and conduct the bulk of their research work unassisted. Researchers in better-resourced environments are more likely to have staff to assist them with many of the activities that are required to write and submit papers for publication (e.g., literature reviews, data entry, data analysis).

Some researchers from LAMI countries might at times fear that the standard of their work does not meet the current requirements of certain journals. With the development and utilisation of increasingly sophisticated equipment and statistical techniques in higher-income countries, the perception might arise that any research that is not state-of-the-art is not publishable. This is surely not the case, however. As stated above, research from LAMI countries provides policymakers in the arena of substance use and abuse with culturally and contextually specific data and evidence-based treatments. When implementing laws, treatment policies, or new research projects in South Africa, for example, it is undoubtedly more useful to have an understanding of the research, population, and resources as they have been studied in South Africa versus, for example, Canada. Further, it is important for researchers in Europe, Australia, and North America to have a more global perspective when developing their own research protocols and policies. Finally, exposing researchers from non-LAMI countries to researchers from within LAMI countries might lead to invaluable investigative collaborations by addiction scientists from different countries with similar interests and research goals. By regularly reading journal articles, attending conferences, and making external contacts with more resourced investigators, researchers from lower-income countries can not only gain exposure to the varied types of research that are being conducted internationally, but also gain confidence in the unique value of conducting and publishing research in a less-resourced country.

Supervisors of students and new researchers have an important role to play in the guidance and encouragement of their mentees through the publishing process. Advice on ways of preparing and writing up one's research findings in a manner that is likely to appeal to journal editors and reviewers can be useful to those who are used to writing brief reports, theses, or school papers. Supervisors can also provide valuable input on how to deal with rejections, address reviewers' concerns about submitted articles, and revise and resubmit manuscripts. In the case where one's supervisor might not yet have developed a strong publication record, it might be worthwhile to diplomatically negotiate working alongside a fellow faculty member who is more familiar with the process of publication.

TOPICS TO WRITE ABOUT

Considering the relative lack of studies coming out of many developing countries in a multitude of research areas, there are, theoretically, ample topics on which to publish. For those who have recently completed their dissertation or thesis, the question of what to write about is easily answered. Nevertheless, people in government agencies, clinical settings, and nongovernmental organizations might not have access to research findings to publish. Fortunately, there are many forms of non-research-related articles that may be published, including case studies, letters, and policy and opinion pieces, all of which can potentially stimulate public debate and influence policies. Before writing or submitting a new piece, especially one that is not based on hard data, it might be a good idea to read through the content of some relevant journals and acquaint oneself with their missions, areas of interest, and specific types of articles accepted for publication.

SELECTING AN APPROPRIATE JOURNAL

As indicated in previous chapters (see Chapter 2 in particular), there is a plethora of addiction journals to which one can submit one's manuscript for publication, but the selection of the "right" journal can present special challenges for those from LAMI countries. A number of competing considerations might influence the choice.

First, many academics are under pressure to publish in "high impact" peer-reviewed journals (see Chapter 2 for a discussion of impact factors). In South Africa, for example, this is particularly true for those in academic institutions that receive government subsidies based on the number of peer-reviewed publications produced. Moreover, in many institutions, the "rating" of academics and their potential for promotion is dependent on their publication records.

Second, the audience one would like to reach can influence journal choice, and the journal that best serves that purpose might not always be of a high standard. Authors might be put in a position where they have to choose between publishing in a "high impact" international journal, thereby furthering their research careers, or publishing in a "low impact" journal that reaches the public health audience of interest for the country. In some cases, however, a middle-ground solution can be reached (i.e., publishing one's papers in both types of journals, provided the right conditions are met; see Chapters 2 and 3 for a discussion of this topic). Third, the topical focuses or missions of different journals also influence one's choice. Some journal reviewers and editors might not have an interest in studies of non-American or non-European populations. Prior scanning of the contents of the journal being considered can help one to gauge the likelihood of interest in a non-European or North American health or addiction issue.

LANGUAGE

Many times a manuscript is rejected by a journal not because of the quality of the work itself but because of the authors' failure to express their ideas clearly. For some people whose first language is not English, writing up one's work can be difficult. Writing in English can even be a challenge for individuals who have attended English-language academic institutions, and who have written their theses or dissertations in English. Converting the dissertation or thesis to the shortened format required for most journals is additionally difficult and time-consuming when working in a second or third language, and can considerably slow down the time to publication. To address these language constraints, one could ask someone who is more fluent in English to assist in the editing of one's work. Some journals are willing to provide authors with editing assistance prior to submission. It might also be helpful to invite a native English speaker as a co-author. International conferences, when one has the financial means to attend them, can be a good forum for interacting with potential co-authors. In choosing a native English speaker as a co-author, however, it is important that this person be available and actively involved in the writing process. Chapters 2 and 3 of this volume discuss these issues in more detail.

ACCESS TO LITERATURE AND THE INTERNET

In many academic and other institutions, suboptimal access to journal articles, books, and other relevant literature is a major challenge that can hinder research and publication completion. This is particularly true for researchers in government or non-governmental organizations, where publishing is usually not a priority. Further, many academics do not have easy access to online journals because (a) they have unreliable connections to the Internet, (b) their institutions do not own subscriptions to the required journals, or (c) they might not know that some journal articles can be accessed online for free or at a reduced cost. Even paper copies of articles and other literature often have to be ordered via interlibrary loan systems that may be slow, costly, and unreliable. The Health InterNetwork Access to Research Initiative (HINARI) is one of several programs that have attempted to directly address such difficulties. HINARI provides free or reduced-cost online-journal access to health workers and researchers from local, not-for-profit institutions in low or lower-middle income countries. More information about eligibility criteria, instructions for access, and related initiatives is available on the HINARI website (http://www.who.int/hinari/en/). See Chapter 2 for additional discussion of online resources.

The lack of consistent and reliable access to the Internet also causes problems at the stage of submission of journal articles, which increasingly occurs online. This process can be lengthy even for those with good Internet access. Establishing collaborations with researchers who have better access to these resources might, in some cases, help to address this challenge.

CHALLENGES OF REJECTION

As noted above, it is quite common for manuscripts to not be accepted for publication on first submission. Papers from non-European and non-North American settings are sometimes rejected because the reviewers and/or editors are unfamiliar with the significance of the piece of research for the setting to which it applies. In such cases, authors may exercise their right to appeal the rejection of their paper if they believe it is based on ignorance on the part of the editor and/or reviewers. In preparing such an appeal, it might be helpful for the authors to include information that specifically addresses the significance of the research.

COMMENT: BE OPTIMISTIC

At the present time, despite the significant challenges addressed above, the relative lack of research from LAMI countries might be seen as an advantage for novice addiction scientists from those countries who are setting out to conduct research and begin their publishing careers. These researchers might be able to claim that their research has never been conducted or replicated before outside the developed world. Further, most of the aforementioned difficulties are surmountable, as evidenced by the current productivity of many academics working in under-resourced settings.

CONCLUSIONS: TAKE THE LONG VIEW

A career in addiction science is not for everyone, but it can be very rewarding for those who have the motivation and the aptitude (see Edwards 2002). The best way to start out is to try to publish one's dissertation, work closely with one or more well-published investigators, hone one's writing skills, and find a place for postdoctoral research or clinical training. Full-time research scientists are not the only ones who enjoy the rewards of publishing. Those who work in clinical settings, government agencies. and other organizations often find that journal publications are not encouraged, but neither are they likely to be discouraged. There is no reason not to try, and there are many reasons to proceed with the attempt.

The writing process from student to postdoctoral fellow to junior researcher is generally the same, although the level of autonomy certainly increases with each transition.

Greater autonomy is usually accompanied by more security regarding one's place in the publication process and an increased ease in negotiating authorship order. In this chapter, some basic guidelines have been outlined for inexperienced authors. It is important to keep in mind, however, that there is no magic formula for guaranteed publication. In the simplest of terms, one should find a good mentor and practice, practice, practice.

REFERENCES

American Psychological Association (2002). Ethical principles of psychologists and code of conduct. Website: http://www.apa.org/ethics/code2002.html (Last retrieved on 3 February 2008).

Cham, J. (2005). The author list: Giving credit where credit is due. Piled Higher & Deeper: A Grad Student Comic Strip. Website: http://www.phdcomics.com/comics/archive.php?comicid=562 (Last retrieved on 3 February 2008).

Chamberlin, J. (1999). Unpublished? Try your dissertation. APA Monitor Online, 30 (11). Website: http://www.apa.org/monitor/dec99/ed1.html (Last retrieved on 3 February 2008).

Edwards, G., ed (2002). Addiction: Evolution of a Specialist Field. Oxford, UK: Blackwell Publishing.

Fine, M. A., & Kurdek, L. A. (1993). Reflections on determining authorship credit and authorship order on faculty-student collaborations. American Psychologist, 48, 1141-1147.

Harvard Medical School Office for Research Issues (1999). Authorship guidelines. Website: http://www.hms.harvard.edu/integrity/authorship.html (Last retrieved on 3 February 2008).

Luey, B. (2004). Revising your dissertation: Advice from leading editors. University of California Press.

McGill University Research Policy Committee of the Faculty of Graduate Studies and Research (1995). McGill University policy on research ethics: Collaborative research. Website: http://www.mcgill.ca/researchoffice/policies/sponsored/policies/ethics/ (Last retrieved on 3 February 2008).

Murray, B. (1998). The authorship dilemma: Who gets credit for what? APA Monitor, 29(12). Website: http://www.apa.org/monitor/dec98/credit.html (Last retrieved on 3 February 2008).

Rudestam, K. E., & Newton, R. R. (1992). Surviving your dissertation: A comprehensive guide to content and process. Newbury Park, CA: Sage Publications.

Shore, B. M. (2007). Mutual expectations regarding research supervision (Contract). High Ability and Inquiry Research Group, Department of Educational and Counselling Psychology, McGill University. Electronic copy retrieved directly from author.

University of Alberta Faculty of Graduate Studies and Research Council (1996). Intellectual property policies: Guidelines for authorship. Website: http://www.uofaweb.ualberta.ca/vpres_policies/nav02.cfm?nav02=11203&nav01=11159 (Last retrieved on 3 February 2008).

University of Cambridge (2002). Good research practice: Dissemination and publication of results. Website: http://www.rsd.cam.ac.uk/about/policies/practice/ (Last retrieved on 3 February 2008).

University of Pennsylvania's Graduate Council of the Faculties (1998). Policy on fairness of authorship credit in collaborative faculty-student publications. Website: www.upenn.edu/grad/authorpolicy_alpha.html (Last retrieved on 3 February 2008).

Washington University in St. Louis (2002). Policies and procedures: Policy for authorship on scientific and scholarly publications. Website: http://www.wustl.edu/policies/authorship.html (Last retrieved on 3 February 2008).

Wuensch, K. (2006). Thesis authorship: Karl Wuensch's policy. Website: http://core.ecu.edu/psyc/wuenschk/thauth.htm (Last retrieved on 3 February 2008).

Appendix 4.1 EXAMPLE OF A RESEARCH SUPERVISOR-SUPERVISEE CONTRACT (EXCERPTED FROM SHORE, 2007)

Mutual Expectations Regarding Research Supervision
High Ability and Inquiry Research Group
Department of Educational and Counselling Psychology, McGill University

These notes are designed as guidelines to facilitate positive and mutually beneficial student-supervisor relationships, and to avoid problems on matters such as authorship and credits on publications, the extent of participation in activities other than the Thesis, Research Project, or Special Activity, and future access to data collected in the course of our work together. Some of the activities described below may be conducted in groups. Where these notes hinder rather than help, they should be amended to meet mutually acceptable needs, in general or as occasions arise.

A. Supervisor's Responsibilities

1. Meet regularly with students and be contactable at other times.
2. Arrange substitute supervision during extended absences.
3. Advise on course selection.
4. Assist in the preparation for comprehensive or oral examinations.
5. Help prepare conference and journal presentations based on work done in the program and assist with applications for support to attend suitable conferences at a reasonable distance and on whose programs students can earn a place.
6. Help apply for funds to cover direct research costs and to provide stipends to full-time students.
7. Provide feedback within a mutually agreed time-frame on written work submitted for review.

B. Students' Responsibilities

1. Regularly pursue work and keep the supervisor informed of progress or problems.
2. To a mutually agreed degree that respects other responsibilities and priorities, contribute to advancing team activities that further the common good of all of us working together -- e.g., workshops for teachers, parent contacts, library orders, data bases, maintaining bibliographies and mailing lists, convening meetings, maintaining computers and supplies. These tasks will be equitably distributed.
3. Join in the preparation of conference presentations and publications on research and other activities done with faculty members.

4. With appropriate guidance, prepare a draft version of the thesis or major report, normally within 3 months of its final presentation for master's degrees, or 6 months for doctoral degrees; after that point the supervisor may take over such preparation and the order of authorship may be changed (with APA and McGill authorship guidelines).
5. Apply for scholarships and bursaries, especially FQRSC, McGill, and SSHRC (where eligible).
6. Participate to a mutually agreed extent in teaching-related activities such as the TA course.
7. Take a professional role in one's discipline by undertaking at least one student or regular membership in an appropriate professional or academic organization.
8. Keep at McGill a copy of raw data, coding sheets, instruments, and subject-identification data.
9. Upon graduation, leave with the supervisor a printed copy of the main research report, and an electronic copy in modifiable form (e.g., not PDF) of any data and the text of the thesis or project.
10. Use Microsoft Word and APA style for written submissions.
11. Report annually in writing on progress and contributions (department and university forms).
12. Regularly attend and participate in research-team meetings.

C. Joint Responsibilities

1. Give full credit for the contributions of others and to research funding in all products.
2. Assign authorship according to the latest APA publication guidelines. (For example, if a thesis topic or report is entirely the student's original contribution, then the advisor's contribution is due a footnote. Shared scientific responsibility calls for co-authorship, with the student as first author on the main points of the student's research or those for which the student took primary creative responsibility, and the advisor as first author on any specific subpoints which the advisor contributed or a broader study of which the student is part.)
3. Both have unlimited access to the data collected on or about the topic of a thesis or project during the time worked together, plus any other that may be agreed to, giving due credit to its origin either by footnote or reference to previous publications.

D. Degree Covered by this Agreement

E. Comments, Additions, or Special Notes

F. Signatures

We agree to work together in an advisory relationship in accord with the above guidelines.

Supervisor	Date	Supervisor	Date
Printed name ______________________		Printed name ______________________	

CHAPTER 5
HOW TO WRITE A SCIENTIFIC PAPER FOR A PEER-REVIEWED JOURNAL
PHIL LANGE

INTRODUCTION

All of the chapters in this book speak to our aspirations to contribute to addiction science and to have a role in the scientific life of this field. In large part, this role comes through being published in peer-reviewed journals.

Susan Savva (2007)

A career in addiction science is largely built on the (perceived) quality of publications that a researcher (or a team of researchers) offers his or her colleagues. If these publications are numerous and of high quality, they lead to research funding and employment. To gauge the contribution of a researcher to addiction science, fellow researchers may consciously or unconsciously compute the number of worthwhile publications that a colleague has produced in relation to the number of years she has published. The greater speed of release for journal articles when compared with books, typically months versus years, means that those who wish to influence their field of study need to publish in peer-reviewed journals in order to communicate quickly their research results.

This chapter offers the novice author a step-by-step guide to prepare a paper for publication. Annotated bibliographies and references listed at the end suggest further readings worth consulting about specific problems. The chapter begins with the proviso that good paper written by a graduate student or a junior investigator may be highly praised by faculty and colleagues and yet fall short of being publishable. Indeed, editors regularly receive poor papers that are accompanied by a letter from a graduate student saying that his or her professor recommended submission. Yet praise from a professor or colleagues does not set aside the need for the novice author to scrutinize every aspect of her text to see that it conforms with the demands of a scientific article.

This chapter offers suggestions on how to use the style guide for the journal of your choice (for which there is additional information in Chapter 2), explains how to use a publication manual, and offers step-by-step guidance on the writing process itself. It also offers advice about working with colleagues, writing strategies, and how to maximize the worth of your paper for your selected journal. Some of the steps mentioned here are described in more detail, and sometimes with a valuable differing viewpoint, in Chapter 9.

This chapter is written for the reader who has completed several years of post-graduate education and has completed a research project that she wants to publish in a peer-reviewed journal, but is unsure of some of the basic steps in preparing the paper for submission.

This chapter is also appropriate for the reader who is already proficient in another field of science but wants to add papers in addiction science to her list of publications. For this scientist we advise caution: terms with everyday meanings may have different meanings for addiction scientists. For example, the word *recovery* connotes in the popular press and in everyday life that someone has undergone a course of clinical treatment, or perhaps an affiliation with Alcoholics Anonymous. But in addiction science, *recovery* means achieving precise behavioural goals or a given score on a measure and by a given point in time. There are enough such special concepts built around everyday language that the converting scientist is advised to gather a group of colleagues to advise her research from the beginning.

We assume here that the reader is already competent in all areas of writing a scientific paper. This chapter aims to fine tune competence in writing, not to teach the basics of science. At the other end of the continuum, a researcher whose papers are already often accepted in the journals of her choice will likely find little of interest here. Authors from developing or non-English speaking countries may wish first to read Chapter 3, which explores some of the special challenges encountered by researchers from developing and/or non-English speaking countries.

A successful publishing career means writing for a highly specific scientific audience and it takes most authors years to discover how to do this in a way that results in a high percentage of accepted papers. An early decision is whether to work alone or with colleagues. To acquire these skills you can work alone, in isolation from colleagues, and hope to learn from rejection letters and from harsh peer reviews. Or, you can build an informal team of fellow scientists who are both critical and supportive and who will read and comment on your papers. This is often a quicker, more efficient, and more stimulating path. If you are new to a centre or department and you want to sort out quickly who will be supportive of your aims versus who may be less than helpful (i.e., those who have reputations for being always harshly critical, for promising and then failing to read and critique papers), ask people you trust this question: "If you were writing on my topic of __________ whom would you trust to critique in a helpful way?" A novice author can learn much from established authors by passing them drafts for their assessment and their recommendations for getting published.

Writing a scientific paper for a peer-reviewed journal can be as creative an act as writing the great Suomi novel, but less constrained than composing iambic pentameters. Some people write beautifully and effortlessly while others feel like they are sweating out each word. But over time authors with both writing styles make successful contributions to science.

This chapter presents one way to write such a paper; it is not the only way, of course, but it does offer the advantage of a clear step-by-step method that helps you to plan ahead. If you follow these steps, you will finish with a paper worth submitting to the journal of your choice. At the end of this chapter we also present an annotated bibliography describing other approaches to preparing scientific papers for peer review.

Being methodical, let's start with a checklist and begin with all of these items handy within arm's reach.

CHECK THE STYLE GUIDE FOR YOUR JOURNAL OF CHOICE

Each journal has its own specific style configuration and to be accepted by a journal you must write to *its* requirements, not those of another style format and not to your own personal preferences. To do this, have all information on all of the parameters required for the one journal that you have (initially) chosen (see Chapter 2 for more information). Many journals offer a one-page style guide. But even the minimal style guides for undergraduate papers typically run to many pages, so clearly a lot will have been left out of a one-page summary. Contemplate that the *Publication Manual of the American Psychological Association* (APA, 2002, pp. 3-76) has seventy-three pages on style alone. Much can be said for simply sitting down and reading these seventy-three pages for a quick and complete overview of essential topics that are left out of most brief style guides. Read these APA paragraphs and you will emerge an enlightened initiate knowing what topics to be sensitive to even if you must use a different style guide than this manual.

Alongside the official parameters given by your journal of choice, you may also have calculated or astutely teased out other style parameters that will affect your paper, such as the preferred length of the paper and its abstract; gender-neutral or other styles of preferred language; the maximum number, length, and style of footnotes or endnotes; and the maximum size of tables.

A brief warning about tables and figures: journals may not specify the size limits on tables and figures yet these have a huge effect on what information you can include in them and how you organize your writing. Beginning researchers have a tendency to send wider, longer, and less interesting tables than seasoned researchers. To create tables that will fit the page in those cases where the journal gives no guidance, (a) estimate the typeface in the table when compared to the textual typeface, and (b) build model "trial" tables (one row, the number of columns needed, longest possible data lines per table cell) that fit the page like tables in the journal and within the journal's required page margins. Then build your tables. This alone may save you from immediate rejection or the work of rewriting the text and reorganizing the table. If you have tables that require more than one page, check the journal to see if it publishes tables of that size or check with the editor. Editors have horror stories of good papers that arrive with huge tables that could never fit on a page. (The tricks authors use to accomplish this include tiny typefaces, margins of less than a centimetre, formatting rows that run off of the edge of the page, and carrying on for several pages with landscape orientation with a journal that does not accept that format. Don't consider any of these as you will only infuriate the editor.)

ıeck the style guide for requirements governing the presentation of figures and make re that they fit within the journal's page parameters and technical requirements. There a danger in looking to old copies of a journal to assess table and figure design. Find :urrent copy for up-to-date formatting. If you cannot get a current copy on-line or at ıniversity library, write to the editor explaining the situation and the editor --- surely ›ased at your concern --- will likely send a sample copy. Figures are often easily ed by click-and-drag formatting to fit a given space within the correct margins.

Box 5.1 THE IMPORTANCE OF JOURNAL GUIDELINES

Editors agree that far too many authors ignore the crucial step of reading and following the journal's submission guidelines. Ask yourself, "Am I 100% confident that I've followed every one of even the smallest details in the journal's guidelines?" If your silent answer to yourself is "Hmmm, certainly yes, probably 90% or 95%," then your next step is to accept that this is not good enough: go back and fix those few items so that they are correct.

Read and follow the journal's instructions.

) A THOROUGH LITERATURE REVIEW

: literature review is a crucial portion of your paper. Many beginning researchers 'e problems with the scope and structure of the literature review. By studying mples of good literature reviews you can improve your understanding of current ıdards. Wikipedia offers an introduction to the basic points of literature reviews at ›://en.wikipedia.org/wiki/Literature_review. Kathy Teghtsoonian offers a useful actic example explaining alternatives in a review of the literature on smoking at ›://web.uvic.ca/spp/documents/litreview.pdf. An example of a thorough literature iew paper that serves as a model for shorter reviews within a paper, with exemplary kground, definitions of terms and variables, treatment conditions, and results, is this er on quasi-compulsory drug treatment in Germany by Wolfgang Heckmann, toria Kerschl, and Elfriede Steffan published by the European Institute of Social ›nces at the University of Kent: http://tiny.cc/KNeKC. (But avoid the one-sentence ıgraphs frequent in this otherwise fine review; most editors and reviewers hate them complain about even one or two.) Cochrane Group reviews also deserve your ntion. Not only may a review from the Cochrane Group spark improvements in r research, but reading a collection of reviews can also help you to develop a model your work. See http://www.health.qld.gov.au/phs/documents/cphun/32103.pdf.

: reviewers will be much more familiar with the literature than you are, and so your ature review needs to read as informed and critical, not naïve and accepting of all is cited.

One way to improve your literature review is with a step-by-step approach. Have these materials handy:

- All of the relevant literature needed to establish the theory and/or hypothesis that you will examine. (It will help to outline your paper and to see what background or literature reviews you need for each section.)

- All relevant literature for each of the measures that you have used (the initial paper describing each measure, crucial papers describing challenges, alterations, refinements, including statistics on validity, reliability, and all other relevant attributes).

- All of the data needed for your Methods, Procedures, and Results sections. A good way to assess if you need more literature for a given section is to ask yourself, "If I were challenged to support why I chose this [measure, method, statistic], what literature supports my choice?"

If you are writing about qualitative research (QR) for a journal that publishes little of your specialty, be sure to have the latest work on rigor in QR and link it solidly to your work, for the probability is high for a rough ride from reviewers who know little about QR and may be more biased than they realize. ("I have seen a few good qualitative papers; but very few," they tell me.) Also, please read Chapter 6, which explains how to write about qualitative research.

WRITING STEP #1

Contact your chosen journal with a draft title and abstract, ask if your paper is of interest and relevant to the journal's mandate, and ask any awkward questions (…flexibility on paper length? average time for peer review time?). Now is the time to learn if your paper is acceptable to this journal, not after you have spent days writing a paper to a specific format when that journal is unlikely to accept it. If the answer is favourable, you are ready to start writing. If the response is unfavourable, look for another journal. Alternatively, you might consider asking knowledgeable colleagues what journal(s) they feel are the best choice(s) for your paper.

WRITING STEP #2

Now settle down to write for colleagues and your posterity your unique contribution to addiction science. Here are a few specific guidelines for each section of your paper:

Title: You should know the overall writing style of your chosen journal well enough to know intuitively what is a suitable title for your paper. If in doubt, (a) read the 'Table of contents' of several issues to get a feel for their style of titles, and (b) make up a couple of possible titles and ask for reactions from colleagues who know this journal well.

Mistakes to avoid: Trendy and cute titles soon look trivial and dated. An editor may allow such a title (especially if rushed), but years from now it will look embarrassing in your CV as reviewers read it to evaluate if you deserve research funding.

Box 5.2 THE IMPORTANCE OF ORIGINALITY

A frequent mistake made by beginning researchers is to not make clear to the editor and reader what is the *original* contribution of a paper. It is easy to forget that scientific journals exist mainly to publish original knowledge. Describe the originality of your research analyses in your initial letter to the editor to see if she is interested in your paper, so that if it later appears on her desk she will remember it for the innovative understanding that it offers. For the reader's benefit, your original contribution(s) should be clear from the Title (if possible), mentioned in the Abstract, and described in the Introduction and in the Discussion (and/or Conclusion).

Abstract: The abstract summarizes how you carried out your research and what you learned. Even if you don't use the structured abstract (Objective, Methods (or) Design, Sample, Results, and Conclusion) it can serve as a guide to a succinct unstructured abstract. As an example of structured abstracts, the *British Medical Journal* requires structured abstracts within a sound framework: objectives, design, setting, participants, interventions, main outcome measures, results, and conclusions.

Mistakes to avoid: Don't go beyond what is established in your paper: offer no non-significant results, no speculation. Don't use telegraphic style (i.e., omitting articles and other parts of speech to achieve brevity) unless allowed by the journal. Don't go over the abstract size limit set by the journal.

Introduction: A good introduction tells the reader why the paper is important in terms of the problems to be investigated, the context for the research question, what place this research question has in understanding addictions, and what is original about the endeavour.

Mistakes to avoid: Don't simply describe the substance or behaviour under study. Authors who see this as sufficient too often feel that the problem substance or behaviour itself implies what research is needed. This is almost never true. At no point should the volume of loosely related information make the reader feel lost and wonder, "Why is all of this information here?" Avoid archaic arguments that have been resolved or that are not pertinent to your paper, even though you may have spent months researching these and you have a fascinating solution to the debate. Avoid formulaic first lines; a sentence like "Access to legalized gambling has increased greatly in the last two decades" begins at least one third of papers on gambling. An occupational hazard of editing is to receive by the dozens papers with opening lines such as "Alcoholism (or drug dependence, or tobacco use) is a significant public health problem." The editor's eyes glaze.

Literature review: The literature section of a dissertation is an entire chapter. For a paper it should briefly summarize only the most important references that lead directly to understanding the importance of this paper in addressing crucial questions in the addictions and this specific research process. For detailed guidance on which papers to cite, check in this volume Chapter 7, "Use and Abuse of Citations." When completed, compare your draft with the literature reviews in your journal of choice.

Mistakes to avoid: If several authors have been involved in writing the literature review then it is likely too long and detailed, for each author adds what she knows are essential works.

Method: After a reader has gone through this section she should know the research methods in such detail that she could replicate the study in full with another sample. One way to check the completeness of this section is to have a colleague read it and ask her to verify if she could carry out this research project wholly from the Methods section. If there are previously released papers using the same methods (whether yours or others, and especially if described in more detail) then you should cite these. This may allow you to shorten the Method section.

Mistakes to avoid: If some aspect of your methods is suboptimal it is better to mention it here with the comment "see the Limitations section" and then be straightforward in the limitations section. Don't try to hide or disguise poor methods; reviewers will pounce on them. If your research involves randomized control trials, editors may refer you to the Consort Statement promoting high standards and uniform methods: http://www.consort-statement.org/

Results: Here you describe the outcome(s) from your research. Double-check that each novel finding to be discussed has already been reported here.

Mistakes to avoid: This section especially lends itself either to over-writing (excessive detail beyond what is needed for analysis, excessive weight given to non-significant results) or to under-writing (cursory attention to important aspects and variables). A mistake to avoid here is opening the Results section with a description of the sample and the analyses that are more relevant to the Methods, such as the validity of your measures. Start your results section with the main findings. Beginning researchers often take up too much of their paper with non-significant results; be ready to drop a result which colleagues or reviewers suggest is unimportant, even though it seems like a wondrous and magical thing to you.

Discussion and or Conclusion(s): Describe how your specific results fit into the world of addiction science. You may address issues raised in the literature review, you may address policy issues, or you may raise new questions that are either unaddressed or rarely addressed by others.

Mistakes to avoid: A little speculation is allowed, but limit it and ask your supportive colleagues what they think. Restrict your discussion of your future research plans to a line or two. Some authors like to end with the trite conclusion "More research is needed." It always is. If you wish to write in this vein, be as specific and creative as possible in tracing what original work needs to be done and what interesting hypotheses it will test.

Limitations: Describe in brief detail the suboptimal aspects of your research. This new trend has come with demand for more transparency in research publishing. Junior authors are often afraid that being open about the limitations of their research will create prejudice against a paper. Nonsense. Senior researchers (i.e., editors and reviewers) will see flaws in your work that you will likely not see. Reviewers and the editor ask only that you acknowledge limitations. To do so is not a sign of weakness in you or your approach, but much to the contrary; it shows that you are on top of what are best practices, and you are a person who sees the need for better methods (as opposed to those who stumble along pleased with their inadequate work). In short, simple, and unapologetic language, describe the shortcomings that kept your work from being optimal. Some journals allow an author to note limitations throughout the text (i.e., not as a subheading towards the end of the paper); you may wish to check to see if your journal of choice allows or prefers this alternative.

Mistakes to avoid: Don't be ingratiating (i.e., don't apologize, don't promise to avoid these mistakes in the future, don't offer excuses), for this creates the impression of servility. You are not grovelling; you are only signalling to your peers that you know what is better practice in research.

References: It is easy to forget that the function of references is to allow any reader to retrace the evidence that you cite. Electronic sources that close down and unavailable conference papers and reports threaten this openness. You should be totally fluent in the minute details of proper reference style for your chosen journal. Too many errors tell the editor that an author has been careless and this suggests carelessness perhaps elsewhere, too.

Mistakes to avoid: Verify if translation of foreign language titles is required. If it is, translate foreign language titles even in the first version you send to the editor.

Appendices: If your journal of choice seems not to have published appendices, then check with the editor to see if they are allowed. Appendices represent an excellent solution to the problem of presenting background information (legislation, policy statements, questionnaires and measures, speeches, protocols) that is too long for the body of the paper. They are also easy for a reader to skip: a blessing. In e-publishing, some journals allow appendix materials such as video files, sound, and URL access that are difficult or impossible to include in print journals, as well as more traditional materials. NOTE: Such data may not have peer review status if not evaluated by the reviewers.

Mistakes to avoid: Omit appendices that you feel are relevant to the paper but that colleagues feel are not linked.

WRITING STEP #3

You have written this first version early enough to allow you to circulate it to several colleagues whom you can trust to read and offer prompt and fair critiques. Once you have their feedback, consider if their assessments warrant rewriting before submitting it to your chosen journal.

WRITING STEP #4

Submit your paper to the editor. Bon voyage on this first step in becoming a contributor to the world of addiction science!

WRITING STEP #5

Your paper has been accepted for review (whether minimal or extensive) and has come back with the reviewers' and the editor's comments. This would be a good time to consult Chapter 9, which describes referees' reports and how to respond to them. If you decide the referees' criticisms are too severe for you to answer, then write the editor and tell her so along with your precise reasons for not revising your paper. This accomplishes several good things to your benefit: (a) it labels you as someone who takes editing a journal seriously, who knows her goals, and doesn't let work slide, (b) it signals to the editor how serious the criticisms were and may lead her to discuss options with you, and (c) she will remember you as someone who didn't leave her hanging and wondering if that paper was ever coming back.

If you decide to revise your paper you have several choices. Authors should not see themselves as helpless in front of their reviewers. To reassure them of their rights, at our journal we offer this paste-in text sent to even experienced researchers so that they all know what their rights are in the face of reviewers' comments:

> As we tell all authors, a reviewer's comments are not orders that have to be carried out. To the contrary, for each point that a reviewer has made an author has these three options:
>
> i) discuss/debate/refute a reviewer's comment(s), or
>
> ii) rewrite the text in response to a comment(s), or
>
> iii) a combination of these so that an author both discusses/debates/refutes a reviewer's comment(s) and rewrites to accommodate some comments by a reviewer. In many of the articles that you see in print, there are several points that are just as the author intended because she debated and defended her approach as written. As editor, I sometimes very much give the author the benefit of the doubt.

The last point in answering the reviewers' comments is practical, but often overlooked. Be crystal clear in accounting for how you responded to each point made by each reviewer. An efficient way to do this is to follow each reviewer's comment with an explanation of how you respond and to key this up in a contrasting and easily read colour (dark blue or dark green are good choices).

If your paper is rejected then carefully read the critiques and see if you feel that submitting it to another journal seems a wise step. If so, be sure to format it thoroughly to that journal's style and revise it in response to the reviewers' criticisms.

WRITING STEP #6

Once your paper is accepted you may have little more involvement until the editor or publisher sends you the proofs to check. When the proofs arrive and you see how the nuances of your careful writing style have been altered, it is easy to feel lonely and unappreciated. But please respect that copyeditors know well what is more readable and credible to the target audience. If you have a hard time deciding on whether to accept a change or not, a criterion is to ask yourself "Has my meaning been respected or has it been changed?" If it has been respected, then let it be as edited and trust the copyeditor. In a year when you read your paper once again you will usually see the wisdom of the copyeditor's changes.

CONCLUSION

When your first addiction paper is published you will have made a contribution to the addiction sciences and to the public arena where the dialectics between what is, what could be, and what will be, are in struggle. A proverb: some Inuit say that a man can only be as good a hunter as his wife's sewing will let him be. In the addiction sciences the effectiveness of our research, treatment methods, policies, and advocacy can only be as good as the literature that we publish.

The author is grateful for invaluable contributions from Susan Savva, Ian Stolerman, Kerstin Stenius, Sheila Lacroix, Thomas Babor, Gerhard Bühringer, and Jean O'Reilly.

FURTHER READING

Below I present a number of annotated bibliographies. If they don't contain a work specific to your needs or the books are unavailable, try searching your local university or professional library using search terms such as *scientific writing* or *publication manual* in the 'title' or 'subject' window.

Yet another technique is to find the library classification codes at your nearest university for books on writing psychology and biomedical science (for example, at the University of Toronto they are mostly among the Dewey decimal codes T11 and R119) and then to peruse the shelves in those sections looking for books that didn't come up in your title or subject search. Some would call this a strategy of desperation, but half of the books in the annotated bibliographies below were found this way.

Some advice about choosing works (books, papers, Web sites) to help you to be a better scientific author: many of the books that I found are written in what I call an exhortatory style in which the title offers to improve your skills and then the text consists in telling you to do something, but without effective teaching. Some, in effect, exhorted "Write clearer!" but had nothing to help the reader select unclear writing and step-by-step guides for how to make it clearly written. Choose works that you can see will be of help to you and whose approach makes sense, not those that promise but don't resonate with your understanding.

To find relevant Web sites try searching on an exact phrase (perhaps *scientific writing*) and then in the 'all of the words' window (where articles and conjunctions are not needed) narrow the search with specifics, perhaps, *avoiding passive* or using *semi-colons* or any writing area in which you would like to improve.

ANNOTATED BIBLIOGRAPHY OF SCIENTIFIC WRITING: BASIC PROBLEMS OF WRITING STYLE AND MOTIVATION

Strunk, W., & White, E.B. (2000). *The elements of style*. (4th ed.) London: Allyn and Bacon. Still one of the best and shortest writing guides, easily read and absorbed. Those learning English find its clarity and brevity helpful.

Rogers, S.M. (2007). *Mastering scientific and medical writing: A self-help guide*. N.Y.: Springer. A compact guide with exercises as solved problems; good for overcoming specific writing handicaps.

Alley, M. (1996). *The craft of scientific writing*. (3rd ed.) N.Y.: Springer.
Lengthy chapters on building competence and curing shortcomings.

Silvia, P.J. (2007). *How to write a lot: A practical guide to productive academic writing*. Washington, DC: American Psychological Association. This breezy guide is especially good for authors who realize that their writing style needs improvement, or who have been told that a component of their paper (abstract, introduction, method, results, analysis, discussion, conclusion) misses the point of what it should communicate. Journal papers have 23 pages of coverage in this book.

ANNOTATED BIBLIOGRAPHY OF SCIENTIFIC WRITING: FOCUSING ON STANDARDS FOR SCIENTIFIC PAPERS AND SPECIFIC SCIENTIFIC AREAS

Huth, E.J. (1990). *How to write and publish papers in the medical sciences*. (2nd ed.) London: Williams and Wilkins. This compact work offers practical advice on how to make decisions about what to write and what to leave out for both novice and experienced researchers. A highly readable source.

Gustavii, B. (2003). *How to write and illustrate a scientific paper*. Cambridge University, UK: The Cambridge Press. This work is oriented to the biological and medical sciences. It is the clearest and most succinct work that I found among all such works at our local university. A marvel of clarity and utility. It is also full of relevant URLs for up-to-date information.

Miller, J.E. (2005). *The Chicago guide to writing about multi-variate analysis*. Chicago: University of Chicago Press. This work shows how specific are the aids available to scientific authors. The book is a mini-course in writing about numbers, i.e., statistical analysis.

REFERENCES

American Psychological Association (APA). (2002). *Publication manual of the American Psychological Association*. 5th ed. Washington, DC: APA.

British Medical Journal. (n.d.) Resources for authors: Research. Accessed June 19, 2007 http://resources.bmj.com/bmj/authors/types-of-article/research

Savva, S. (2007, July 25). Personal communication.

WEB RESOURCES

Several Web-based approaches to writing are available:

Two guides that address basic problems include http://academic.bowdoin.edu/courses/f02/bio105/dissemination/ScientificPaperBasic.pdf
and http://classweb.gmu.edu/biologyresources/writingguide/ScientificPaper.htm

An advanced, comprehensive guide:
http://www.aspsilverbackwebsites.co.uk/RobertWest/resources/checklistarticle.pdf

CHAPTER 6
HOW TO WRITE PUBLISHABLE QUALITATIVE RESEARCH

KERSTIN STENIUS, KLAUS MÄKELÄ, MICHAL MIOVSKY, AND ROMAN GABRHELIK

INTRODUCTION

Conducting and publishing qualitative research requires the same principal skills as quantitative research. In addition, there may be special challenges for the qualitative researcher. She may have to overcome prejudice and communication barriers within the scientific community. This chapter provides advice to authors who wish to publish their research in a scientific journal. The chapter starts with some remarks on special characteristics of the processes of qualitative study that can have an impact on the reporting of the results. It continues by identifying the common criteria for good qualitative research. We then present some evaluation principles used by editors and referees. Finally, we give practical advice for writing a scientific article and discuss where to publish your results.

In quantitative research the observations typically follow a systematic scheme where the classification of the observations is already determined to a large extent when the data collection starts. This makes it possible to gather large data sets for numerical analyses, but the understanding of the findings will be restricted by the concepts on which the collection of data was based. You can argue that in qualitative research, where the observations (e.g., texts, sounds, behaviour, images, etc.) are usually fewer, the researcher's preconception of a social phenomenon does not determine the research results to the same extent as in quantitative research (Sulkunen, 1987). Qualitative research is thus often used for the study of social processes, or for a study of the reasons behind human behaviour, or as Wikipedia puts it: the why and how of social matters, more than the what, where, and when that are often central to quantitative research.

The topics dealt with in qualitative addiction research range from historical processes to treatment outcomes. Qualitative research is used increasingly to answer questions about alcohol and drug policy, including rapid assessment of policy developments (see for instance Stimson et al., 2004). It is used to study program implementation and in the evaluation of various policy measures. And ethnographers have employed qualitative methods to increase the understanding of patterns of substance use in various population groups (see for instance Lalander, 2003).

There is also an important and growing interest in the combination of qualitative and quantitative research, so called mixed methods research, not least within evaluation and intervention research in the clinical and policy fields (Creswell & Plano Clark, 2007). The combination of qualitative and quantitative methods can deepen the understanding of processes, attitudes, and motives.

There is frequent discussion in theoretical mixed method studies of the relation between various kinds of knowledge, or the actual procedure of combining qualitative and quantitative methods (Creswell & Tashakkori, 2007). Box 6.1 presents criteria for good mixed-methods articles.

Box 6.1 CRITERIA FOR GOOD MIXED-METHODS ARTICLES

a) The study has two sizeable data sets (one quantitative, one qualitative) with rigorous data collection and appropriate analyses, and with inferences made from both parts of the study.
b) The article integrates the two parts of the study in terms of comparing, contrasting, or embedding conclusions from both the qualitative and the quantitative "strands."
c) The article has mixed methods components that can enrich the newly emerging literature on mixed methods research.

Source: Creswell & Tashakkori (2007)

In spite of what we believe is an increasing interest in qualitative research, many journals do not publish qualitative studies. In addition, many editors of addiction journals have noted that qualitative manuscripts are more likely to present the editors with problems and are more often declined for publication than quantitative research reports. Some of the problems are related to how the articles are written.

In the addiction field there is no journal dedicated exclusively to qualitative research, and in many journals the format of an article has to follow a strict standard. Qualitative articles tend to break with that format, putting special demands on the reader. Another problem for a comparatively small research field such as addiction research is that it is difficult to find referees who are competent to evaluate qualitative methods and analyses. The journal may have only a small pool of suitable referees. The author can thus run the risk of being judged by someone who is not only unqualified but also may be prejudiced against qualitative research. For all of these reasons, the qualitative researcher has to be particularly professional in her writing.

ON QUALITATIVE AND QUANTITATIVE RESEARCH

Qualitative methods can be used for pilot studies, to illustrate the results of a statistical analysis, in mixed methods studies, and in independent qualitative research projects (c.f. Denzin & Lincoln, 1998). This chapter will focus on the last category: original research reports building on qualitative methods. We will emphasise the similarities and considerable overlap in the evaluation, and effective presentation, of both qualitative and quantitative research.

The first and foremost aim of all social research, quantitative as well as qualitative, is to present a conceptually adequate description of a *historically specific* topic, subject or target. In qualitative research the determination of the subject is as important as the choice of a population in a statistical study. The description of the subject is always, in both types of study, a theoretical task because it requires a conceptually well organized analysis.

The processes of classification, deduction and interpretation are in their fundamental aspects similar in both qualitative and quantitative research. Quantitative analyzing operations, however, are more clear-cut than qualitative operations. Furthermore, the various steps of quantitative research can be more clearly distinguished than those of a qualitative study. The first issue is that, in qualitative work, the collection and processing of data are more closely intertwined than in a quantitative study. Especially when the researcher personally collects the data, she will not be able to avoid problems of interpretation during the collection phase. A specific issue in some qualitative research may be the fact that the methods used can change during the study, depending on interim results. It is a challenge to explain in a short article why this has happened, and why you have used a different method in the final phase of the data acquisition than in the previous parts; or why you changed a classification scheme and encoded the data in a different manner. The researcher must also carefully consider her relations with the study objects. Many qualitative reports often discuss at length the character and psychology of the process of data collection, but are less careful in describing what happened to the interview tapes afterwards. Were they transcribed in whole or in part, how was the resulting stack of papers handled and sorted out? In qualitative research these data processing explications may be necessary to render credibility to the analysis.

A second issue is that qualitative analysis is not restricted to an unambiguously demarcated data set in the same way as a quantitative study. The good researcher may keep a detailed field diary and make notes of all discussions and thus produce a corpus to which she limits her analysis. Nevertheless, during the analysis phase she may recall an important detail which she has not recorded in her notes, but has to take into account in the analysis. The qualitative researcher has to describe this analytical process in an honest and convincing way.

EVALUATION CRITERIA FOR QUALITATIVE ANALYSIS

There are some differences between the evaluation of qualitative and quantitative research. The replicability of a qualitative study cannot be formulated as a problem of reliability, and the accuracy of a qualitative interpretation cannot be compared to the explanatory power of a statistical model. In the following paragraphs we propose three main criteria for evaluating qualitative studies. Since in qualitative research the analyses and reporting are very closely intertwined, the following criteria are as relevant to researchers and authors as they are to reviewers and editors: 1) significance of the data set and its social or cultural place; 2) sufficiency of the data, and coverage of the analysis; 3) transparency and repeatability of the analysis.

1. SIGNIFICANCE OF THE DATA SET AND ITS SOCIAL OR CULTURAL PLACE

The researcher should be prepared to argue that her data are worth analyzing. It is not easy to identify criteria for the significance of data. One precondition can, however, be presented: the researcher should carefully define the social and cultural place (contextualising) and the production conditions of her material.

The production conditions can be discussed at various levels. When the data consist of cultural products, their production and marketing mechanisms should be considered. Texts produced by individuals should be related to their social position. Furthermore, the situational aspect of the data production and the researcher's potential influence on the data should be evaluated. The relationship of cultural products to people's everyday life depends on the production and distribution network. Weekly magazines and movies represent the ambient culture at a number of levels. When doing comparisons over time it is important to bear in mind that the social and cultural place of one and the same genre may vary from decade to decade.

In international comparisons it is important to be able to exclude demographic variation as a factor causing differences. If we wish to identify the distinct characteristics of Finnish A.A. members' stories, we should make sure that we do not compare Finnish farmers to American college Professors. The criterion for selecting the target group is not demographic but cultural representativity .

Additionally, people speak of the same things in different ways on different occasions, and it is the task of the researcher to decide which discourse she wants to study and argue for her decision in the article. Informal interviews are often advocated instead of questionnaires on the grounds that they will produce more genuine information. But, on the other hand, an in-depth interview is a more exceptional situation for a present-day person than completing a questionnaire. Possible effects of the power structures and gender relations present in every social situation should be considered in the discourse analysis, since it could affect the outcomes of the qualitative research.

Study of the variations of discourse, i.e. the incorporation of the production conditions into the study design, can be rather laborious. Members of A.A. emphasise various sides of their story according to the composition of the audience, and depending on whether they talk at a closed or an open A.A. meeting. Furthermore, the life story will change in relation to how long the speaker has been in A.A. Even when variation cannot be incorporated into the actual study design, it is important to consider and discuss the conditions under which the material was produced and their place in the potential situational variation of the discourse.

2. SUFFICIENCY OF DATA AND COVERAGE OF ANALYSIS

For statistical studies we are able to calculate in advance the extent of data needed to estimate the parameters accurately enough for the purpose of the analysis. We have no similar methods for estimating the extent of qualitative data required. We usually speak about data saturation: data collection can be terminated when new cases no longer disclose new features (Strauss & Corbin, 1998).

The difficulty here, of course, is that the limit is not always known in advance, and the collection of data is rarely a continuing process which could be terminated or extended at will.

Only in very special cases can you base your analyses on just a handful of observations. In most cases you will need to be certain that you cover the variation of the phenomenon you are studying. On the other hand, a loose but useful rule is that one should not collect too much data at a time. It is better to analyze a small data batch carefully first and only then determine what additional data will be needed. To divide the analyses into smaller parts also helps to end up with manageable results for a publishable report.

It is often advisable to group the collection of data according to factors which may prove important as production conditions. The goal is not to explain the variation but to make sure that the data are sufficiently varied. For example, it would be helpful to stratify the collection of A.A. members' life stories according to the members' social position, sex, age and length of sobriety (Arminen, 1998). The only difficulty is that we will have no advance knowledge of which characteristics will decide the type of life stories; they may depend more on drinking experiences than on external circumstances, and within A.A. there may be various narrative traditions which have an influence on the life stories.

A proper coverage of the analysis means that the researcher does not base her interpretations on a few arbitrary cases or instances but on a careful reading of the whole material. Qualitative reports are often loosely impressionistic because the excessive amount of material has made it unfeasible to analyze it carefully enough.

3. TRANSPARENCY AND REPEATABILITY OF THE ANALYSIS

Transparency of the analysis means that the reader is able to follow the researcher's reasoning, that he is given the necessary information for accepting her interpretations -- or challenging them. The repeatability of an analysis means that the rules of classification and interpretation have been presented so clearly that another researcher applying them will reach the same conclusions. We may identify three ways of improving the transparency and repeatability of qualitative analysis and the report: 1) enumerating the data; 2) dividing the process of interpretation into steps; and 3) making explicit the rules of decision and interpretation.

The best method to decrease arbitrariness and increase repeatability is to enumerate all units on which the interpretation is based. To do this an analytical unit must be specified and it should be as small as possible: in other words, not a movie or a group discussion but a scene, a statement or an adjacent pair. The identification of the unit of analysis is in itself part of the process of interpretation.

The process of interpretation and analysis can never be fully formalized. It is above all a question of working step by step so that the process of interpretation can be made visible to both the researcher herself and the reader.

Qualitative analysis is of necessity more personal and less standardized than statistical analysis. Thus it is even more vital that the reader is given as exact a picture as possible of both the technical operations and the chain of reasoning that have led to the reported results. The reader must not be left at the mercy of the researcher's intuition alone. The demand for transparency in qualitative research is of crucial importance.

EDITORS' AND REFEREES' ASSESSMENT OF QUALITATIVE RESEARCH REPORTS

A discussion of the evaluation criteria for peer review of qualitative research can start with evaluation principles for quasi-experimental research or natural experiments. The *American Journal of Public Health* recently published an evaluation system for these types of study (Des Jarlais et al., 2004) entitled TREND (Transparent Reporting of Evaluations with Nonrandomized Designs). TREND was designed specifically for research results where the randomisation principle was somehow restricted. The criterion of *transparency*, which is central to this evaluation system, emphasises a detailed description of all steps and procedures, as well as a detailed justification of the choice and manner of application of the individual methods and theoretical background (see also Mayring, 1988, 1990).

Mareš (2002) analysed quality criteria for research using pictorial documents and summarized the findings with the concepts of *completeness* -- how well the data captures the phenomenon examined, *transparency* -- the accuracy, clarity and completeness of the description of the individual phases of the study, *reflexivity* -- the ability of the researcher to reflect upon her different steps and measures during the study and how she may have influenced the research situation, and *adequacy* of interpretation and *aggregation* of contradictory interpretations -- the identification and weighting of alternative interpretations and other validity control techniques.

Des Jarlais, et al. (2004, pp. 363-365) have drawn up a 22-item list to serve as a general assessment guide for authors and evaluators. Box 6.2 shows some of the requirements and recommendations.Additional recommendations proposed by Gilpatrick (1999) and Robson (2002) are summarised in Box 6.3.

It is true to say that the qualitative paper, both in its entirety and in its constituent parts, will be evaluated by and large according to the same criteria and expectations as those applied to a quantitative report.

BOX 6.2 ASSESSMENT CRITERIA FOR QUALITATIVE STUDIES

a) An article should be provided with a structured abstract (as a minimum: background, aims, sample, methods, results).

b) The sampling should be described and justified, including an explanation of criteria used.

c) The theoretical background of the entire study, or individual methods, should be described, to show that the sample and data collection were consistent with the study's theoretical background.

d) The context (setting) in which the study was carried out should be described. The author must describe the characteristics of the field in which the study was carried out, and what made it different from other settings.

e) A detailed description of the research intervention should be included, and of how study participants responded during that intervention.

f) A detailed description of the analytical methods applied, how they were used, including the tools used for minimising bias, and a validation of the results should be presented.

g) A description of the manner of data processing (e.g., technical aspects and procedures) is needed.

h) Description of outcomes and their interpretation are obviously necessary. This includes a discussion of limitations (contextual validity of results), and an analysis of how the design of the study reflects these limitations.

Source: Des Jarlais et al. (2004)

Box 6.3 EVALUATION CRITERIA FOR QUALITATIVE STUDIES

a) The research issue and the research questions and goals derived from it, should be properly presented.

b) The goals should be contextually embedded and put into a theoretical framework, with an analysis of the present state of knowledge.

c) The author should argue for the importance of her study against this background (e.g. what questions or issues the results should contribute to, how they will move the field forward).

d) Control tools (e.g., research logs, control points) should be reported and how ethical problems were handled (e.g., use of informed consents, careful adherence to research protocols, manner of preparing the research team to manage risky or problem situations).

Sources: Gilpatrick (1999) and Robson (2002).

PRACTICAL ADVICE FOR WRITING A PUBLISHABLE QUALITATIVE ARTICLE

A good way to start the process of improving both your writing skills and your chances of publication is to become familiar with the common reasons why editors reject qualitative articles (see Box 6.4), and then carefully read some examples of well written qualitative articles (see Box 6.5).

Based on our experience as journal editors, referees and researchers, we now present nine recommendations for potential authors of qualitative articles.

1. CONSIDER THE FORMAT AND STRUCTURE OF YOUR PAPER

When you get acquainted with various addiction journals, you will realize that qualitative articles can look very different, depending on their topic but also on where they are published. You can choose to target a specific journal and try to follow closely the format used in that publication. But if you want a greater choice of potential journals for your manuscript and in particular if you are not a very experienced researcher, it may be wise to choose a traditional structure for your research report.

Box 6.4 COMMON REASONS WHY EDITORS DECLINE QUALITATIVE PAPERS

1. the author has not related the study to earlier (international) literature,
2. the research question is not clearly stated,
3. the structure of the paper is not clear or does not respond to the expected structure of papers in the journal,
4. theories, methods and data analyses are not consistent,
5. the central concepts are not clearly presented or used in a consistent way,
6. the methodology is poor,
7. the size of the dataset is not defended in a convincing way,
8. the data set is not sufficiently contextualised or there is a clear selection bias,
9. the data collection is poor and there is a lack of validity control,
10. the methods and the analyses are not explained clearly enough, which may lead the referees and the editor to regard the article as too descriptive and the analyses based too much on intuition,
11. the author makes unsound conclusions or unfounded generalisations,
12. ethical rules are violated or ethical issues are not mentioned or adequately discussed,
13. the text is too long.

Primary source: Drisko (2005)

Box 6.5 EXAMPLES OF WELL WRITTEN QUALITATIVE ARTICLES

Amos, A., Wiltshire, S., Bostock, Y., Haw, S., & McNeill, A. (2004). 'You can't go without a fag . . . you need it for your hash'-a qualitative exploration of smoking, cannabis and young people. *Addiction*, 99 (1), 77-81.

Demant, J. & Järvinen. M. (2006). Constructing maturity through alcohol experience - Focus group interviews with teenagers. *Addiction Research and Theory*, 14 (6), 589-602.

Herd, D. (2005). Changes in the prevalence of alcohol use in rap song lyrics, 1979-97. *Addiction* 100(9), 1258-1269.

Maher, L., & Hudson, S. L. (2007). Women in the drug economy: A metasynthesis of the qualitative literature. *Journal of Drug Issues*, 37(4), 805-826.

Miovský, M. (2007). Changing patterns of drug use in the Czech Republic during the post-Communist era: A qualitative study. *Journal of Drug Issues*, 37(1), 73-102.

Phillips, D., Thomas, K., Cox, H., Ricciardelli, L. A., Ogle, J., Love, V., & Steele A. (2007). Factors that influence women's disclosures of substance use during pregnancy: A qualitative study of ten midwives and ten pregnant women. *Journal of Drug Issues*, 37(2), 357-376.

2. MAKE SURE THAT THE TITLE OF THE ARTICLE CORRESPONDS TO THE CONTENT

The title of an article is very important. Drisko (2005) gives the following advice: present the research question reshaped into the manuscript title. A title that indicates what you are interested in will generate more readers who really are interested in your research -- and probably more citations of your article (see Chapter 7). Sometimes it is possible to formulate the title so that it also describes what kind of data you have used. A title should not promise too much or be too fancy. If the title of the article is "The commercial discourse on alcohol," the reader expects that the theoretical contribution will be substantial. If it is "An analysis of alcohol marketing" and you only deal with beer advertisements in a short period in Greece, the reader may be disappointed.

3. STATE THE RESEARCH QUESTION EARLY AND CLEARLY

It is a common failure in qualitative reports that the research question is so embedded in the text that the reader cannot find it. The best way to avoid this is to include at the beginning of your manuscript a subtitle called "Research question" or "Aim of the study." An alternative is to present the question at the end of the Background or Introduction section.

It is not unusual for the reader of a qualitative article to find several different, sometimes even contradictory, research questions presented throughout the various sections of the article: one question in the introduction, another in the methods and data section and a third in the discussion (Drisko, ibid.). Even if the research process in qualitative research often is more unpredictable than in quantitative research, and you gain new insights during the research process that will affect your perspective, the aim of a research report is as a rule not to report on this exploratory process, but on specific findings answering a specific question. The reader does not want to be taken through the whole story of the researcher's mistakes and new choice of questions. Focus on a single clear question that will orient the reader's interest and prepare him for the text to come. It may be that your research project will in fact be able to answer many questions. Perhaps then you should consider producing several shorter and focused articles, rather than trying to squeeze it all into one text.

If possible, phrase the research question in a way that reflects the scientific ambition of the study: is it an article that explores a topic, aims at discovering a new social phenomenon, presents a new perspective, seeks to raise consciousness about a problem, evaluates a project, or tests a theory (Drisko 2005)?

4. CONDUCT A THOROUGH REVIEW OF EARLIER RESEARCH

A good review of earlier research on the topic is essential for your claim that you are contributing something new. It also shows that you want to take your place in the research community, in serious dialogue with other researchers. If the referees find that you have overlooked important literature, particularly if it is their own work (and since qualitative addiction research is a small field, you will often have a referee that has contributed to your topic), or that you have misinterpreted them, they will read your study with skepticism. Do not limit yourself to literature from your own country, but be sure to cover what has been written from your own culture.

The literature review should not be solely descriptive. Use it to position yourself in relation to other researchers and to demonstrate you are doing something new. What conclusions about your questions can already be drawn from earlier research? State why you think that earlier studies have missed a certain aspect, or taken a perspective that can be complemented with a new one. Alternatively, say why and in what way you would like to use an approach or develop a line of thought presented by someone else.

When you have presented a good review of earlier research you will also have defended your theoretical and methodological position and your choice of data. Be certain to choose the right body of literature with theoretical relevance for your question. If you are studying gender differences in advertisements for tobacco, be sure to cover the literature on gender and media: do not focus exclusively on what we know about gender differences in smoking patterns.

A thorough review where you position yourself will also be a practical way to avoid unfavorable referees. If you state that you disagree with X who has not taken Y into account, the editor will in all probability not send your text to X, to avoid a conflict of interest. Since the number of possible referees available to the editor usually is limited, this is an important consideration.

5. PRESENT THE METHODS AND DATA

According to Drisko (2005), inadequate methods are among the most common reason for qualitative articles being declined by editors. It is important to justify the choice of methods. If you want to be really convincing, explain your choice in relation to alternative methodologies. If you use several methods, explain how they complement each other. For instance, it is not enough simply to state that you use focus group interviews and a post-structuralist text analysis: you should describe how and why you use them.

Remember that many readers of addiction journals will not be familiar with qualitative methods. Therefore you must describe the content of the method quite explicitly. Show that the research methods are suitable for the purpose of the study. It is important to convince the reader that you have used your method(s) systematically and on the entire data set. This includes the consistent use of crucial concepts.

You must argue that the size of the sample is sufficient for your purpose. As noted above, a small sample is one of the factors that raise skepticism among readers of qualitative research. How extensive was your data set? How many interviews with how many persons, how many meetings or observations? The sample should be clearly positioned. Sometimes however, the positioning can be too long. Try to focus on the essential features which will help an uninitiated reader to understand what you are analyzing and what the sample represents.

It is important to explain why your data set is the most illustrative and useful to answer the question you are posing. Be careful to describe how you picked your sample. What criteria did you use? Can you compare the data set to other alternatives and why did you choose this one? Describe the important variations within the data set (for instance age and gender distributions) so that the reader gets a good picture of it. If you have used only a part of the data you have collected within a project, describe the rest of the data briefly to illustrate the context; or refer to another, already published article, where these data are presented.

For the interpretation and transparency of your reasoning it is crucial to describe how the data were produced and collected and how these conditions may have influenced the data. What special conditions, for example, come into play if you collect data from AA members where anonymity is important? Do they affect the research participants' willingness to be interviewed or how they talk during an interview? Tell the reader how (or whether) you presented the study to the participants. If you used focus groups, describe the groups' dynamics.

Describe carefully each step in the analysis to make it possible for the reader to believe that your conclusions are correct -- or argue against them. A good rule is to present the analysis of one observation/item/response in detail. Describe your interpretations during the analysis in a systematic way, in small identifiable steps. Show the fruitfulness of your concepts. Show how you argued for saturation, and how you handled diversity and contradictions in the data.

A thorough description of how the data were handled is also important. It should be clearly stated, for instance, how and whether the interviews were transcribed, coded and grouped.

6. RESULTS

For the reader, the presentation of the results is easiest to follow if the structure is directly linked to the research question, moves in logical steps according to the theory and method, and consistently uses the concepts presented earlier in the article.

Present your data in a systematic way in the body of the text, so that quotations, field notes and other documentations are easily identifiable. The reader must be certain, for instance, whether you are using direct citations or if you are analyzing interpretations of what the observed or interviewed persons said. The citations or other illustrations must be clearly contextualised. If it is observational material, state whether you collected the data yourself or if you used data collected by someone else.

Give enough raw data, for instance direct citations, but not too much. Avoid very short quotations. If you run out of space, find out from the editor if you can use online appendices for additional material. Do not refer in the results section to data that you have not already presented in the data and methods section; if you state that you are going to use interviews, do not in the results section refer to observations. If the results are contradictory, declare that openly and explain how this may have occurred and what it may mean.

If you use grounded theory, you should be able to present a theory as a result. Descriptive statements are not enough. The theory should be a product of the analyses and not just confirm or illustrate earlier theories (Glasser & Strauss, 1967/99).

7. DISCUSSION

The structure of the discussion in a qualitative article can follow the same structure as in quantitative research reports. After a very short summary of your research question (check that it is the same as in the Introduction) and the motivation for your wish to explore it, you can repeat in one sentence the main result of your study.

Following this, you can discuss how your findings relate to earlier research: do they fill out the picture of what we already know, or possibly challenge or even contradict earlier findings? In this section you can also, if possible, refer to earlier quantitative research. In what way has your study been important for the research community or for a larger audience? Can the results change the picture of similar phenomena in other cultures? Discuss the extent to which the findings with this data set may be relevant to the understanding of other situations. What are the concepts that can be transferred to other settings?

As noted in Chapter 9, a good discussion will also contain a consideration of the limitations of your study. What problems with the sample and data collection restricted the possibility of getting a full answer to your research question? With what other data could the answer have been more complete? Could you have used an additional or alternative method?

Finally, consider giving recommendations for further research that will improve knowledge about the topic you have studied.

8. ABSTRACT

Most addiction journals require the authors to write very short abstracts, covering background, aims, data and methods, results and discussion. It is a good idea for the author of a qualitative article to write a preliminary abstract at an early stage of the writing process, to make sure that the text will be coherent and logical.

9. AND FINALLY, SOME GENERAL ADVICE

First of all, it is sensible for a qualitative as well as for a quantitative researcher to save your good data for scientific articles. Many qualitative researchers publish their results as reports, sometimes in series that will have limited distribution, or as longer articles in monographs. If you want to spread your findings to a larger audience it is often more efficient to publish one or more articles in a scientific journal.

Second, choose the right journal -- a crucial success factor if you want to get your article published. The first step is to choose among an addiction journal, a journal for qualitative research or a scholarly journal for sociology, anthropology, history, etc. (see Chapter 2).

If you choose an addiction journal or a disciplinary journal, find out if they accept qualitative reports. Box 6.6 presents a list of English language addiction journals that publish qualitative research. Non-English language journals as a rule accept submissions of qualitative articles. Check if the journal has particular demands on article length that will make it difficult for your submission to be accepted. Look at the editorial board and determine whether it includes members who are familiar with qualitative methods. Finally, look at the content of the journal: to what extent do they publish qualitative articles? Bear in mind that many addiction journals are open to various research methods, even if they have a predominantly quantitative orientation.

Box 6.6 ENGLISH LANGUAGE JOURNALS THAT PUBLISH QUALITATIVE ARTICLES

Addiction	International Journal of Drug Policy
Addiction Research and Theory	Journal of Addictions Nursing
Addictive Behaviors	Journal of Alcohol and Drug Education
African Journal of Drug and Alcohol Studies	Journal of Drug Education
Alcohol and Alcoholism	Journal of Drug Issues
Alcohol Research and Health	Journal of Ethnicity in Substance Abuse
Alcoholism Treatment Quarterly	Journal of Gambling Issues
American Journal of Drug and Alcohol Abuse	Journal of Smoking Cessation
Contemporary Drug Problems	Journal of Social Work Practice in the Addictions
Drug and Alcohol Dependence	Journal of Studies on Alcohol and Drugs
Drug and Alcohol Review	Journal of Substance Abuse Treatment
Drugs: Education, Prevention and Policy	Journal of Substance Use
European Addiction Research	Substance Abuse Treatment, Prevention, and Policy
Harm Reduction Journal	Substance Use and Misuse
International Gambling Studies	Tobacco Control

Finally, consider if it would be good to suggest a suitable referee for your article. Some journal editors may find it difficult to identify experienced referees for your manuscript. As an author, you can always suggest someone whom you would like to review your text, without, of course, any guarantee that the editor will follow your advice.

CONCLUSIONS

In this chapter we have emphasized that the similarities between doing and writing up quantitative and qualitative research are greater than the differences. We have presented some quality criteria, particularly for qualitative research, discussed criteria for evaluation of journal articles and given some practical advice to authors.

To publish qualitative research is as least as challenging as to get quantitative reports accepted. However, it is apparent that the addiction field as a whole is increasingly coming to realize the value of qualitative studies. We believe that in the future there will be an even greater interest in good qualitative research, and a growing demand for mixed methods studies. Those who have dug themselves down into the qualitative or quantitative trenches will come out and start communicating, for their own and everybody's mutual benefit.

ACKNOWLEDGEMENTS

The authors want to thank Tom Babor, Phil Lange, Tom McGovern, Peter Miller, Jean O'Reilly and Betsy Thom for valuable comments on earlier versions of the text.

REFERENCES

Arminen, I. (1998). Therapeutic Interaction. A Study of Mutual Help in the Meetings of Alcoholics Anonymous, Vol. 45. Helsinki: The Finnish Foundation for alcohol studies.

Creswell, J.W., & Plano Clark, V.L. (2007). Designing and conducting mixed methods research. Thousand Oaks, CA: Sage.

Creswell, J.W. & Tashakkori, A. (2007). Developing Publishable Mixed methods Manuscripts. Journal of Mixed Methods Research 2 (1): 107-111.

Denzin, N.K., & Lincoln, Y. S. (Eds.) (1998). The Landscape of Qualitative Research: Theories and Issues. Thousand Oaks, London, New Delhi: SAGE Publication.

Des Jarlais, D.C, Lyles, C., & Crepaz, N. (2004). Improving the Reporting Quality of Nonrandomized Evaluations of Behavioral and Public Health Interventions: The

TREND Statement. American Journal of Public Health 3 (94): 361-366.
Drisko, J. (2005). Writing Up Qualitative Research. Families in Society: The Journal of Contemporary Social Services 86 (4): 589-593.

Gilpatrick, E. (1999). Quality Improvement Projects in Health Care. London, Thousand Oaks, New Delhi: SAGE Publications.

Glaser, B. G., & Strauss, A. L. (1967). The discovery of grounded theory: Strategies for qualitative research. New York: Aldine.

Lalander, P. (2003). Hooked on Heroin: Drugs and Drifters in a Globalized World. London/New York: Berg Publisher.

Mareš, J. et al. (2002). Sociální opora u d?tí a dospívajících II [Social support of children and adolescents]. Hradec Králové: Nukleus.

Mayring, P. (1988). Qualitative Inhaltsanalyse: Grundlagen and Techniken. Weinheim: Deutcher Studien Verlag.

Mayring, P. (1990). Einführung in die qualitative Socialforschung. München: Psychologie Verlag Union.

Robson, C. (2002). Real World Research. Oxford: Blackwell Publishing.

Stimson, G.V., Fitch, C., Des Jarlais, D., Poznyak, V., Perlis, T., Oppenheimer, E. Rhodes, T. (2004). Rapid Assessment and Response Studies of Injection Drug Use. Knowledge Gain, Capacity Building, and Intervention Development in a Multisite Study. American Journal of Public Health 96 (2): 288-95.

Strauss, A., & Corbin, J. (1998). Basics of qualitative research: Techniques and procedures for developing grounded theory, Second Edition. Thousand Oaks, CA: SAGE Publications.

Sulkunen, P. (1987). Sosiologian avaimet (The Keys to Sociology). Porvoo, Helsinki, Juva: WSOY.

CHAPTER 7
USE AND ABUSE OF CITATIONS
ROBERT WEST AND KERSTIN STENIUS

INTRODUCTION

Research output in the form of papers, books, and book chapters is there to be used by other researchers to inform subsequent research, influence policy decisions, and improve clinical practice. Authors need to consider how to make appropriate use of their previous publications and the work of others, and to ensure that their own work will be used appropriately.

A research paper, book, policy document or treatment manual should refer to other writing that is relevant to its message. Citation is the formal vehicle for doing this. It involves explicit reference to a piece of research output which can in principle be anything from an article in a journal to a web-site. Conventions applying to citation practice regulate the transmission of information. Citation conventions vary from one research field to another. The following text focuses primarily on what might be termed 'cumulative research' in which the goal is to accumulate enduring knowledge and understanding.

There are two main types of citation (Box 7.1). In this chapter we use the term *referential citation* to refer to the situation where a piece of research output (which may be empirical or conceptual) is being used for what it contributes to the field. The term *critical citation* is used when the citing piece points to what is considered a flaw in some research output.

The citation serves one or more essential functions; it enables the reader to examine the cited work to check the veracity of a statement that it is being used to support, or the correctness of the use of a concept or interpretation of a process. When citing in support of a statement being made in one's own article, it also acknowledges the contribution made by the cited work. Both the *verification function* and the *acknowledgement function* are important. One may also use citations to document how a political debate or historical process or a specific concept has developed and has been defined. We can call this *the documentation function*[1].

As regards the verification function and the documentation function, the scope for intentional and unintentional distortion of research through unfounded assertions or misleading statements is enormous. In principle every non-obvious factual claim should be supported in some way: either by direct evidence or by tracing a link through citations and/or inference to that evidence. Similarly every hypothesis, conceptual analysis, or statement of a theoretical position that is not advanced for the first time in a given paper should trace a link to its source. Citation offers the reader an opportunity to determine for himself or herself: a) whether the original source of a claim was justified, and b) whether that claim is being accurately represented in the current piece.

---

[1]We are grateful to Klaus Mäkelä for this insight.

Box 7.1 TYPES AND FUNCTIONS OF CITATIONS

Types of citations	Functions of citations
Referential citation: a work or part of a work is cited for what it contributes to the field	*Verification function*: the reader should be able to check the source for its accuracy and the accuracy with which it is reported
Critical citation: a work or part of a work is cited because it is believed to mislead the field	*Acknowledgement function*: the source is given credit for its contribution
	Documentation function: the source is identified as the object of the research in its own right

As regards the acknowledgement function, it is right and proper that a researcher should receive credit for his or her work and citation is the primary means by which this is achieved. This is not merely a matter of etiquette; employment and promotion of individual researchers are built on reputation, and citations play a crucial role in this. The institutions that employ researchers achieve kudos and in many cases funding on the basis of the reputations of their employees. Moreover, charities and government bodies that fund research must receive credit for the work they support. Their own income may well depend on it.

DEVIATIONS FROM IDEAL CITATION PRACTICE

Citation practice often falls far short of the ideal (for a discussion see Reyes (2001)). There are a number of sources one may use to find out about good practice in the use of citations in systematic reviews (e.g. Chalmers, Enkin et al. 1993; Cook, Sackett et al. 1995; Bannigan, Droogan et al. 1997; Moher, Cook et al. 1999; Sutton, Jones et al. 1999; Reeves, Koppel et al. 2002). Use of citations in less formal reviews, such as to introduce research reports, is subject to greater variability. The following paragraphs examine common deviations from ideal practice (as summarised in Box 7.2).

BOX 7.2 TERMINOLOGY RELATED TO DEVIATIONS FROM IDEAL CITATION PRACTICE

Convenience citation	Selects citation material that is easy to find
Discovery paper	The article that first puts forward a new concept
Grey literature	Unpublished matter, such as conference presentations, submitted articles, and in-house papers and reports
Publication lag	The time between an article's acceptance by a journal and its publication
Reputation citation	Cites a work or part of a work with a view to enhancing one's own reputation or that of a colleague
Review article	An article that summarizes the research on a specific topic
Viewpoint citation	Cites a work or part of a work because it supports a given hypothesis or idea

SELECTIVE CITATION THROUGH NEED FOR CONCISENESS

A legitimate reason to depart from ideal practice arises from the need for conciseness. Many times in a given field, a large number of studies may be cited in support of a given statement. In the absence of other constraints, the acknowledgement function might dictate that all relevant studies are cited. However, this would be impracticable. This raises the question of which article or articles to cite. There is a case for citing what we might call the *discovery paper*: the first article to record the finding. However, this may be impossible to determine. Moreover, it may not represent the most robust support for the assertion in question. There is a case for citing a *review article* (an article that summarizes the research on a specific topic). This has the advantage of pointing the reader, at least indirectly, to a body of work rather than one or two studies that might be unrepresentative. The disadvantages are: a) the increased danger of misrepresentation because of hearsay, and b) failure to acknowledge the contribution of the original source.

A possible rule of thumb in determining policy relating to a specific finding is to aim to cite the discovery piece and no more than five other original sources that testify to the generality of the finding unless there is an authoritative and non-contentious review which can be cited instead. When referring to a conceptual or theoretical exposition, the first major presentation of the current version should be used.

SELECTIVE CITATION IN SUPPORT OF A VIEWPOINT

A common bias in reporting the literature is to select only (or primarily) studies that support a given hypothesis or idea (*viewpoint citation*). This is harder to avoid and to detect than one might imagine. If there were a well defined body of literature that examined a particular hypothesis, and numerous high-quality studies conflicting with the hypothesis were ignored in a review, that would amount in the eyes of some to scientific misconduct. A reader who was not familiar with the area would be misled as much as if the author had fabricated data.

Less straightforward is the case where there are doubts about the methodological adequacy of conflicting studies. For example, studies that fail to detect the effect of an intervention may be small or involve inadequate implementation of the intervention. Unless one is explicitly attempting a comprehensive review where there is the space to explore these issues, the citing author has to make a judgement about how far to go in ignoring weak studies. Given the realistic possibility that the citing author is not wholly disinterested in the matter, it is good practice to alert the reader to conflicting findings and make a brief comment about the weight that might be attached to these and why.

Even less straightforward is the case where it is extremely difficult to determine what the corpus of findings on the topic is. This can happen for findings which typically do not form the main focus of papers. In the smoking literature, for example, it has been noted, and is widely believed, that depressed smokers are less likely to succeed in attempts to stop than non-depressed smokers. There are certainly studies showing such an association (Glassman, Helzer et al. 1990; Covery 1999).

However, often buried in reports of clinical trials and other studies are numerous reports of failures to find such an association and indeed a recent meta-analysis has reported no association (Hitsman, Borrelli et al. 2003). No doubt there are even more instances where the association has been looked for, not found and no report has been made. At the very least, scientific prudence dictates that findings that are susceptible to this kind of phenomenon be cited with suitable caveats.

SELECTIVE CITATION TO ENHANCE REPUTATION

Self-citation or citation of colleagues with a view to enhancing one's own or the colleague's reputation (*reputation citation*) is clearly unacceptable. It distorts science and the process of science and is personally damaging to individuals in less powerful positions or those who do not engage in that practice. One may debate how widespread this practice is but there can be little doubt that self-serving bias runs at some level throughout the scientific literature.

Self-citation can also apply to journals (articles in journals tending to cite articles from the same journal). This may arise for reasons other than reputation citation, some of which may be legitimate, but it can distort the literature. One study found significant difference in self-citation rates among journals of anesthesiology (Fassoulaki, Paraskeva et al. 2000).

It may be thought that a bias of this kind would be easily detected and an appropriate correction could be applied. However, this is probably optimistic. First of all, it is not unreasonable that one's own name should feature prominently in a reference list given that one's research is presumably to some degree programmatic. A similar principle would hold true for one's close colleagues. It can be difficult therefore to tell when this bias is operating. Secondly, the agencies that count citations (such as the Institute for Scientific Information, see later in the chapter) would only exclude a citation from an index if the same name appeared as *first* author.

SELECTIVE CITATION FOR CONVENIENCE

Using citations that are easy to find or happen to have come to the attention of the author is not good practice but is probably very common. There may be many ways in which *convenience* citation can distort the literature. Insofar as more accessible articles may not represent the literature it would create a biased impression. Searchable electronic databases could in principle mitigate the problem but they can also lead to their own kind of distortion. It would be expected that they would favour English language articles in journals indexed by the main databases. One would also expect more recent articles to gain preference because of the way that electronic databases sort the results of searches. Convenience citation would also be expected to favour the more popular journals. One might argue that this is no bad thing because it would be the better articles that would in general find their way into these journals; however, this is not necessarily so.

SELECTIVE CITATION BY COUNTRY OF ORIGIN

It goes without saying that a tendency to cite articles simply because they are from one's own country of origin is not good practice. Many researchers are under the impression that this occurs, however. Naturally, the greatest suspicion falls on the US as the main producer of research output and many non-US researchers can probably recount cases where a US author has cited predominantly or exclusively US references even when more appropriate ones from other countries exist. In fact this bias has been found among both UK and US researchers publishing in major medical journals (Campbell 1990; Grange 1999). Another study found North American journals to cite North American journals to a greater extent than did journals from other regions (Fassoulaki, Paraskeva et al. 2000) but the opposite has also been found (Pasterkamp, Rotmans, de Klein, and Borst, 2007).

CITING INACCESSIBLE SOURCES

It is quite common for authors to cite conference papers or their abstracts, submitted articles, in-house papers or unpublished reports (the so-called *grey literature*). The problem with this kind of citation is that it does not fulfill the verification function of citation. Therefore it is generally to be discouraged. There may be cases where it is the only option and important in fulfilling the acknowledgement or documentation role, but if this is not obvious the use should be justified. If that citation is more than a few years old the use becomes increasingly problematic. It is often reasonable to presume that if it is a paper or an abstract and the finding was robust it would have found its way into the peer reviewed literature.

It is becoming common to cite web sites. This is reasonable but will pose increasing problems over time as web sites move or become inaccessible. In general, for any statement intended to have lasting significance this practice is best avoided until a system is devised for ensuring the longevity of web-based scientific literature. In policy analyses or descriptions of historical processes, though, references to sources such as web-sites and government documents may be a key part of the research process

CITING UNEVALUATED SOURCES

When a citation is used to support a substantive statement, the implication is that the cited reference reports evidence in support of that statement. Inadequate though it is, peer review is the primary gatekeeper for this kind of report. However, it is commonplace for statements of fact to be supported by citations to book chapters, letters, conference presentations, abstracts, opinion pieces and other material that has not been peer reviewed. Although in principle the reader can track down the source and make his or her own evaluation, this is often impracticable. The only thing that comes close to a safeguard is the fact that the report has been through a peer review process. Within the social sciences, though, even non-peer reviewed books still remain a main source for new analytical concepts. In some cases, however, the review process for books is as rigorous as the peer review process for journal articles.

CITING WITHOUT READING

There is a great temptation to cite a work or part of a work on the strength of a report of what it says without going to the original source. Thus, if a paper or book chapter that we have access to makes a statement which is relevant to our work and cites another article in support of it, it is tempting to repeat the assertion and the citation without reading the original source material. This is clearly unacceptable because of the risk of misrepresentation. Equally, having identified an abstract of an article using an electronic database, there is a temptation to cite the article without going to the full text. This is risky practice because one has not taken the opportunity to evaluate the research being cited by reference to the methods and analyses used.

As a general principle, authors should not make reference to research output without having read and evaluated that output directly.

OVERUSE OF CITATIONS

Much of the earlier discussion concerned selective use of citations. Quite a common problem is the reverse: providing a long list of citations to support a single statement when fewer would be sufficient. If it is important that the work of the authors of all the various works be acknowledged, or if the intention is to provide a comprehensive review, than a long list of citations is appropriate. Otherwise it can make a paper unwieldy and the rule of thumb of selective citation described earlier could be adopted.

GETTING CITED

All the above should suggest that the process of citation is subject to considerable bias and, while there is a duty on researchers to minimize this, it is unlikely that it will ever be eliminated. This being said, if one is writing an article that one believes is important it would seem reasonable to try to ensure that it is drawn to the attention of its intended audience, and that means being cited. The choice of journal is obviously of relevance (see Chapter 1). And it may not be the most prestigious journal that offers the best chance, but rather the best quality *specialist* journal. The most prestigious journals tend to be generalist and as such may be not be routinely read by many potential users of the research. Whatever outlet one uses for one's research it can often be a good idea to take other steps to publicise the findings. Some researchers email or send copies of their papers to colleagues. Others post them on list-serves. Conference presentations and web-sites are also potentially useful sources of publicity.

CITATION INDEXES

We mentioned earlier that citations are often used as a marker of quality. There is a presumption that the more often an article is cited, in some sense the better it is. This extends to journals, for which the single most widely used measure of quality is the 'Impact Factor'. The Impact Factor for a journal in a given year is calculated as the average number of citations in indexed journals in that year to articles in the preceding two years. Thus, if a journal published 50 articles in 2005 and 2006 and there were 100 citations to these articles in 2007, the journal's Impact Factor for 2007 would be 2.0. Self-citations are included, so clearly the more prolific an author is and the more that authors cites his or her own work, the more useful that author is a to a journal wanting to maximize its impact factor!

Researchers are often judged by the citation counts of their articles and by the Impact Factors of the journals in which they publish. Funding decisions in many institutions and departments are based in part on members of those institutions publishing in 'high impact' journals. Unfortunately there are many problems associated with using citation counts as a marker of quality and even more with using the Impact Factor (Opthof 1997; Seglen 1997; Hecht, Hecht et al. 1998; Jones 1999; Semenzato and Agostino 2000). Some researchers have suggested that it may be possible to use them with appropriate caveats and corrections (Rostami-Hodjegan and Tucker 2001; Fassoulaki, Papilas et al. 2002; Braun 2003) while others have argued that they should be abandoned (Bloch and Walter 2001; Ojasoo, Maisonneuve et al. 2002; Walter, Bloch et al. 2003).

As regards citation counts, the various biases in the use of citations discussed earlier should give an indication of the problem with using counts as a marker of quality. In addition, it should be recalled that *critical citation* is quite commonplace; therefore an article might be cited precisely because it is weak or misleading. A recent article examined the association between peer ratings of quality and the numbers of citations between 1997 and 2000 to articles appearing in the journal *Addiction* in 1997 (West and McIlwaine 2002). Although two independent reviewers agreed moderately in their ratings of the papers, the correlation between these ratings and the number of citations was almost zero. One factor that was correlated with citation count was the region of origin of the first author of the paper: papers from English speaking countries received more citations than those from continental Europe, which received more than those from the rest of the world. A larger analysis of citations to articles in emergency medicine revealed that the citation count of articles was predicted to some extent by the impact factor of the journal in which they appeared and to a more limited extent by quality of the articles (Callaham, Wears et al. 2002). A further study of citations to papers reporting randomized trials in hepato-biliary disease found a significant association with a positive outcome but no association with adjudged quality (Kjærgard and Gluud 2002).

Apart from the biases already discussed, the fact that only a small proportion of predominantly US journals is indexed in the Institute of Scientific Information (ISI) databases would lead to a bias, particularly against non-English speaking countries. One study reported that exclusion of core journals in emergency medicine had led citation counts in the field to remain low despite considerable expansion of the field (Gallagher and Barnaby 1998). Another noted that the way to improve the Impact Factors of journals in dermatology was to increase the number of them indexed by the ISI (Jemec 2001). Another bias arises from the fact that some fields, such as biosciences, use a lot more citations than others. This will disadvantage authors in low citing fields, typically the social sciences. There are a range of other factors that make citation counts potentially misleading as a marker of quality (Box 7.3).

Additional problems arise from the two-year time window used by the Impact Factor score. The *publication lag* (the time between the acceptance of an article by the journal and its publication) in many journals, particularly social science journals is at least a year. This means that for an article to be read after it has been published and then used to inform new research would normally take at least two years. Citations made within the Impact Factor window may therefore not have been used to generate new research ideas but more likely be part of a programme involving a community of authors with reciprocal knowledge of each others' research.

Box 7.3 WHY CITATION COUNTS ARE OFTEN MISLEADING AS A MARKER OF QUALITY

Articles are sometimes cited in order to be criticised

Papers describing important original studies are often neglected in favour of reviews

There is a bias towards citing articles from one's own country or research group, or that are easily accessible

Some fields of study generate more citations than others irrespective of how important they are: e.g. fields with high levels of activity and mature fields

The importance and quality of a work or part of a work may relate to its policy or clinical implications rather than its use by other researchers

Other researchers may fail to grasp the importance of a work or part of a work

The citation indexes are biased towards English-speaking and US journals

CONCLUSIONS

Citations are the primary formal means by which scientific findings are communicated. Ideal citation practice would involve comprehensive and objective use of the whole corpus of published literature. Clearly, this is impossible. However, it should still be possible to approximate this ideal by adopting a few guidelines. These recognize that citation serves the dual function of enabling verification of statements and acknowledging contributions.

In the case of formal reviews, the principles are well-documented: the sources searched and the search rules should be clearly specified, as should the inclusion and exclusion criteria for articles; the sources should go beyond ISI databases and include searching reference lists of papers in the search domain. With regard to informal reviews, such as those used to introduce research reports, the following principles can be applied:

1. Support all non-obvious, substantive claims by citation or direct evidence.
2. Do not support statements of the obvious by citation.
3. If there is an authoritative review on a well-supported statement, this may be used in place of original papers.
4. When citing original papers, cite the discovery paper together with a small number of other papers that illustrate the generality of the phenomenon.

5. Resist the propensity to:
    a. prefer citations from one's own country unless the finding is country-specific,
    b. prefer citations from oneself and one's colleagues,
    c. limit citations to those that support a contention, when in fact there are others that conflict with it,
    d. cite output which is readily retrievable if there are more appropriate references, and
    e. provide an unnecessarily large number of citations for a single statement.
6. Avoid citing inaccessible sources wherever possible.
7. When using citations in support of substantive statements, either use references that have been through some kind of peer review process or provide an appropriate caveat.

Citation counts are widely used as an index of quality. Given that few if any researchers are able to follow all the above principles, together with the fact that many other factors influence the number of times a piece is cited, citation counts are a highly problematic index of quality. Journal Impact Factors are even more problematic. Authors should be aware of this and not be beguiled by their apparent objectivity. Ultimately there is no substitute for peer evaluation of research output, however flawed and subjective this might be.

REFERENCES

Bannigan, K., J. Droogan, et al. (1997). "Systematic reviews: what do they involve?" *Nurs Times* 93(18): 52-3.

Bloch, S. and G. Walter (2001). "The Impact Factor: time for change." *Aust N Z J Psychiatry* **35**(5): 563-8.

Braun, T. (2003). "The reliability of total citation rankings." *J Chem Inf Comput Sci* **43**(1): 45-6.

Callaham, M., R. L. Wears, et al. (2002). "Journal prestige, publication bias, and other characteristics associated with citation of published studies in peer-reviewed journals." *Jama* **287**(21): 2847-50.

Campbell, F. M. (1990). "National bias: a comparison of citation practices by health professionals." *Bull Med Libr Assoc* **78**(4): 376-82.

Chalmers, I., M. Enkin, et al. (1993). "Preparing and updating systematic reviews of randomized controlled trials of health care." *Milbank* Q **71**(3): 411-37.

Cook, D. J., D. L. Sackett, et al. (1995). "Methodologic guidelines for systematic reviews of randomized control trials in health care from the Potsdam Consultation on Meta-Analysis." *J Clin Epidemiol* **48**(1): 167-71.

Covey, L. S. (1999). "Tobacco cessation among patients with depression." *Prim Care* **26**(3): 691-706.

Fassoulaki, A., K. Papilas, et al. (2002). "Impact factor bias and proposed adjustments for its determination." *Acta Anaesthesiol Scand* **46**(7): 902-5.

Fassoulaki, A., A. Paraskeva, et al. (2000). "Self-citations in six anaesthesia journals and their significance in determining the impact factor." *Br J Anaesth* **84**(2): 266-9.

Gallagher, E. J. and D. P. Barnaby (1998). "Evidence of methodologic bias in the derivation of the Science Citation Index impact factor [see comments]." *Ann Emerg Med* **31**(1): 83-6.

Glassman, A. H., J. E. Helzer, et al. (1990). "Smoking, smoking cessation, and major depression." *Jama* **264**(12): 1546-9.

Grange, R. I. (1999). "National bias in citations in urology journals: parochialism or availability? [see comments]." *BJU Int* **84**(6): 601-3.

Hecht, F., B. K. Hecht, et al. (1998). "The journal "impact factor": a misnamed, misleading, misused measure." *Cancer Genet Cytogenet* **104**(2): 77-81.

Hitsman, B., B. Borrelli, et al. (2003). "History of depression and smoking cessation outcome: a meta-analysis." *J Consult Clin Psychol* **71**(4): 657-63.

Jemec, G. B. (2001). "Impact factors of dermatological journals for 1991 - 2000." *BMC Dermatol* **1**(1): 7.

Jones, A. W. (1999). "The impact of Alcohol and Alcoholism among substance abuse journals." *Alcohol Alcohol* **34**(1): 25-34.

Kjaergard, L. L. and C. Gluud (2002). "Citation bias of hepato-biliary randomized clinical trials." *J Clin Epidemiol* **55**(4): 407-10.

Moher, D., D. J. Cook, et al. (1999). "Improving the quality of reports of meta-analyses of randomised controlled trials: the QUOROM statement. Quality of Reporting of Meta-analyses." *Lancet* **354**(9193): 1896-900.

Ojasoo, T., H. Maisonneuve, et al. (2002). "[The impact factor of medical journals, a bibliometric indicator to be handled with care]." *Presse Med* **31**(17): 775-81.

Opthof, T. (1997). "Sense and nonsense about the impact factor." *Cardiovasc Res* **33**(1): 1-7.

Pasterkamp, G., Rotmans, J.I., de Klein, D.V.P. and Borst, C. (2007) "Citation frequency: A biased measure of research impact significantly influenced by the geographical origin of research articles." *Scientometrics* **70**(1), 153-165.

Reeves, S., I. Koppel, et al. (2002). "Twelve tips for undertaking a systematic review." *Med Teach* **24**(4): 358-63.

Reyes, H. (2001). "[The references in articles published in biomedical journals]." *Rev Med Chil* **129**(4): 343-5.

Rostami-Hodjegan, A. and G. T. Tucker (2001). "Journal impact factors: a 'bioequivalence' issue?" *Br J Clin Pharmacol* **51**(2): 111-7.

Seglen, P. O. (1997). "Why the impact factor of journals should not be used for evaluating research." *Bmj* **314**(7079): 498-502.

Semenzato, G. and C. Agostini (2000). "The impact factor: deeds and misdeeds [editorial]." *Sarcoidosis Vasc Diffuse Lung Dis* **17**(1): 22-6.

Sutton, A. J., D. R. Jones, et al. (1999). "Systematic reviews and meta-analysis: a structured review of the methodological literature." *J Health Serv Res Policy* **4**(1): 49-55.

Walter, G., S. Bloch, et al. (2003). "Counting on citations: a flawed way to measure quality." *Med J Aust* **178**(6): 280-1.

West, R. and A. McIlwaine (2002). "What do citation counts count for in the field of addiction? An empirical evaluation of citation counts and their link with peer ratings of quality." *Addiction* **97**(5): 501-4.

CHAPTER 8
COIN OF THE REALM: PRACTICAL PROCEDURES FOR DETERMINING AUTHORSHIP

THOMAS F. BABOR AND DOMINIQUE MORISANO

> *Like a coin, authorship has two sides: credit and responsibility. One receives professional credit from his/her publications and takes responsibility for their contents.*
>
> Biagioli et al. (1999, p. 2)

INTRODUCTION

Authorship credit is conceivably the most important and least understood area of professional life for members of the scientific community. Because promotion, prestige, and productivity are judged largely by publication activity, authorship credit has become the 'coin of the realm' in the scientific marketplace (Wilcox 1998). Beyond the value of authorship to individual investigators, the assignment of individual credit to a publication implies certain ethical and scientific imperatives that are of tremendous importance to the scientific enterprise. These imperatives include the certification of public responsibility for the truth of a publication and the equitable assignment of credit to those who have contributed in a substantive way to its contents.

The need for clear and consistent procedures for the determination of authorship credits comes from two considerations. First, many journals are now demanding that papers be prepared in a way that is consistent with the principles of responsible authorship. Second, a clear consensus about the conditions governing authorship decisions would make the work of individual authors much easier.

Numerous professional organizations (e.g., American Psychological Association 2002), expert panels (International Committee of Medical Journal Editors 1991; 2003), and individual commentators (Rennie et al. 1997) have developed policies and procedures dealing with individual, group, and corporate authorship. In this chapter, we review some of these guidelines from both the practical and ethical perspectives, in an attempt to develop workable procedures that authors can follow during the course of preparing and publishing a scientific article. In addition, we consider authorship problems that sometimes arise in the course of a publication cycle.

These problems seem to be occurring with increasing frequency (Wilcox 1998) and include failure to involve potential collaborators; failure to credit collaborating authors; undeserved authorship credits; relaxed policies for students, research assistants and post-docs; and excessive numbers of co-authors. Although these are all serious problems, the pervasiveness of some of them in the publication process is suggested by the extent to which most scientific readers can be amused by the satirical humor epitomized in the 'Ode to multi-authorship' quoted in Box 8.1.

Box 8.1 ODE TO MULTI-AUTHORSHIP: A MULTICENTRE, PROSPECTIVE RANDOM POEM (Quoted from Horrowitz, et al., 1996)

All cases complete, the study was over
the data were entered, lost once, and recovered.
Results were greeted with considerable glee
p value (two-tailed) equaling 0.0493.
The severity of illness, oh what a discovery,
was inversely proportional to the chance of recovery.
When the paper's first draft had only begun
the wannabe authors lined up one by one.
To jockey for their eternal positions
(for who would be first, second, and third)
and whom 'et aled' in all further citations.
Each centre had seniors, each senior ten bees,
the bees had technicians and nurses to please.
The list it grew longer and longer each day,
as new authors appeared to enter the fray.
Each fought with such fury to stake his or her place
being just a 'participant' would be a disgrace.
For the appendix is piled with hundreds of others
and seen by no one but spouses and mothers
If to 'publish or perish' is how academics are bred
then to miss the masthead is near to be dead.
As the number of authors continued to grow
they outnumbered the patients by two to one or so.
While PIs faxed memos to company headquarters
the bees and the nurses took care of the orders.
They'd signed up the patients, and followed them weekly
heard their complaints, and kept casebooks so neatly.
There were seniors from centres that enrolled two or three
who threatened 'foul play' if not on the marquee.
But the juniors and helpers who worked into the night
were simply 'acknowledged' or left off outright.
'Calm down' cried the seniors to the quivering drones
there's place for you all on the RPU clones.
When the paper was finished and sent for review
six authors didn't know that the study was through.
Oh the work was so hard, and the fights oh so bitter
for the glory of publishing and grabbing the glitter.
Imagine the wars when in six months or better
The Editor's response, 'please make it a letter'.

RPU = repeating publishable unit; PI=principal investigator

CONVENTIONS IN ASSIGNING ORDER OF AUTHORSHIP

One of the difficulties in determining the criteria for authorship comes from the different traditions and practices that have been used to distribute authorship credits. Box 8.2 provides definitions of common authorship terms and ethical issues, some of which are also discussed in Chapter 4. Authors are sometimes listed in alphabetical order to avoid controversy about the relative contributions of different authors, especially when the contributions have been fairly equal. A related convention is to list authors in reverse alphabetical order, presumably to avoid the preference given to persons whose surname begins with a letter that appears early in the alphabet.

Box 8.2 FORMS OF AUTHORSHIP

Coercion authorship	Is a gift authorship that is demanded rather than voluntarily awarded
Contributorship	Advocates listing the contributions of each person involved in the project, and avoiding the attribution of authorship entirely
Corporate authorship	Lists the name of a project as author, along with a separate acknowledgement describing the contributors and the corresponding author (as an alternative to long author lists in multi-authored reports)
Corresponding author	The first author listed on an article, assumed to be the main researcher and writer of the article and responsible for corresponding with the journal editor. In some cases the corresponding author is not listed first when the writing and corresponding functions are divided.
Ghost authorship	The failure to include as co-author of a work a person who satisfies the criteria for authorship (e.g., a science writer employed by a drug company)
Gift authorship	Awards authorship credit because of a person's power or prestige rather than for substantial contribution to the work
Guarantor	The person who takes responsibility for the contents and integrity of the work as a whole
Honorary authorship	See 'gift authorship'
Mutual admiration authorship	Occurs when two or more researchers agree to list each others' names on their own papers despite the others' minimal involvement.
Mutual support authorship	See 'mutual admiration authorship'

Another convention is to list the laboratory director, center director, or other prominent person last. As noted in other parts of this chapter, this convention is not ethical unless that individual has made a substantial contribution to the publication and is not being listed merely to flatter the powerful or to add to the prestige value of the authorship list.

The convention followed most frequently in the addiction field is to list authors according to their relative contributions, with the first author assumed to be responsible for writing the paper, corresponding with the journal editor, and making the most substantive contributions. The first author in such a system is sometimes called the corresponding author. In some cases a senior researcher who is not the first author is designated as corresponding author to facilitate the progress of the manuscript through the peer review process. This practice is not acceptable if the main purpose is to take advantage of the influence and prestige of the corresponding, rather than his or her publishing experience.

Although the main-author-first convention is assumed to be based on the equitable distribution of authorship credits, the relative ordering of authors is often dependent on the first author's judgment of others' contributions. In the absence of conducting an inventory of contributions, effort, and follow through, it is likely that some contributors will receive more credit than they deserve, and others less, because of the ambiguity and arbitrariness of the process.

With the growth of multi-center clinical trials and other 'big science' collaborative projects, corporate authorship has also increased. This convention lists a team name as the author, with a footnote or acknowledgement describing the contributors and the corresponding author. One reason for this convention is to make citations and referencing more efficient in cases where there are large numbers of contributors. Corporate authorship may also help to avoid the difficulties associated with determining who contributed what to a multi-authored paper, and how much credit each author should receive. Some journals require contributors to formally name at least one person in the masthead, however (e.g., Alexander Bloggins for the Addiction Research Group).

Because of the problems associated with determining who merits authorship credit, one editor (Smith 1997) proposed the concept of 'contributorship'. This involves listing the contributions of each person involved in the project, and avoiding the attribution of authorship entirely. Although some journals now request all contributing authors to list their contributions when an article is submitted, and some publish a summary in a footnote or acknowledgement, this convention has not been adopted by any journal in its pure form (probably due to the problems it causes with referencing).

In summary, a variety of conventions have been used to arrange the names of individual contributors in multi-authored papers. Some conventions are used more than others, with the 'main author first' convention used most often. Other conventions (e.g., corporate authorship) tend to be used in special situations as the case demands. The purpose of these conventions, particularly more recent variants, is to assure that proper credit is assigned so that individual responsibility for a publication can be inferred by the reader.

PUBLICATION POLICIES AND PUBLICATION MISCONDUCT

Over the past 25 years, journal editors, research administrators, and funding agencies have devoted increasing attention to the ethical and practical issues of scientific authorship. Concern about authorship has been heightened by a number of events and situations that have at times compromised, and at other times embarrassed, the entire scientific enterprise.

The most flagrant examples involve scientific misconduct. In a number of well-publicized cases (Broad and Wade 1984), investigators have published scientific papers that have been retracted because the data were fraudulent or the contents plagiarized from other sources. What is remarkable about many of these cases is that in addition to the person directly involved in scientific misconduct (e.g., John Darsee, who was the lead author on numerous fraudulent articles), there have typically been a number of co-authors who apparently had no idea that the senior author was fabricating data or copying others' ideas. This implies that in some cases, co-authors are not in a position to take public responsibility for the contents of a scientific report, which is now considered to be one of the main criteria for authorship credit. In its updated statement on authorship standards for submissions to biomedical journals, the International Committee of Medical Journal Editors (2003) indicated that some journals now request that one or more authors, referred to as 'guarantors', be identified as the persons who take responsibility for the contents and integrity of the work as a whole.

Extreme cases aside, the abuse of scientific authorship has been suspected in an even greater number of cases where the scientific misconduct is much more subtle. Examples include the addition of authors to curry favour, conferring co-authorship by virtue of status or power, rewarding students or junior faculty with co-authorship to advance their careers, and adding a prominent name to a list of co-authors to receive a more sympathetic editorial review. Related to these problems and to the ever-growing importance of 'research productivity' are disturbing trends toward the proliferation of authorship credits attached to publications, a growth in the number of mediocre quality publications ('paper inflation'), and the multiplication of reports using the 'least publishable unit' (LPU) in order to maximize the output from a single study (see Lafollette 1992).

In part to prevent these kinds of problems, many journal editors and other individuals in scientific publishing have promoted policies designed to both detect misconduct and prevent the more blatant forms of authorship abuse. These policies include the requirement that all authors sign a statement of authorship responsibility, descriptions of the criteria for scientific authorship, limitations on the number of authors listed on the masthead, and requests that co-authors provide a written explanation of their individual contributions to a publication.

How does all of this apply to individual authors? Even if most authors in the addiction field have never encountered an instance of data fabrication or plagiarism, they are likely to encounter the more subtle forms of irresponsible authorship and publication misconduct, such as 'gift authorship' and 'ghost authorship' (Flanagin et al. 1998). Honorary or gift authorship consists of awarding authorship credit because of the person's power and prestige, rather than for time, effort, and substantial contributions to the work. When someone demands (and receives) an honorary authorship, it is sometimes called a coercion authorship (Claxton 2005). Closely related to gift authorship is mutual admiration or mutual support authorship, in which two or more researchers agree to list each other as authors despite little involvement in each other's papers, usually as a means to expand their individual publication histories (Claxton 2005). Ghost authorship refers to the failure to include as co-authors those who satisfy the criteria for authorship (Sheikh 2000). This happens most often in the publication of pharmaceutical company trials where an industry-paid scientific writer drafts the article but is not listed as a co-author to avoid the perception of conflict of interest.

In the remainder of this chapter, we review guidelines that have been developed to deal with publication misconduct before describing some practical steps that can be taken by individuals, project teams, centers, departments, and professional organizations to ensure responsible authorship.

FORMAL GUIDELINES

In order to develop a more coherent, equitable, and ethical set of guidelines for addiction journals, various policies and procedures have been set forth in the recent scientific literature. These policies include the guidelines recommended by the Council of Science Editors (Biagioli et al. 1999), the Sigma Xi standards for responsible authorship (Jackson and Prados 1983), the statement of the International Committee of Medical Journal Editors (2003), and a variety of proposals from individual commentators (e.g., Fine and Kurdek 1993; Broad and Wade 1984). Box 8.3 describes the general guidelines developed by the American Psychological Association (2002). These have been the subject of a considerable amount of interpretation and discussion in the psychological literature, and some attempts have been made to develop operational definitions of the specific criteria.

In an interesting variant of the APA guidelines, Winston (1985) developed a system in which points are earned for various professional contributions to the scholarly publication, with research design and report writing assigned the most points. A certain number of points must be earned to qualify for authorship credit, and the individual with the highest number is granted first authorship.

One of the most cited sources on authorship is the 1985 consensus statement of the International Committee of Medical Journal Editors (ICMJE 1985). The statement indicated that only those in a position to take public responsibility for the work could claim authorship. Although this definition would preclude gift authorship and help to minimize ghost authorship, there were problems with these criteria, such as the requirement that all authors be prepared to take public responsibility for its contents and the definition of a 'substantial' contribution (see Yank and Rennie 1999). In addition, there was a problem with the distribution of recognition to collaborating

Box 8.3 AUTHORSHIP GUIDELINES PROPOSED BY THE AMERICAN PSYCHOLOGICAL ASSOCIATION

Psychologists take responsibility and credit, including authorship credit, only for work they have actually performed or to which they have substantially contributed. Principal authorship and other publication credits accurately reflect the relative scientific or professional contributions of the individuals involved, regardless of their relative status. Mere possession of an institutional position, such as department chair, does not justify authorship credit. Minor contributions to the research or to the writing for publications are acknowledged appropriately, such as in footnotes or in an introductory statement. Except under exceptional circumstances, a student is listed as principal author on any multiple-authored article that is substantially based on the student's doctoral dissertation. Faculty advisors discuss publication credit with students as early as feasible and throughout the research and publication process as appropriate.

Source: Section 8.12, American Psychological Association (2002)

investigators who band together on a project in order to take advantage of expertise that is unlikely to be concentrated in one individual. These problems were corrected in a 2003 revision to this statement (see http://www.icmje.org/). ICMJE now indicates that 'each author should have participated sufficiently in the work to take public responsibility for appropriate portions of the content', and that one or more authors ('guarantors') should take responsibility for the integrity of the work as a whole, from inception to published article. In addition, all authors must have made substantial contributions in each of the following areas: 1) conception and design, or acquisition of data, or analysis and interpretation of data; 2) drafting the article or revising it critically for important intellectual content; and 3) final approval of the version to be published. Additional changes were made by ICMJE to deal with contributors who do not meet the authorship criteria, such as people who provide technical help or writing assistance, or general support for a project. These individuals and their contributions should be listed in an acknowledgements section. To the extent that a listing of such persons could be interpreted as an endorsement of the data or conclusions, all persons listed must provide written permission to be acknowledged.

PRACTICAL STEPS TO DETERMINE AUTHORSHIP

The foregoing discussion of conventions, problems, and policies suggests that authorship of an article or paper is first and foremost a social process that requires a considerable amount of negotiation, influence, and persuasion. If there is a general perception that the current procedures for attributing authorship credits are inadequate and ineffective (see Yank and Rennie 1999), then it may be because the social nature of authorship has not been taken into account in the design of policies and procedures for responsible authorship. Most guidelines focus on individual accountability in relation to abstract ethical principles, with bureaucratic controls and punitive sanctions emphasized instead of practical guidance about what to do at the level of the group where real influence and control are concentrated. In this section we describe a model process to demonstrate how many of the helpful suggestions provided in the literature on scientific authorship can be implemented in a practical, systematic and open way. The process is based on the assumption that because authorship on a multi-authored article is a social process, responsibility, accountability, and the equitable distribution of credit reside in the group of individuals most responsible for conducting the research and writing the article. This process can be easily implemented by an external agency or even within an institution, department, or research centre. It needs to be conducted in an open, democratic, and ethical way so that all collaborating investigators agree to accept the basic values of scientific integrity.

As in any group process, one or more individuals need to take a leadership role. There is general agreement in the scientific community that the person most closely associated with the project should take responsibility for drafting the paper and being first author. Exceptions to this rule are possible, such as when the investigator who conceived and directed a project cedes responsibility to a junior investigator who made special contributions and who is capable of carrying the written report to a successful conclusion. A critical skill that should be taken into account in the choice of one or more leaders for a scientific publication is familiarity with the authorship issues described in this chapter. If the person has had no formal training in research ethics, the papers cited in the reference section of this chapter should be reviewed, giving special attention to several key sources (e.g., International Committee of Medical Journal Editors 2003; Fine and Kurdek 1993).

To avoid conflict, misunderstandings, and publication misconduct, both the leader and the group should be guided by generally accepted procedures that are characterized by openness and transparency. In the following paragraphs we provide an outline for such a model that can be modified to fit the needs of a project team.

The model requires the completion of specific tasks at each of three stages in the publication process. As described below, periodic discussions about authorship and accountability should be conducted at the planning stage, the drafting stage, and the finalization stage of a publication. According to Lafollette (1992, p. 107), 'The issue is absolutely clear. Who did what and how much? Answering those questions early on - and continuing to ask them as projects change - can help to prevent disputes or embarrassment later'.

PLANNING STAGE

The planning stage of the publication process begins when a scientific investigation or other project (e.g., a review paper) has advanced to the point where it is likely that a scientific article is appropriate or warranted. This decision is usually made by the project leader, who either takes direct responsibility for the direction of the publication or designates one or more individuals to initiate the publication planning process. The following tasks and activities are suggested:

- One or more senior members of the research or writing team take responsibility for developing an outline of the paper, a timetable for the completion of the article, and a list of potential co-authors, based on actual contributions to date and expected contributions in the future. The outline is distributed to all prospective authors, with the understanding that authorship will depend on substantive contributions, as well as effort and follow-through, as described in relevant policies and publications (including this chapter).

- It is explained that there will be a periodic reassessment of the contributions of the research team throughout the planning, drafting, and finalization stages. If it is found that previous expectations are not being met, then assignment of authorship credit may have to be modified, based on the actual contributions at the completion of the publication.

- Relevant policies and publications (including copies of this chapter) are distributed to prospective authors along with the outline.

- A meeting is called to discuss the proposed publication and the distribution of responsibilities for its completion. Assignments are made for data analysis and writing sections of first draft. A timeline of key tasks should also be distributed and discussed.

DRAFTING STAGE

After the first draft of a paper is completed, or as relevant sections are finished, the drafting author(s) circulate the article for comments. At this stage potential authors again need to be reminded not only about their rights to possible authorship, but also about their responsibilities.

A crucial task at this stage is the process of identifying who qualifies for formal authorship credit according to generally accepted criteria for responsible authorship. One way to accomplish this task is to ask all potential contributing authors (including the lead author) to describe their contributions to the project. Box 8.4 provides a checklist of possible contributions that prospective authors should be asked to complete by the lead author in order to determine eligibility for authorship at this stage in the process. Disclosure checklists like this one have been found to be feasible and to provide important information that is relevant to the determination of authorship credit (Yank and Rennie 1999).

Once the checklist is completed, the lead author calls a meeting to discuss authorship and other matters related to the proposed publication. At the meeting, each person is asked to describe his or her contributions to the project to date. In such a setting, individuals often reveal contributions that others were not aware of, and in other cases describe activities that may not be considered substantial in comparison to those of others. At this time it is important to discuss generally accepted criteria for authorship, such as those listed in Box 8.4, to make sure that everyone agrees on the standards to be used to determine who should be listed on the paper and in what order the names

Box 8.4 CHECKLIST FOR CONDUCTING AN INVENTORY OF MAJOR AND MINOR CONTRIBUTIONS TO A SCIENTIFIC PAPER

Instructions: Use the checklist to describe your contributions to the project to date. Under each item you have checked, describe the nature of your contribution, the amount of effort you put into it (e.g., hours, days, months), and whether your contribution fulfilled all of the requirements for that task or some of the requirements (e.g., in collaboration with others you wrote part of the paper, or collected part of the data).

Conception (planning meetings, drafting of research proposal, etc.)
Review of literature
Obtained funding or other resources
Assembling the project team
Coordinated study (5) by assigning responsibilities and tasks
Training of personnel
Supervision of personnel
Human (or animal) subjects approvals
Design of methodology or experimental design (2)
Advised on design or analysis (9)
Writing the research protocol
Collection of data (4), including follow-up data
Clinical analysis or management (6)
Performed randomization or matching
Statistical analysis of data (8)
Interpretation of data (3)
Economic analysis of data
Managed data (10)
Provision of technical services (coding questionnaires, laboratory analyses (7), etc.)
Provision or recruitment of patients
Provision of materials or facilities
Present and defend findings in a public forum
Writing draft of paper
Writing final version of paper (1)
Submitting report for publication
Responding to reviewers' comments
Other activity or service (describe)

Note: numbers in parentheses refer to the top 10 overall categories of contribution identified by Yank and Rennie (1999) in a content analysis of articles according to the most frequently mentioned contributions to authorship.

should be arranged. To provide authority to the process, it may be advantageous to mention that most journals now require a similar process of asking authors to sign a statement attesting to the fact that they have met minimal criteria for authorship, and some journals (e.g., *Lancet*, *British Medical Journal*, *American Journal of Public Health*) require authors to describe their individual contributions in a footnote that is published along with the article.

One of the most difficult decisions in the assignment of authorship credit is the distinction between major (or substantial) and minor contributions.

A major contribution usually involves the independent development or interpretation of ideas that are critical or essential to the advancement of a scientific study or scholarly article. It may also involve the use of special skills to perform a complex task without which the project could not have been done. The emphasis in these definitions is more on quality than quantity. All persons making major contributions should receive authorship credit, provided that they also participate in the writing of the article and any revisions required by the editor. Such individuals should also be capable of taking public responsibility for both general and specific aspects of the publication, recognizing that opinions differ as to what this means. Although the checklist provided in Box 8.4 was compiled from a variety of sources, we borrowed heavily from Yank and Rennie (1999), who distinguished between 'major' and 'partial' contributions, and also reported the 10 major contributions that were observed in a content analysis of articles where authors provided a description of their roles in the publication process. A major contribution meant that the contributor fulfilled a majority of the activities for a given category. A partial or minor contribution refers to a more limited role, presumably in terms of time, effort, or substance.

According to Yank and Rennie (1999), examples of major contributions that fulfill their 'lenient' interpretation of the ICMJE criteria (ICMJE 1991) for authorship are: a) conception of the idea for the study or article; b) design of the study; c) statistical analysis or interpretation of data; d) laboratory analysis; e) management or analysis of clinical aspects; and f) performance of field work or epidemiology. Anyone who wrote or revised the paper (even sections) fulfilled the second part of the criteria (i.e., drafted the paper or revised it critically for important intellectual content).

In considering the relative importance of major contributions, we believe two additional factors should be taken into account by the leader and the group. These factors are effort and follow-through. Effort pertains to the amount of time spent on the particular contribution. Follow-through involves active participation at various stages throughout the project. For example, if a person has participated in a study in a minor way, or has made a major contribution that involves minimal effort (e.g., the development of an idea for the study, or a novel hypothesis) and/or follow-through, this does not necessarily entitle the individual to authorship if other persons have made greater contributions with respect to effort and follow-through.

Non-substantive considerations should not determine the order of authorship or whether or not to include an individual as an author. Examples of non-substantive factors include rank or status, need for publication credits to justify advancement, involvement in the project as a consequence of routine duties for which the individual is paid (e.g., collecting lab samples), or ability to provide access to experimental subjects. The person who is named as the principal investigator (PI) of a project or a grant for adminstrative reasons may not qualify for authorship under these circumstances if she or he had no role in the design and conduct of a particular project (e.g., the secondary analysis of data collected for another purpose).

Members of a research team also need to recognize that individuals will be expected to contribute to projects in a collegial fashion without necessarily receiving credits in all publications from that project. In some cases it may be justified to award authorship to individuals who have made minor contributions to several papers, but who may not qualify as having made a substantive contribution to all of them. And, as noted in Chapter 4, the group may want to give consideration to the special situation of students and post-doctoral fellows. Taking all of this information into account, it should not be difficult in most cases to reach consensus about who qualifies for authorship, and what the most equitable relative ranking of contributions should be. When contributions are discussed in an open forum in relation to generally accepted criteria and ethical principles, secondary (nonsubstantive) considerations tend to be difficult to defend, especially when there is a written record of each individual's perceived contributions. If there are discrepancies between what an individual perceives to be his or her contributions, and the perceptions of others, these differences often can be resolved through open discussion.

FINALIZATION STAGE

Before an article is formally submitted to a journal, there is a need to designate a corresponding author. This person is usually the first author, but sometimes it is also the senior project leader in cases where the first author is young or inexperienced. A prominent or senior co-author should never be designated as corresponding author solely to influence the review process. If there is general agreement about the order of the contributing authors, this can be reviewed at the final stage to determine whether the process of preparing and revising the paper altered the relative order of the contributions enough to require further changes.

CONCLUSION

Intellectual honesty is a fundamental ingredient of scientific integrity, and this extends to the need for complete accuracy and transparency in representing contributions to research reports and other scientific writing. The contributions of colleagues and collaborators need to be recognized in all scientific publications, but authorship must be assumed or awarded only on the basis of substantive contributions to an article and the ability of its authors to take public responsibility for its contents, or at least for major parts of the contents. Decisions regarding authorship should be seen as part of a process that begins with the development of a publication plan and ends with the final revision of an accepted paper. In between, it is best to have all potential contributors to a publication participate in an open process of stating their perceived contributions to a given project in the context of generally accepted criteria for authorship. Such a process is likely to prevent publication misconduct as well as misunderstandings and conflicts. To the extent that authorship credit continues to be seen as the 'coin of the realm' in addiction science, both sides of the coin (credit and responsibility) need to be valued.

ACKNOWLEDGEMENTS

The authors would like to thank Ian Stolerman for his helpful comments and suggestions.

REFERENCES AND ADDITIONAL READING

American Psychological Association's (APA's) Ethics Committee (2002) Ethical principles of psychologists and code of conduct. Website: http://www.apa.org/ethics/code2002.html (Last retrieved 16 August 2004).

Biagioli, M., Crane, J., Derish, P., Gruber, M., Rennie, D. and Horton, R. (1999) Council of Science Editors (CSE) Task force on authorship draft white paper. Website: http://www.councilscienceeditors.org/services/atf_whitepaper.cfm (Last retrieved 16 August 2004).

Broad, W. (1982) Crisis in publishing: credit or credibility? BioScience, 32, 645-647.

Broad, W. and Wade, N. (1984) Betrayers of the truth. New York: Simon and Schuster.

Burman, K. D. (1982) Hanging from the masthead: reflections on authorship. Annals of Internal Medicine, 97, 602-605.

Claxton, L. D. (2005) Scientific authorship part 2: history, recurring issues, practices, and guidelines. Mutation Research, 589, 31-45.

Editor (1982) Authorship from the reader's side. Journal of Internal Medicine, 97, 613-614.

Editor (1983) Responsibilities of co-authorship. Annals of Internal Medicine, 99, 266-267.

Editor (1983) Who should be an author. British Medical Journal, 287, 1569-1570.

Editor (1992) Instructions for authors. New England Journal of Medicine. 267, 41-44.

Fine, M. A. and Kurdek, L. A. (1993) Reflections on determining authorship credit and authorship order on facultystudent collaborations. American Psychologist, 48, 1141-1147. Website: http://www.apa.org/journals/amp/kurdek.html (Last retrieved 16 August 2004)

Flanagin, A., Carey, L. A., Fontanarosa, P. B., Phillips, S. G., Pace, B. P., Lundberg, G. D., et al. (1998) Prevalence of articles with honorary authors and ghost authors in peer-reviewed medical journals. Journal of the American Medical Association, 280, 222-224.

Horowitz, H.W., Fiebach, N.H., Levitz, S.M., Seibel, J, Smail, E.H., Telzak, E.E., Wormser, G.P. Nadelman, R.B., Montecalvo, M., Nowakowski, J. and Raffalli, J.

(1996) Ode to multiauthorship: a multicentre, prospective random poem. Lancet. 348, 1746. (21/28 December.).

International Committee of Medical Journal Editors (1985) Guidelines on authorship. British Medical Journal, 291, 722.

International Committee of Medical Journal Editors (1991) Uniform requirements for manuscripts submitted to biomedical journals. New England Journal of Medicine, 324, 424- 428.

International Committee of Medical Journal Editors (2003) Uniform requirements for manuscripts submitted to biomedical journals: writing and editing for biomedical publication. Website: http://www.icmje.org/ (Last retrieved 16 August 2004).

Jackson, C. I., and Prados, J. W. (1983) Honor in science. American Scientist, 71, 462-464.

Lafollette, M. C. (1992) Stealing into print: fraud, plagiarism, and misconduct in scientific publishing. Berkeley, CA: University of California Press.

Murray, B. (1998) The authorship dilemma: who gets credit for what? APA Monitor, 29 (12).

Rennie, D. Yank, V. and Emanuel, L. (1997) When authorship fails: a proposal to make contributors accountable. Journal of the American Medical Association, 278, 579-585.

Sheikh, A. (2000) Publication ethics and the research assessment exercise: reflections on the troubled question of authorship. Journal of Medical Ethics, 266, 422-426. (1 December).

Smith, R. (1997) Authorship: time for a paradigm shift? BMJ, 1997, 314-992. (5 April).

University of Pennsylvania's Graduate Council of the Faculties (1998) Policy on fairness of authorship credit in collaborative faculty-student publications. Website: www.upenn.edu/grad/authorpolicy_alpha.html. (Last retrieved on 16 August 2004).

Wilcox, L.J., ed. (1998) Authorship: the coin of the realm, the source of complaints. Journal of the American Medical Association, 280(3), 216-217. (15 July).

Winston, R. B. (1985) A suggested procedure for determining order of authorship in research publications. Journal of Counseling and Development, 63, 515-518.

Wuensch, K. (2002) Dr. Wuensch's authorship tips. East Carolina University (Department of Psychology). Website http://core.ecu.edu/psyc/wuenschk/thauth.htm. (Last retrieved 16 August 2004).

Yank, V. and Rennie, D. (1999) Disclosure of researcher contributions: a study of original research articles in The Lancet. Annals of Internal Medicine, 130, 661-670.

CHAPTER 9
PREPARING MANUSCRIPTS AND RESPONDING TO REVIEWERS' REPORTS: INSIDE THE EDITORIAL BLACK BOX

IAN STOLERMAN

INTRODUCTION

This chapter describes how the peer review process works and presents suggestions to authors of manuscripts. It is based upon the experiences of scientists and clinicians who have many years of involvement as editors of prominent addiction journals. The task of the editor is to publish manuscripts appropriate to the journal and to assist would-be authors in the production of suitable material. Many of the problems facing authors writing for scholarly peer reviewed journals in the addiction field are similar to those in other fields. Therefore, it is recommended that readers consult one or more of the full-length books that have already been published in this general area. Numerous books and articles have been published, as can be seen by searching amazon.com or PubMed for 'scientific writing'. For example, a search of PubMed on 1 July 2008 yielded 144 hits, many of which were relevant. A short list of recent books is provided at the end of this chapter in Appendix 9.1.

TRIAGE: THE FIRST SELECTION

The author's quest to find a suitable publication outlet ends with a letter stating 'I am pleased to inform you that your manuscript is acceptable for publication …'. The first step is to get the manuscript into the peer-review system. This is not the inevitable consequence of submitting to a peer-reviewed journal. Some journals state formally that they operate a system of 'triage' whereby the editor or his or her assistants decide which submitted articles will be entered into the peer review process. In practice, it is likely that all journals have such a system to protect the profile of the journal and to avoid bothering authors and peer reviewers with a long and laborious process when it is easy to predict a negative result (see Box 9.1). Thus, if something is received that clearly has no hope of acceptance it may be rejected without review. Here, the difference between journals is quantitative rather than qualitative: in the journals of highest impact in science and medicine generally, it may be that more than half of the submissions are rejected at this stage. In contrast, in very specialised journals such as those in the addiction field, it may be a fairly rare occurrence for submissions to be rejected without review. Nevertheless, this rate can be as high as 20% for some addiction journals.

There are some aspects of manuscript preparation that are so easy that everyone should get them right. To ensure your manuscript has the best chance at triage (and beyond), make sure you do all these things as set out in the Instructions to Authors that every journal provides. Follow all advice and recommendations to the letter, format your submission precisely as requested, check to make sure that all sections are complete, and that no tables, figures, or figure legends are missing. Check the reference list to ensure that all cited references are in it, and no others. Check the accuracy of each citation. Look in the journal to see exactly how they are styled. Then check them over again, after you have made the corrections, until no more errors can be found. This sort of work is tedious but does not need expensive resources, profound knowledge of the subject or outstanding intellectual ability. If the editor sees at a glance that you do not even get these straightforward, mechanical things right, he or she may well develop a jaundiced view about your capability to deal with more complex matters. Try to look at the manuscript as an editor might. If you do not bother to do the easier things required of an author, the editor might reasonably conclude that you will not be able to do complex revisions either and you may not be given the opportunity to revise and resubmit.

Box 9.1 REASONS FOR REJECTION BY TRIAGE

- The submission is outside the scope of the journal (e.g., it is about an abused drug but it is not relevant in any discernible way to abuse of or dependence on it)
- The manuscript type is not appropriate (e.g., a case report is submitted to a journal that does not publish case reports)
- Clear ethical problems such as apparent violation of current generally accepted standards for the treatment of human or animal subjects
- The article is poorly organized
- The report is purely descriptive, has no hypotheses, or reaches no conclusions
- There are major methodological weaknesses
- The article appears to offer nothing new
- Instructions to Authors are flagrantly ignored in some way not covered by the above

Note: The editor has a duty to reviewers as well as to authors, and tries not to waste their time by requesting reviews of work that has no chance of acceptance for one or more of the reasons above.

COMMUNICATION WITH MORE EXPERIENCED WRITERS

Would-be authors may seek the advice of more experienced colleagues at almost any stage of the publication process. When planning a publication, discussion with colleagues after a presentation of the work at a seminar in the home institution may yield some tips as to the type of journal that may be interested in the study. Subsequently, during preparation of the manuscript, it may be appropriate to seek the advice of local colleagues on technical aspects such as statistical analyses. When a manuscript exists in a complete form, it can often be immensely helpful to ask at least one person to read through it and make comments and suggestions. People are very often willing to help if authors make clear they value an expert opinion on aspects such as coverage of the literature, clarity, style, language and validity of conclusions. If there is no person in the author's own institution, it is possible to approach outsiders and ask if they would be willing to comment.

Both people whom you know personally and others who have published in the area are likely to feel flattered and pleased that you value their opinion and may well provide advice. The manuscript that cannot be improved has yet to be written, and even experienced authors often seek the opinions of colleagues because after working on a manuscript for months, through revision after revision, it can be difficult to spot the little problems that spring to the attention of a new reader.

WRITING IN A FOREIGN LANGUAGE

It is an unavoidable fact that many authors have to write in a language other than their own, and to convey complex scientific ideas with clarity and precision can be a difficult task even in one's native language. Authors may therefore find it worthwhile to seek the assistance of colleagues with more experience of writing in the chosen language and, if possible, enlist a native speaker of the language to correct the manuscript. If that is not possible, it may be necessary to obtain the assistance of a professional translator to suggest corrections. Journals provide varying amounts of assistance in the correction of errors after accepting a manuscript for publication, but they cannot do anything to assist reviewers of poorly written manuscripts. A fuller consideration of language issues may be found in Chapter 3.

THE PEER REVIEW PROCESS: SELECTION OF REVIEWERS

The next step for the editor is selection of reviewers who will advise him or her of the strengths and weaknesses of the work and recommend whether or not it should be accepted, reconsidered after revision, or rejected outright. Reviewers are also expected to make constructive suggestions for improving the manuscript in a report that can be sent to the authors. The criteria used for selecting reviewers are diverse and probably few if any journals have tightly defined procedures. Box 9.2 shows the main criteria used by editors to identify reviewers. The number of reviewers for each article varies within and between journals, but most commonly there are two. The editors of some journals may work with only one reviewer but this seems to be increasingly rare. Occasionally, three or more reviewers are used, depending upon the journal and the editor's perception of the complexity and significance of the work. For example, multi-disciplinary manuscripts may require more than two reviewers to ensure sufficient expertise. Similarly, if a study seems likely to have major practical impact, for example upon policy or treatment, the editor may wish to be especially certain that it is assessed thoroughly. If the two reviewers selected initially disagree about the paper an editor may seek additional advice from a third person if needed to reach a decision.

For all reports, regardless of whether they are quantitative or qualitative, each journal has its own set of instructions for reviewers; journals differ with respect to the attributes of their 'ideal' manuscripts. There will sometimes be a requirement for reviewers to complete a questionnaire as part of the review, with ratings of the manuscript according to criteria such as importance and likely impact on the field, as well as technical competence. The reviewers are usually also asked to make a recommendation on the fate of the manuscript, and to justify it in confidential comments to the editor. Finally, reviewers are in all cases expected to produce a report that the editor will forward to the authors. The main purposes of this report are (1) to make suggestions enabling the author to improve the manuscript and (2) to list criticisms that the reviewer believes need to be addressed if the paper is to be published. The report to the authors should not include specific recommendations for acceptance or rejection of the manuscript because that decision is in the hands of the editor. Chapter 10 provides further advice on how to become a competent reviewer.

Box 9.2 SOME METHODS EDITORS USE TO IDENTIFY REVIEWERS FOR A PARTICULAR MANUSCRIPT

- Recognised expertise in the specific field of the manuscript as noted in the journal's database of previous reviewers and authors.
- Previous invitations to reviewer for the journal have resulted in thorough, well written, polite reviews submitted in a timely manner.
- Record of recent publications in the field as determined by searches of databases such as MEDLINE and PsycINFO.

The following criteria are used to *exclude* reviewers from consideration:

- Persons who are known to have a very close connection to the authors or to have a conflict of interest with the authors will be avoided.
- People who are currently reviewing another manuscript for the same journal or have reviewerd one within a set period (e.g., three months) will be avoided.
- Excessive praise or criticism of the reviewer's work in the manuscript to be assessed.

Note: Different criteria will be used in combination to reach a decision on whom to invite and there will inevitably be appreciable variations between journals with respect to the use of these different methods of selection.

Reviewers are asked to act according to ethical guidelines that are presented and discussed elsewhere in this book (see Chapters 11 and 12). The task of the editor is to reconcile sometimes conflicting reports from different reviewers and to make a personal judgement based on this and additional considerations. The task is made more difficult if the reviews contain conflicting recommendations for publication.

CRITERIA FOR EVALUATION OF MANUSCRIPTS

If the journal has published its Instructions to Reviewers, or put them on a website, they will give you an idea about the features at which both editors and reviewers will look. Many journals probably look for the same desirable features of highly-rated studies.

If it is a *quantitative* study, the criteria include the use of a sufficiently large and suitably representative sample of the population under study, a high response rate among invited participants, valid measures, absence of procedural biases and minimal confounding of one independent variable with another, and the use of appropriate controls.

Similarly, reviewers will look for as full a description of the methods as available space allows, with referencing of earlier publications that provide more detail and establish the validity of the methods and measuring instruments (where applicable). Results must be described in a clear and logical sequence, with all necessary information presented. No more detail should be provided than can be covered in the discussion section. The discussion should bring out the importance of all the main findings, and indicate how the work advances the state of knowledge and understanding in the relevant sub-field. Additionally, alternative interpretations of the data may be given, thus acknowledging limitations of the study. Reviewers pay attention to all the preceding points, and to many others.

In quantitative research, the data analysis section is prone to several problems. These include:

- failure to deal adequately with confounding variables
- claims to have shown something without performing a (statistical) test that supports it directly and unequivocally;
- failure to control for multiple comparisons;
- drawing inappropriate conclusions from non-significant associations or differences: we probably all realise that lack of significance means only that we have failed to find an effect and does not prove that no effect exists, but we don't always remember this in our enthusiasm to explain how our results fail to support the ideas of a scientist whose theory we dislike.

Authors developing reports of randomised controlled trials may wish to follow the CONSORT (Consolidated Standards of Reporting Trials) checklist, which includes 22 items considered essential to judge the reliability or relevance of the findings (presented in Appendix 9.2 to this chapter in slightly abbreviated form).

The criteria for the evaluation of *qualitative* reports vary depending on the type of data and methods of analysis (e.g., participant observation and ethnography, qualitative interviews, content analysis, textual analysis, discourse analysis, ethnography and conversation analysis). Chapter 6 provides more information about how to write and publish articles using qualitative methods. The following issues should be addressed in most types of qualitative report:

- Give clear criteria for the selection of data or subjects. Position the material carefully in the social and cultural space. For example, different genres of fiction represent different segments of the culture.
- Present a detailed account of where and when data were collected or which existing data sets were used. In studies based on fieldwork, describe the relation between the fieldworkers and the subjects and discuss the possible influence of the data collection on the phenomenon under study. Keep careful records of the data so that they can be provided for independent examination if necessary.
- Clearly state how the analysis was done, with an indication of whether reliability was assessed, for instance by replicating the analysis.

- Describe any themes, concepts and categories derived from the data. Divide the interpretation process into short steps, specifying rules of classification and interpretation.
- Outline steps taken to guard against selectivity in the use of data; discuss exceptions and deviant cases. Ideally, the reader should be able to apply the same classifications, take the same analytic steps, and reach the same kind of results with another dataset.
- Present data systematically so that quotations, field notes, and so on are easily identifiable.
- Offer enough primary evidence to show a relation between evidence and conclusions, but avoid the presentation of too many illustrations; the focus should be on the most representative examples.

COMMON PROBLEMS WITH MANUSCRIPTS

All parts of a manuscript are open to criticism from the title onwards. The first requirement for gaining the confidence of an editor or a reviewer is to describe the findings objectively and in a sober style without the use of hyperbolic language. If your data are good, they will speak for themselves. It is always better for the reader to find that the results themselves are stronger than you claim, instead of being obscure and unconvincing in relation to your description.

Every 'data not shown' statement may raise the suspicions of reviewers that the authors are trying to hide something. If there really is not enough space to show important data graphically or in tabular form, then give some examples of the more important of such results in the text (with means, standard errors or other indicator of variance and numbers of subjects, if it is a quantitative study).

The discussion section is the most difficult part of a manuscript to write, and it often shows. Sometimes the opening paragraph is only a summary of the results, which is not satisfactory. One approach is to decide which are the main new findings, mention only them, and summarise two or three important conclusions that follow from them. It is also common to find that the discussion does not focus on the aims as stated in the introduction, and sometimes discusses issues on which no background was given. Such a failure to place findings in the context of previous knowledge means that the case for publication is not made. Reviewers and editor want to know what is new, what is confirmatory, and of any important failures to confirm previous findings. Instead, authors may attempt to extract too much from their data, in the sense of trying to address too many different issues. The effect of this error is to dilute strong conclusions with weakly supported ones, giving an overall unfavourable impression leading to rejection.

The discussion should also consider alternative interpretations of the study and acknowledge major limitations. These may arise from methodological weaknesses or unexpected findings that could not be pursued to a firm conclusion, due to practical limitations such as the project period coming to an end, or a financial constraint (these non-scientific reasons do not need to be stated). If the reviewers discover these weaknesses they will consider themselves smart and are likely to make sure you know it; if you show that you are aware of the limitations and understand the implications, they will perceive *you* as smart and honest, which counts for a lot.

Don't waste time and space discussing 'trends' that are not statistically significant; if the effect is not there, its implications do not need discussing. Remember that there are more than enough 'significant' effects that do not replicate and there is no need to create new myths. If it is believed that a real and important difference was undetected due to lack of statistical power the study needs to be repeated, and then there may be something to discuss.

Particular but somewhat different problems are associated with reviews and theoretical articles. If a review claims to be comprehensive, it is now common practice to state in it the way that the literature search was carried out, and to define criteria for including articles. Articles that do not claim to be integrative reviews but rather argue the case for a particular theoretical viewpoint or set of ideas are often less comprehensive. In such instances authors often cite publications that support their own position in a rather uncritical manner, and they may refer to few or no articles that oppose it. Editors may then firmly but politely ask the author to state the assumptions made and ensure that the article clearly indicates any controversial issues. Alternatively, where the intention is to let a distinguished writer express a personal view based on his or her selective citation of the literature, it should be made clear that a case is being made for a theory and that a balanced assessment of the state of the field is not being attempted.

Finally, remember you are writing a scholarly paper and not running a campaign! Do not enter into politics and polemics. For example, if your main finding is that a widely used intervention is less favourable than another which lacks some sort of official approval for general use in your country, make the case for their relative merits and if appropriate argue for a policy change, but don't abuse the politicians and don't keep repeating the argument in more and more florid and emphatic language. Political battles are not won in the pages of academic journals.

THE EDITOR'S DECISION

The much-anticipated and sometimes feared letter from the editor finally arrives on the corresponding author's desk, together with the statements from the reviewers. The editor will often need to reach a decision based upon the balance between innovation and quality of work. The perfect manuscript would have important new ideas with far-reaching importance backed up by sound data obtained by means of thoroughly validated methods. In reality, such manuscripts are seen only rarely, if ever, and the editor and the reviewers have to make judgements. If the approach to a problem is highly novel or the study is a potential stimulus for further valuable work, a manuscript may be accepted with data that are less than wholly convincing. On the other hand, if there is not very much that is really new, but the study is the first one to address a particular methodological weakness of previous work, then clear data of high quality will probably be essential.

The reviewers' reports and recommendations inevitably and appropriately influence the editor's decision but they are not the sole determining factors. Editors may study a manuscript in varying amounts of detail and may have concerns that are not reflected in reviewers' reports. These concerns may relate to any of the whole range of issues that the reviewers also address, but especially to the appropriateness of the subject matter for the journal; whether there are any ethical problems; and whether the importance of work is sufficient to justify publication in his or her journal rather than in a publication of lesser status that may be struggling to fill its pages. Studies may be technically competent and presented well, but may be unimportant because they merely confirm well-known facts or because they focus on apparently trivial issues. When the reports of reviewers are in agreement with each other, the editor will most frequently accept the recommendations made. It is a brave editor indeed who overturns the opinions of two independent experts, not least because reviewers will soon stop assisting an editor who consistently ignores the advice given. When reviewers disagree, the editor may seek to sort out the matter by studying the manuscript and coming down in support of one or other reviewer; this is the ideal method if the editor can reach a clear view because he can reach a decision quickly without wasting another expert's valuable time. However, sometimes reviewers reach opposing conclusions on the basis of equally well-argued cases and then the editor may feel it is essential to obtain advice from a third person. This is especially likely to occur if the work is outside the editor's main area of expertise.

When a third reviewer reaches a definite view supporting one or the other of the earlier reviewers, then the way forward is clear, but this does not always happen. If the first reviewer supports publication strongly and the second reviewer recommends rejection, the third reviewer quite often says the manuscript is weak but may reach publication standard after major revision; in such cases the contribution of the third reviewer may swing the decision one way or the other depending upon the journal's needs at the time. If the journal is trying to raise the standard of published items, such marginal manuscripts will probably be rejected, whereas if the study is in a field that is under-represented in the journal, the editor may wish to include it. An editor may also seek to publish the article in a shorter form that reflects its lesser merits.

The abusive reviewer is a particular annoyance to editors. The most commonly identified, although happily quite rare form of abuse occurs when a reviewer attempts a review of the author instead of the manuscript. It is one thing, and perfectly acceptable, to state that an argument is constructed poorly and is unconvincing, that it is presented badly, or does not take account of previous knowledge; it is quite another thing to assert that the author is stupid, careless or ignorant. Editors have a duty to alter or remove such inappropriate remarks from a reviewer's report, so that unnecessary distress is not caused and the author will be encouraged to improve the manuscript. If the reviewer is young and inexperienced, the editor may also inform him or her about the problem with the report, whereas a senior person will more likely not be invited to review again. Additional advice for inexperienced reviewers may be found in Chapter 10 of this volume and at www.parint.org.

A particularly difficult situation arises if the review process generates suspicion that the author has engaged in scientific misconduct or other forms of unethical behaviour. Such misconduct may be either minor or major in nature and the editor typically has available a range of sanctions to apply. These may include refusing to consider further work from the author, reporting the matter to the author's institution or employer, and publishing a statement in the journal to alert the scientific community to the issue. The availability of a code of practice by which editors can abide in such circumstances is very helpful (see http://www.parint.org/isajewebsite/farmington.htm for the ethical practice guidelines developed by the International Society of Addiction Journal Editors). Editors are also wary of trying to resolve contentious ethical issues because they do not have the resources to conduct a full investigation; equally important, they cannot simply brush the matter aside by refusing to publish suspect material but must take reasonable steps to ensure that appropriate action is taken. These and other related issues are discussed in greater detail in Chapters 11 and 12, which deal with ethical considerations in scientific publishing.

RESPONDING TO REVIEWERS' REPORTS: GENERAL RULES OF CONDUCT

Authors who achieve immediate acceptance of a manuscript as submitted are rare indeed. Revisions are almost always required prior to acceptance, and in many cases a final decision cannot be reached until the revised version has been assessed. Therefore, the way in which authors respond to the reports of reviewers and to the editor can have a major influence upon the outcome. If editors invite resubmission, it means they expect to receive the manuscript back again.

An invitation to resubmit is not a half-hearted and cowardly way of saying the work is unpublishable, but rather an implicit suggestion that the editor remains interested in the paper and that it is likely to be accepted if the author is responsive to the questions and recommendations of the reviewers. In such cases, it is nearly always worth resubmitting unless there is some clear and unavoidable requirement with which you cannot possibly comply. The remainder of this section offers guidance for authors on how to navigate through this maze successfully.

The overriding aim of the response is to engender trust among editors and reviewers. Authors should never claim to have made changes that in fact they have not done. If the covering letter says all requested changes have been made and an editor or reviewer checks two or three points at random and finds nothing much has changed, they may reject the manuscript without looking carefully at the rest of it. If you have made major changes by rewriting whole sections of the manuscript, state that is the case and identify the sections. Alternatively, if just a few words have been inserted or deleted, make clear which words were changed so that reviewers can see what has been done. If you were asked to shorten something, you should almost always do so and perhaps state by how much (i.e. by how many words or pages). Don't try to fool the editor by printing the new version in smaller type or by other stylistic changes! Be polite, even if you feel that the reviewers have not understood your intentions. When you have been through all the points of criticism, you should have an idea of the changes you think are appropriate. Will they be enough?

If after reading the reports, you have concluded that none of the recommendations is worth accepting and you don't want to make any changes, it is common sense to take a break from the job and look at it again on another day! It is simply not realistic to expect editors and reviewers to accept that none of the changes they request and the criticisms they make is well founded. Reviewers spend anything from an hour to a full day preparing their reports. If you dismiss all this effort out of hand you will get nothing published. You must therefore aim to make changes to deal with as many as possible of the points raised, and preferably with a clear majority of them.

Occasionally authors may feel that an editor's decision to reject their manuscript was unnecessary because the criticisms made could be answered through revisions. In such cases, where there was no other clear reason given for rejection, authors may wish to seek approval to resubmit. For example, there may be no criticism of the conduct of the study or analysis of the data, but the reviewer may feel that the interpretation is seriously flawed so that the conclusions are not supported by the data. The manuscript might therefore be publishable if the authors are willing to revise their conclusions. Resubmission after rejection should be preceded by a carefully considered letter to the editor explaining why you believe that you can deal with the criticisms made. The editor will then decide whether to alter the previous negative decision and may agree to consider a revised version. Seek approval before resubmitting because if a rejected manuscript is resubmitted without prior agreement, it is very likely that the editor will refuse to consider it. Some journals have stated their appeals procedure whereas others deal with appeals on an *ad hoc* basis.

THE COVERING LETTER: MAKE LIFE EASIER FOR THE EDITOR

Once you complete the changes to the manuscript, write a detailed reply to the reviewers. It is worth spending a significant amount of time getting your reply to reviewers as near perfect as you can. Sometimes constructing the letter takes as long as revising the article, but it will not take as long as botching the job and then being obliged to reformat the manuscript for another journal in order to start the whole process over again. Nevertheless, it is best to keep this reply as short as possible. Typical successful replies will be in the range of 1-3 single-spaced pages. If the reviewer makes a point in just three lines and you need a page to rebut it, it is likely you have not got straight to the heart of the matter and your reply will probably not be convincing. It is best to write the minimum needed to refute the criticism.

If the reviewer cannot understand a point that you made in the manuscript, it may be because he or she is lacking in intellectual capacity (as we often think when we encounter such comments on our own work). However, if one person does not follow what you have written, the same may apply to others. Reviewers are all published research workers and are often the very people whom you might hope would read your paper; if a reviewer cannot understand your point, try to analyse your text to see how the misunderstanding may have arisen. Then make changes to ensure it will not happen again.

Do remember that if a reviewer asks a question, other readers may want to know the answer to it too. The answer should therefore usually be contained in the revised manuscript and not in the covering letter. The latter need only refer to the sections of the manuscript where the question is addressed. Save the reviewers' time and they will love you; don't get them to read the answer to a question in the letter and then refer them to the manuscript where they have to read the answer over again to check if it is really there!

If possible, reply in numbered sections that correspond with the reviewers' numbered points. Explain the revisions you made to deal with most of the criticisms and also explain why you did not deal with the rest. Describe briefly each change you made, referring to the relevant page or paragraph in the revised manuscript. Try not to respond in a combative, overly-assertive style. If there are major and important changes recommended that you are sure are wrong, then present a concise, logically-argued rebuttal. If there are minor changes requested that you feel don't really improve matters, do them anyway because it helps a lot if you can truthfully claim to have dealt with the majority of points. At all stages, remember that although reviewers and editors may appear to be distant, self-opinionated and arrogant, they are also human beings with their own feelings, emotions and problems. If you want acceptances, make life easy for them by writing clearly, and don't antagonise them with criticisms or gratuitous insults, however unwise and misguided you think they may be.

It is sensible to maximise and stress agreements with what reviewers write and to acknowledge their contribution when they have made suggestions that improve the manuscript. Don't build minor disagreements into major issues. You probably only need to make minor changes to accommodate them, and then mention the changes in the cover letter, instead of wasting time arguing and putting the reviewer's back up in the process. However, it is not necessary or appropriate to minimise disagreements to the point of dishonesty; they should be dealt with by logical rebuttal in the cover letter and, sometimes, by acknowledging and discussing the point in the manuscript.

Perhaps the most difficult case occurs when you feel that a reviewer shows a bias towards a theoretical approach that differs from yours, and therefore undervalues the work. Here you can explain in the cover letter that there are different approaches to the problem (state what these are), that yours is equally valid, that there is a genuine difference of opinion and that you have a different but scientifically legitimate point of view. However, this strategy is probably unwise unless you have a strong case and there is no other way to deal with the issue. In the end the editor will have to decide and what one person perceives as objective and unbiased looks very different from another viewpoint. At the end of the day, the editor wants to have papers to publish. The number of acceptances rather than of rejections is therefore the mark of success and of an editor's job well done. Authors, editors, reviewers and publishers must all work together to ensure the production of a journal of high quality that achieves its intended objectives.

ACKNOWLEDGEMENTS

I would like to thank Klaus Mäkelä and Kerstin Stenius for assistance with drafting the material about qualitative research.

Appendix 9.1 GENERAL PUBLICATIONS ON SCIENTIFIC AND MEDICAL PUBLISHING

Many additional works may be found by searching biomedical databases such as PubMed or on-line booksellers.

Albert T, 2000. *The A-Z of Medical Writing*. BMJ Books. ISBN 0727914871.

Iverson, C., ed. *American Medical Association Manual of Style*, 1998. 9th ed. Williams & Wilkins. ISBN 0683402064.

American Psychological Association, *Publication Manual*, 2001. 5th ed. American Psychological Association. ISBN 1557987904.

Huth EJ, 1990. *How to Write and Publish Papers in the Medical Sciences*. 2nd ed. Williams & Wilkins. ISBN 0683042718.

McInerney DM, 2001. *Publishing your Psychology Research*. Sage. ISBN 0761973370.

Peat J, 2002. *Scientific Writing*. BMJ Books. ISBN 0727916254.

Publishing Addiction Research Internationally. www.parint.org. ISAJE develpoed this website to provide a wide range of resources for authors, editors and reviewers of addiction research.

Richardson P, 2002. *A Guide to Medical Publishing and Writing*. Quay Books. ISBN 1856422224.

Appendix 9.2 CHECKLIST OF ITEMS TO INCLUDE WHEN REPORTING A RANDOMISED TRIAL

This section consists of a slightly shortened version of the checklist of Moher et al. (2001).

Title and abstract	How participants were allocated to interventions (e.g., 'random allocation', 'randomised', or 'randomly assigned').
Introduction	Scientific background and explanation of rationale.

Methods

Participants:	Eligibility criteria for participants and the settings and locations where the data were collected.
Interventions:	Precise details of the interventions intended for each group and how and when they were actually administered. Objectives Subjective objectives and hypotheses.
Outcomes:	Clearly defined primary and secondary outcome measures and when applicable, any methods used to enhance the quality of measurements (e.g., multiple observations, training of assessors).
Sample size:	How sample size was determined and, when applicable, explanation of any interim analyses and stopping rules.
Randomisation:	Method used to generate the random allocation sequence, including details of any restriction (e.g., blocking, stratification).
Allocation concealment:	Method used to implement the random allocation sequence (e.g., numbered containers or central telephone), clarifying whether the sequence was concealed until interventions were assigned.
Implementation:	Who generated the allocation sequence, who enrolled participants, and who assigned participants to their groups.
Blinding:	Whether or not participants, those administering the interventions, and those assessing the outcomes were aware of group assignment.
Statistical analysis:	Statistical methods used to compare groups for primary outcome; methods for additional analyses, such as subgroup analyses and adjusted analyses.

Results

Participant flow:	Flow of participants through each stage (a diagram is strongly recommended). Specifically, for each group, report the numbers of participants randomly assigned, receiving intended treatment, completing the study protocol, and analyzed for the primary outcome. Describe protocol deviations from study as planned, together with reasons.
Recruitment:	Dates defining the periods of recruitment and follow-up.
Baseline data:	Baseline demographic and clinical characteristics of each group.
Numbers analysed:	Number of participants (denominator) in each group included in each analysis and whether the analysis was by "intention to treat". State the results in absolute numbers when feasible (e.g., 10/20, not 50%).
Outcomes and estimation:	For each primary and secondary outcome, a summary of results for each group, and the estimated effect size and its precision (e.g. 95% CI).
Ancillary analyses:	Address multiplicity by reporting any other analyses performed, including subgroup analyses and adjusted analyses, indicating those prespecified and those exploratory.
Adverse events:	All important adverse events or side effects in each intervention group.

Discussion

Interpretation:	Interpretation of the results, taking into account study hypotheses, sources of potential bias or imprecision and the dangers associated with multiplicity of analyses and outcomes.
Generalisability:	External validity of the trial findings.
Overall evidence:	General interpretation of the results in the context of current evidence.

CHAPTER 10
REVIEWING MANUSCRIPTS FOR SCIENTIFIC JOURNALS

ROBERT L. BALSTER

INTRODUCTION

One of the main moral principles of virtually all major religions and cultures is the ethic of reciprocity, sometimes known as the Golden Rule: Treat others as you would like to be treated. Show mutual respect. This Golden Rule is also a fundamental principle of the process of peer review, including the review of manuscripts submitted to professional journals. If you have been asked to review someone's paper it is very likely the case that you are an author yourself and will have been subjected to the same peer review process. Keeping in mind how you expect your own journal submissions to be reviewed, you could readily derive from that experience nearly all of the advice I will be offering you in your role as a reviewer.

GOAL

The goal of this chapter is to provide rather specific principles and suggestions on how to be a competent reviewer. Most editors of peer reviewed journals see the peer review process similarly, even if some of their specific journal policies differ. It is those commonalities that I will address here, approaching the topic in my various roles as Editor-in-Chief of *Drug and Alcohol Dependence*, member of several editorial boards for other journals, and reviewer for many others. Interested readers may also want to consult prior publications on peer review in general (Godlee and Jefferson, 2003) and on peer review of journal submissions specifically (Girden, 2001; Enckell, 2003a, 2003b; Hames, 2007). Chapters 5, 6 and 9 in this book also consider certain types of information relevant to journal reviewing.

I should mention that reviewers of journal submissions are sometimes referred to as referees. I am not aware of any distinction between being a reviewer and a referee. I have always preferred the term *reviewer* because being a referee conjures images of a sporting contest with winners and losers. When you are a good reviewer, everybody wins -- authors, editors and the scientific community -- because reviewing is fundamentally a constructive process. Yes, reviewing involves making judgments and recommendations, but reviewers are not the decision makers in the process. This responsibility falls to the editor. Thus, I will use the words *reviewing* and *reviewer* throughout, but just as a matter of personal preference. It seems likely that the words used for the reviewer function in non-English languages have nuances of their own to consider, but that is a matter for another discourse by someone with greater language skills than I.

BRIEF OVERVIEW OF THE JOURNAL REVIEW PROCESS

If a journal declares itself to be a "peer reviewed" journal, this normally means that all papers that are eventually published in that journal have been reviewed. Peer review implies review by outside reviewers as well as the editorial staff. Of course, journals differ in their application of the peer review process and it is common for journals to publish editorials, commentaries, book reviews and similar content without peer review, reserving that form of assessment for research reports and critical reviews.

Before moving on to a more detailed discussion of journal reviewing, I want to give a brief overview of the process so readers can appreciate the steps involved. Table 10.1 outlines the basic steps of the review process used by most journals, keeping in mind that editorial structure differs among journals. For *Drug and Alcohol Dependence*, all submissions are made using an interactive internet-based system whereby they are all received in a centralized editorial office. I then decide whether to edit the paper myself or assign it to one of the Associate Editors (six at this writing). Other journals may have more than one submission site, depending on the geographical location of the author or the general topic of the paper. Some journals may have more than one editor look at the submission before assigning it to reviewers, while others may have an editorial team that considers the recommendations of the reviewers. To simplify this discussion, I will assume there is one "Decision Editor" who assigns reviewers and makes decisions, as is the case with *Drug and Alcohol Dependence*. I will refer to this individual as the Editor, regardless of the specific editorial title assigned by the journal.

Table 10.1 STEPS IN THE JOURNAL REVIEW PROCESS

1.	Editors develop a reviewer database.
2.	Authors submit manuscripts to the journal.
3.	Editor(s) make initial assessment if paper is suitable for the journal and if peer review is warranted.
4.	Editor(s) select reviewers and invite them to review.
5.	Editor(s) monitor the timeliness of peer review and send reminders or invite new reviewers if necessary.
6.	Reviewers complete the review and provide recommendations and comments to the editor and authors.
7.	Editor makes decision to accept the submission, ask authors for a revision or reject the submission.
8.	Most journals notify reviewers of the editor's decision.
9.	If required, authors revise submissions and return to editor.
10.	Editor decides if further review is needed; if so, the process recommences at Step 4.

The first step in the peer review process is the assignment of reviewers. In the next section I will discuss reviewer databases and how editors select and invite reviewers (Steps 1 and 4). All journals have some procedure for monitoring the review process after reviewers have been assigned (Step 5). This has become easier with computer-based systems that notify the editorial team when assigned reviewers decline the invitation to review, when reviews are completed, and when they are late.

At some point the Editor stops the review process and decides whether or not to accept the manuscript for publication (Steps 6 and 7). Editors carefully consider the recommendations of the reviewers and their comments on the paper, but ultimately they must make the decision themselves based on both the reviews and their own assessment of the submission. Usually, Editors inform reviewers of their decisions (Step 8). There are three basic options open to the Editor. First, the Editor may accept the submission for publication as submitted. For many journals it is rare to accept a first submission of a paper without asking for any revisions at all, but it does happen.

Second, if the submission seems to the Editor to be potentially publishable, he or she will ask the authors to make revisions (Step 9). Most journals divide revisions into minor and major categories. Minor revisions do not change the paper very much, and the resubmission usually does not require additional outside reviews. Major revisions typically require significant changes to the paper, such as the collection of additional data, a change in the way the existing data are analyzed or presented, or even changes to some of the conclusions of the report. Manuscripts with major revisions are often returned to the same or different peer reviewers for their comments and recommendations (Step 10).

The third option open to Editors is rejection of the submission. Some submissions may be rejected without peer review (Step 3), such as when the topic is not appropriate for the journal readership or the form of paper (e.g. case report, book review) is not one published by the journal. Editors may also decide that the paper's methods or other characteristics give it little or no chance of receiving a positive recommendation in the peer review process. Giving authors feedback on such papers immediately may be in their best interest since it allows them to submit elsewhere without delay. Rejection without review also saves the time of busy reviewers, who are more useful to the journal when reviewing manuscripts with a greater chance of success. Most often, Editors base their rejections on negative recommendations in the peer review process. In such cases, authors usually receive comments from the Editor or reviewers that describe some of the weaknesses of their submission. Ideally, authors consider these comments and revise the paper before they send it to another journal.

HOW DO EDITORS SELECT REVIEWERS?

Turning to the principle of reciprocity, who do we, as authors, want assigned as reviewers of our papers? To be honest, we probably prefer reviewers who are known to be favorably impressed with our work. But primarily, we want reviewers who are knowledgeable about our field of study and who will be fair in the review process. This is what editors want too; we want competent reviewers with specialized knowledge of the potential advantages and pitfalls of various research approaches. We also want reviewers who are fair and unbiased, without conflicts of interest. Finally, we want reviewers who complete their work on time and who write constructive comments on the submission.

The process of selecting appropriate reviewers usually involves the use of a database. At a minimum, such a database includes postal or email addresses by which to contact reviewers. In the case of a large, multidisciplinary journal, editors also need some means of matching reviewers with submissions. Smaller, more specialized journals often rely mainly on their normal editorial advisory boards for reviews, but ad hoc reviewers carry most of the load for larger journals.

In addition to up-to-date contact information, a typical reviewer database includes some means of identifying their reviewers' areas of expertise. For example, the database may assign to each reviewer one or more key words or classifications (e.g. molecular genetics, pharmacotherapy, prevention, policy). Commercial editorial software systems are particularly adept at matching the key words assigned to both submissions and reviewers to provide editors with a list of knowledgeable reviewers. These programs also tell editors if reviewers are currently assigned other manuscripts, the date of their last review, and the number of reviews they have done lately. It is also possible to see if reviewers have defaulted on prior assignments or how long they have taken to complete their prior reviews. Some systems even allow editors to rate reviewers to help them remember who provided useful suggestions and constructive and timely comments in previous reviews.

There are several ways to get one's name added to a journal's database. Perhaps the most common way is by publishing a paper in that journal. Editors typically prefer reviewers who have themselves published at least several papers as senior or corresponding author. Many Editors do a quick author search using PubMed or a similar database to see if potential reviewers have other publications. Sometimes authors suggest reviewers for their manuscripts. If the Editor agrees with the suggestion and the reviewer is not in the database, he or she will be added. Editors may ask their editorial advisory boards to suggest new reviewers for the database, and most editors are also pleased to receive self-nominations. Finally, an Editor sometimes receives submissions for which no suitable reviewer is available. In such cases, Editors use their knowledge of the field or use authors cited in the submission who are clearly doing related work to add new reviewers to the database.

Selecting the best possible reviewer for a submission is one of the most important responsibilities of an Editor. In my experience, taking time at this step to ensure a good match between reviewer and submission will often save time -- and requests for more reviews -- later on. Reviewers, too, prefer to assess papers in areas in which they feel qualified. Each Editor goes about the matching process in different ways. In addition to seeking reviewers with expertise in the area, editors also may seek to balance their selection of reviewers for a single submission along several dimensions. For example, Editors may seek a methodological balance, in which a reviewer with specific knowledge of a data analytic approach complements another with knowledge of the content area of the work. It is often good to pair a senior scientist with a less experienced reviewer as this can serve to train the junior person who subsequently sees the comments of the senior reviewer. Sometimes one needs a reviewer the Editor knows to be unbiased in a particularly controversial area. Editors usually like to have reviewers who provide a broad perspective on the work, so they may want to ensure geographical, cultural or gender balance.

Generally, only two reviewers are needed for each submission, but there are times when more than two are invited. If the review process becomes delayed because of problems obtaining timely reviews, Editors may at some point add a reviewer they know to be particularly reliable. These and many other subtle factors make the reviewer selection process a difficult one.

In addition to selecting knowledgeable and reliable reviewers, Editors do their best to avoid actual or perceived conflicts of interest (COIs) and bias. As I will discuss later, Editors cannot know about every possible COI or bias that reviewers may have, so we rely on reviewers to tell us. There are some relatively straightforward methods Editors use to try to avoid apparent COIs. We generally exclude as potential reviewers close scientific colleagues, such as reviewers who have co-authored with any of the authors of the submission in recent years, or persons known to be part of the same research team. It is usually wise not to assign reviewers from the same institution as the authors, but with large multi-campus institutions such precautions may not always be necessary. Because Editors are usually experts themselves, they may be aware of longstanding disagreements or controversies and take care to select unbiased reviewers. It is impossible to eliminate potential bias completely, but Editors do the best they can.

The actual process of inviting reviewers differs among journals. Some Editors send a copy of the submission and reviewing instructions directly to the reviewer. Other Editors first invite possible reviewers, usually by sending the abstract by email or FAX and asking them first to agree to do the review by a certain deadline. If they agree, they are then assigned the review and provided access to the full paper, review forms, and instructions. One advantage to this invitation process is that potential reviewers can identify COIs or tell Editors that they lack expertise in the area of study. Some Editors will invite several reviewers and then assign only the first two who agree. Computer technology and the use of email have automated some of these steps, making the process faster. It is now possible to receive a submission, invite reviewers, assign them, and get the review process started all in one day.

WHY HAVE PEER REVIEW?

Before further discussion of how to be a good reviewer, I will explain why we use peer review and why anyone would want to be a peer reviewer. Peer review has four primary objectives:1) advise the editorial decision-making process; 2) justify rejections; 3) improve the quality of acceptable manuscripts; 4) identify instances of ethical or scientific misconduct.

EDITORIAL DECISION MAKING

The most obvious reason to seek reviews of journal submissions is to help the Editor make a decision about the paper's acceptability for publication in that journal. One should always remember that reviewers only make recommendations; it is the Editor's choice whether or not to follow those recommendations. This fact often frustrates reviewers, who may feel that the Editor ignored their advice. A consideration of some of the factors that affect the Editor's decisions can relieve some of that frustration. Editors must make decisions based on all of their reviewers' input, and sometimes reviewers give conflicting recommendations. The Editor may feel that a problem identified by a reviewer could be addressed in a revision or that the author has good arguments for why the problem is not an important consideration. Indeed, the Editor may read the paper and disagree with the reviewer's interpretation. An Editor may feel that the importance of the paper mitigates some problems identified by the reviewers. On the other hand, reviewers may not find any fault with a paper that the Editor decides is unimportant or belongs in a different journal. Many journals receive more submissions than they can publish and thus Editors must choose among potentially publishable papers with no major flaws. All of these factors and others go into the editorial decision-making process. Editors who choose not to follow a reviewer's recommendations may still consider the review to be excellent. Reviewers who are provided access to the Editor's decision letter, or to the comments of the other reviewer, can usually glean the basis for the Editor's decision.

EXPLAINING THE BASIS FOR REJECTION

Nearly all journals ask reviewers to provide comments and suggestions on the submission, which are then sent to the author with the decision letter. When reviewers recommend rejection of a manuscript they should provide the basis for that recommendation in their comments to the authors. Not only does this give authors the feedback they deserve on their submissions, but it also helps the authors to revise their papers for submission elsewhere, and to improve their work in general.

IMPROVING THE QUALITY OF PUBLISHED PAPERS

Certainly, one of the most important reasons for obtaining constructive comments during the review process is to make the papers that are ultimately published in the journal the best they can possibly be. I have seen modest papers transformed during the review process into far better and more important contributions to the field. I have received many statements of appreciation by authors for the improvements in their manuscripts brought about by peer review. Of course, not all authors appreciate constructive criticism or relish doing the extra work required to revise their submissions to satisfy reviewers, but I believe that most authors value expert criticism of their work. I suppose that some contributions could be weakened when authors follow reviewer advice, but I cannot recall a specific example where I know this occurred. It is the responsibility of the Editor to make judgments about major changes reviewers ask authors to make and to tell authors in a cover letter if he or she does not agree with a reviewer's suggestions. Editors should also carefully consider counter arguments made by authors who prefer not to make some recommended changes.

IDENTIFY AREAS OF ETHICAL OR SCIENTIFIC MISCONDUCT

Most journals request reviewers to comment on any subject protection issues or other ethical concerns they detect in a submission. Their careful examination of the data may reveal inconsistencies between reported methods and the ways in which data are presented or analyzed, or highly unlikely data sets (e.g. with no variability) that may lead them to suspect errors in data reporting or outright data fabrication.

Reviewers may know of concurrent submissions of the same manuscript to two or more journals or prior publications by the authors that present the same data. It is important for reviewers to communicate their concerns about possible ethical or scientific misconduct problems to the Editor. Typically this is done in confidential comments to the Editor who then must investigate these concerns. Reviewers do not need proof of these types of problems, just a reasonable basis for concern.

WHY BE A JOURNAL REVIEWER?

There are seven reasons to review manuscripts for scientific journals. I am not even including the most important reason many people do it……they enjoy it. Thinking critically about science, staying informed on the latest advances, and making a contribution to human health are what attracted many of us to science in the first place. Reviewing is a scholarly, creative, focused, important activity that is capable of being completed with a few hours of work. What could be better?

PROFESSIONAL RESPONSIBILITY

The peer review process is a simple application of the Golden Rule. You need people to review your papers, so you should review those of others. A system made up of all authors and no reviewers is doomed to a very short life. Thus, it is your professional responsibility to be part of the process, both as author and reviewer. I do not subscribe to the view that senior scientists can be excused from the peer review process because they "did their duty" earlier in their careers. If you write, you should review. Indeed, the perspective of experienced scholars can be particularly important to the peer review process.

IMPROVE YOUR UNDERSTANDING OF THE PEER REVIEW PROCESS

Younger scholars particularly need to learn the peer review process, as much of their career success will depend on it. Many faculty mentors include in their training a gradual exposure to doing peer reviews. A good strategy is for a mentor to ask a junior colleague to prepare a review of a manuscript that has been assigned to the mentor. The mentor should explain fully the confidentiality issues surrounding the review process when asking a junior colleague for help. The novice reviewer then returns the review to the mentor who modifies it as needed and gives feedback to the trainee. The mentor then submits the review to the journal. In such instances of guided peer review, mentors should tell the Editor the name of the junior colleague who helped with the review. Mentors might even recommend that the junior colleague be added to the reviewer database once they feel the colleague is ready to do independent work.

IMPROVING YOUR CRITICAL THINKING.

The review of other people's work improves your critical thinking about your own work. Good reviewers attempt to articulate both the strengths and weaknesses of a particular scientific approach. You may be using a similar approach in your own work without thinking about it critically as often as you should. Perhaps you are considering the employment of methods similar to those in the paper you are reviewing. Thinking about some of that paper's weaknesses can lead you to make improvements on the approach.

One of the most useful ways to evaluate your own critical thinking is to see what the other reviewer(s) and Editor say about the work. I strongly believe that journals should make all comments to authors and decision letters available to reviewers on an anonymous basis, although not all journals do. When another reviewer or the Editor identifies a serious flaw in experimental design or data analysis that you missed, it can be both instructive and a little embarrassing.

IMPROVE YOUR OWN WRITING AND DATA PRESENTATION

Reviewing a manuscript (and comments from other reviewers and the Editor) gives you new insights into how to improve your own writing, presentation, and data analyses. By seeing how authors make revisions and respond to reviewer comments, you can improve your own approach to revising papers. Reviewers often advise authors on how papers can be shortened and more sharply focused. I suspect this is partly because reviewers are not as enamored with the author's lengthy rambles and speculations as the authors themselves are. As reviewers help authors focus their writing they likewise learn to do this with their own papers. In addition, proofreading other manuscripts for errors improves the proofreading of your own writing.

LEARN MORE ABOUT RESEARCH IN THE FIELD

Reviewing a scientific paper can give a reviewer a much better understanding of the work than just reading it because of the critical thinking involved in doing a review. In addition, you will probably be asked to review papers that you would not normally read because they are a little outside your specific area of work. The comments and suggestions of the Editor and other reviewer(s) are sometimes more interesting and important than the paper you reviewed. Some of the best scientific writing I have encountered has taken the form of reviews. After all, reviewers are experts in the field who are asked to summarize the salient strengths and weaknesses of a scientific study or new hypothesis in a few paragraphs. One of the major rewards of being an Editor is the education we receive in the form of manuscript reviews and author replies.

BUILD RELATIONSHIPS WITH JOURNALS

The databases that include you as a reviewer generally will also include you as an author. Persons who are regular authors and reviewers for a journal and who are successful in these roles build a relationship with a journal, becoming a good "journal citizen," as it were. The editorial team comes to know who you are, appreciate better your areas of expertise, and develop confidence in your work. Your good relationship with a journal may result in your being asked to join its editorial advisory board or take on editing roles yourself.

FULFILL SERVICE OBLIGATIONS FOR PROMOTION

As scientists our work is constantly being evaluated. This includes assessment for promotion and tenure. Everyone understands that, for most scholars, service to the profession is one of the areas where we are evaluated and judged. As mentioned above, journal reviewing is an important service that should be acknowledged and rewarded. I know that reviewers typically report their journal reviewing activities on their *curricula vitae* and include them in regular activity reports. Simply being invited to review a manuscript is evidence that you are known in the field and that an editor has some confidence in your expertise. Many journals regularly publish lists of who has recently reviewed for them and some use additional incentives (such as small gifts or reduced costs for the publisher's books and journals) to reward good reviewers.

HOW TO BE A GOOD REVIEWER

Much of the advice in this section stems from the goals of the review process, as described above. Simply stated, a good reviewer helps the Editor achieve the goals of peer review. Another guiding principle is our friend the Golden Rule. You should be the kind of reviewer that you would want to review your work. It is important for reviewers always to try to take an author's perspective and to remember that publishing is vitally important to authors. Sometimes an author needs one more publication to ensure a promotion or to receive a favorable review on a grant application. Authors may be performing research in a highly competitive area where having a paper accepted for publication is critical evidence of their precedence. Reviewers should easily be able to imagine an author's response to a careless review or one that is delayed by months. Reviewers often offer excuses to the Editor for late or cursory reviews, but the author feels the delay -- and the curt treatment -- even more keenly than the Editor. I suggest placing this aphorism on your desk as you participate in the review process: Review others as you would be reviewed.

Below I present what could be viewed as one editor's advice on being a good reviewer. I have ordered this section pretty much in the order of steps in the review process as presented in Table 10.1.

RESPOND PROMPTLY TO INVITATIONS TO REVIEW

As I mentioned above, many journals now use email or FAX to invite reviewers for a submission. The invitation typically includes only basic information about the paper and an abstract. The worst thing you can do with an invitation is ignore it. It takes only a minute or two to decide if you are able to accept the invitation and then notify the Editor. If you want to do the review but cannot complete it by the deadline, contact the Editor and see if this is acceptable. If you decide you cannot accept the invitation, you can help the Editor with some suggestions for other reviewers, but the main thing is to tell the Editor promptly. Failure to reply puts the Editor in the difficult situation of deciding how long to wait until contacting other potential reviewers, and the review process is already behind schedule. To avoid delays with this invitation step, some Editors invite several qualified reviewers and hope that the required number will agree promptly.

Reviewers decline invitations all the time, so Editors are used to this. If you are too busy at the moment, have other review assignments to complete, do not feel competent to review the paper, or have a COI, Editors will understand, especially if you regularly agree to write reviews for that journal. If you will never agree to do a review for that journal, it's best to tell the Editor so you can be removed from the reviewer database.

NOTIFY EDITOR OF ANY POTENTIAL CONFLICTS OF INTEREST OR PREVIOUS REVIEWS YOU DID OF THE PAPER

If you have an obvious COI you should decline the invitation to review. Often reviewers are uncertain if they should declare what appears to be a slight COI, such as a small collaboration with an author or a collaboration that occurred many years ago. In these cases it is best to tell the Editor about your concerns and he can then decide if it represents a real conflict. Putting such ambiguous conflicts on the record can often lessen an Editor's concern. On the other hand, if you feel a conflict that might affect your ability to give a fair and unbiased assessment, then you probably are in conflict and should not accept the invitation to be a reviewer.

More often than one might expect, a reviewer is invited to review a paper he or she has already reviewed and rejected for another journal. Many reviewers are in more than one reviewer database and these journals match reviewers to submissions in pretty much the same way. Some reviewers prefer to decline the second invitation, often stating that they do not want to place the author in double jeopardy. In such instances, I recommend asking the Editor what to do. I personally have no problem with reviewers assessing the same manuscript for two different journals. If the new paper is identical to the one reviewed earlier and the reviewer feels that the same recommendation and comments are in order, then he or she should submit them again. But if the author has made improvements before resubmitting, the recommendation should address those changes. Authors should be advised that they take a risk if they submit a rejected paper to another journal without addressing any of the concerns raised with the initial submission; their manuscript may be assigned to the same reviewer.

MAINTAIN CONFIDENTIALITY

Submissions to journals are confidential information. Reviewers should scrupulously respect the secrecy of the information, including even the fact that the submission exists. Reviewers who solicit input on a review from a colleague or trainee must first inform the colleague or trainee about the confidentiality of the information. The reviewer is responsible for any disclosures by his or her consultants.

The most unethical use of information in manuscripts under review occurs when the reviewer uses the information to facilitate directly the reviewer's own work, for example by using a new methodology before it has been published or citing the work in his or her own publication or grant application. Failure to maintain confidentiality and misuse of information obtained in the review process is considered scientific misconduct.

I strongly advise reviewers not to contact author(s) with questions or offers to negotiate some changes in the manuscript or for any other reasons related to the submission. This applies even if the journal uses an unblinded review process whereby the authors know the identities of their reviewers. Such communications usually go badly for both reviewer and author, who can end up arguing about the paper, and they improperly exclude the Editor from the decision-making process, perhaps concealing from him or her important aspects of the review process.

COMPLETE THE REVIEW ON TIME

Editors give reviewers a fixed period of time within which to return a review recommendation. Reviewers who are late ultimately disrespect the author. When a reviewer accepts an invitation to review with a specified deadline, there is little excuse for tardiness. If you know you are going to be late with a review, notify the Editor, who can decide whether to wait for your review or invite someone else. One of the most disagreeable aspects of being a journal editor is the need to remind reviewers, often several times, of late reviews. Computerized reviewer databases keep track of how long it takes reviewers to complete reviews so that chronically late reviewers can be removed from the database.

WRITE A GOOD REVIEW

Completing a review requires at least two steps: making a publication recommendation and writing comments to the authors (and Editor when needed). Both are important. I will devote most of this section to the process of writing comments, but I begin with some advice about making recommendations.

Read the reviewer instructions carefully to learn on what basis the journal wants you to make a recommendation. How does the Editor want you to balance technical merit vs. importance to the field, etc? Most journals ask for your overall recommendation based on the review criteria specified. Although journals differ on this, they usually want one of four possible decisions: accept, minor revision, major revision, or rejection. Because many journals receive more technically acceptable papers than they can publish, Editors want recommendations that also consider the importance of the information and whether it covers new ground or applies a novel perspective. In my experience reviewers are least comfortable with judging the importance of submissions, but as experts in the area, they may be in the best position to make this judgment.

PROVIDE COMMENTS TO THE EDITOR

Nearly all journals give reviewers the option of providing comments to the Editor. These comments are confidential and not shared with the author or other reviewer(s). There is no need to reproduce your comments to the author in this space, but do include things you believe the Editor should know in addition to what should be seen by the author. The following are some of the matters you would want to bring to the confidential attention of the Editor.

Identify COIs not previously reported. If you have some relationship to the authors or have some financial or personal interest in the work you are reviewing, you should tell the Editor. The Editor will take this information into account when making decisions based on your recommendations. If the Editor believes the COI precludes you from being a reviewer, your review may not be considered in making a decision and your comments to authors may not be sent on. Situations like this are rare, but it is better to tell the Editor too much than too little.

Identify your areas of expertise. There may be some aspects of the paper about which you do not feel competent to provide a review. As I mentioned before, you may have been invited to complement another reviewer who lacks expertise in your area. Tell the Editor if there are parts of the paper for which another expert is needed. It's far better to place statements about your areas of expertise in the comments to the Editor than in your comments to the author.

Concerns about ethics or scientific misconduct. As I have already mentioned, you need not be certain of ethical problems to report your suspicion. If you have sufficient cause for question, tell the Editor.

Other comments. Reviewers may have additional information or some options the Editor should consider that are not appropriate for sending to the authors. Reviewers should feel free to help Editors in any way they can to make the right decision and seek changes in a submission. Examples include when a reviewer is familiar with a controversy surrounding the reported research or when there is excessive overlap with other reports coming from the same research group.

COMPLETE QUESTIONNAIRES

Most journals ask reviewers to complete questionnaires, which may include items about COIs, ethics, technical merit, significance, language usage or other matters. Some of these items (e.g. COI and subject protection) may be critical to the review process. It should not take you long to complete the questionnaire, and the information you provide will help the Editor.

PROVIDE COMMENTS FOR AUTHORS

Here again, the Golden Rule tells us how to act. As an author, you would undoubtedly want to know the basis for an Editor's decision; so, too, do the authors of the papers you review. Comments to authors are a critically important part of the review process and should be written for the edification of both the author and the Editor. There is no standard length for these comments. In my experience 1-2 pages is usually sufficient, but if the key basis for your recommendation can be stated in a paragraph or two, that is fine. Some reviewers do fairly detailed page-by-page suggestions for improvements; these are much appreciated by Editors if they are constructive. Below are guidelines for writing a good review.

State the paper's main strengths and weaknesses. Start the comments to authors with your views of the main strengths and weaknesses of the manuscript. Generally, after reading this section the Editor should understand the basis for your final recommendation (which you should not include in the comments to authors). Make your statement of weaknesses as constructive as possible and suggest possible avenues by which the author might address the problems in a revision. Those weaknesses that are inherent in the design and execution of the study cannot be fixed in a revision, so you can expend less effort in telling authors how they should have done their study. Even if you recommend rejection you should provide constructive suggestions for improving the paper in the event that the Editor gives the author an opportunity to address the weaknesses. Many reviewers organize the comments to authors by describing the strengths and weaknesses of each of the sections of the paper (e.g. introduction, methods, results, and discussion).

Try to balance technical merit with scientific significance. This balance has been the subject of debate in the grant review process for many years, with many believing that technically competent but scientifically unimportant or uncreative proposals have an advantage, even though they may lack significance (e.g. National Institutes of Health, 1996). It is important for reviewers of journal publications to identify particularly important or creative papers and, conversely, to indicate if in their judgment a paper represents only a minor advance in the field.

Provide specific suggestions for improvements. Detailed suggestions for improving the writing in the paper, the figures or the tables are very helpful to both the Editor and the author. Identify paragraphs or sentences that are unclear, point out areas where information is missing and explain how the writing can be clearer. If you have trouble understanding the paper there is a good possibility that other readers will as well. Reviewers familiar with the journal's formatting requirements can point out departures for correction. Reviewers can also identify relevant publications that should have been cited by the author.

It is important for reviewers to appreciate that journal space is limited and that articles should be as short as they can be while still covering the necessary material. Reviewers can be especially helpful in pointing out how to shorten papers, perhaps by eliminating tables or figures or summarizing data in text. Introductions are often longer than they need be: point out nonessential background information that can be edited out. Similarly, discussions can be too speculative or focused on minor aspects of the study results. Chapter 9 provides advice on writing papers for addiction journals; reviewers can offer similar advice in their comments to authors. Reviewers are often exceptionally generous with their help, especially to inexperienced authors. I am truly impressed and grateful to the many reviewers who see the peer review process as a mentoring opportunity.

Having advised reviewers to provide both general and specific suggestions for improving manuscripts, I would not want authors to see this as a rationale for submitting rough drafts or papers that have not been proofread so they can get reviewer feedback. Submission of unpolished drafts shows a lack of respect for the reviewers and Editors and is not a good application of the Golden Rule. Authors should submit papers that they would be happy to review. Reviewers often become exasperated when reviewing sloppy submissions -- it colours their recommendations and discourages them from providing detailed suggestions. Authors are well advised to turn in their very best work.

Comment on language issues. Chapter 3 presents the problems faced by authors having to submit their papers to English-language journals when English is not their first language. Reviewers cannot be expected to correct language problems. When assigned a paper obviously written by a non-English speaker, reviewers should do their best to focus on the science being presented and simply point out areas where language usage needs to be improved. There are various means by which authors and editors can handle this problem, so reviewers should not be biased in their recommendations based on poor English language usage. For example, some journal publishers provide language assistance, or the Editor can request that the author seek help from a native English speaker if the paper is likely to be accepted.

Avoid unconstructive comments. There are some things that do not belong in comments to authors. First and foremost are pejorative comments about authors or the work. Reviewers should strive to be constructive at all times. Editors may remove overly personal criticisms or other material that insults the authors, their institution, or their geographical location.

Jokes and witty remarks also do not belong in comments to authors. Editors may appreciate them in comments to the Editor, but for authors this is serious business. They may perceive such remarks as a lack of serious intent by the reviewer.

Unless the journal uses unblinded reviews, reviewers should not reveal their identity in the comments to authors. Personal pronouns can provide clues to the reviewer's identity ("We did a study that showed...."). Reviewers often provide authors with several of their own publications that they feel should have been cited, leading the author to suspect who the reviewer is.

REVIEWING REVISIONS

Most of what I have said about reviewing applies to reviewing revisions of manuscripts. I feel that reviewers have a special obligation to agree to review revised papers that they reviewed in an earlier version. Reviewers should evaluate how the authors addressed the weaknesses they identified in the earlier version. If authors have failed to address the concerns successfully, it should be stated in the review; on the other hand if the authors were successful in their revisions or, alternately, convinced you that your concerns were unwarranted, this should also be stated in your comments. In any case, you should check to make sure the authors actually made the changes in the manuscript. Addressing problems only in a cover letter is not constructive.

It is also helpful for reviewers to look at the concerns of the other reviewer(s) and see how the authors addressed those. If you disagree with the other reviewer(s) and agree with the authors' explanation and defense of their original article, help the Editor out by discussing these issues. If you feel that another reviewer was way off base, it's probably best to discuss your concerns in the comments to editor rather than sharing your views with the authors.

Sometimes when authors clarify their methods or data analyses you see that the submission is even weaker than you initially thought. If that's the case, state your new observations clearly and make your recommendation accordingly. Sometimes in reading a revision of a paper, reviewers will identify weaknesses they missed in the first review. It is fine to voice these new concerns in your written review, but ideally these problems would have been identified in your earlier review. Depending upon the scope of additional changes you and the Editor request in a second revision, the Editor may return the same paper to you a third time for your recommendation.

WHAT DO EDITORS DO WITH PEER REVIEWS?

After reviews of a manuscript are completed, the Editor evaluates the paper and the reviews and makes a decision. As I mentioned, with some journals this decision-making process may involve multiple editors and/or members of the editorial advisory board; others may involve one Editor's decision. Many factors go into making a decision on a submission. The primary factor is the recommendations of the reviewers, but other factors include the Editor's assessment of the importance of the paper and how well it fits with the journal's area of coverage, additional concerns the Editor may have that were not identified by the reviewers, the likelihood that the submission can be successfully revised to address its weaknesses, and the overall rejection rate for the journal.

Addiction journals differ greatly in their rejection rates with some able to publish much less than half of the submitted papers. Rejection rates are determined primarily by two things: the number of submissions to the journal and the number of printed pages that are allotted for the year. Many journals have an annual page budget determined by the publisher and/or the owners of the journal. There are financial implications to exceeding the page budget, so as the number of submissions climbs, so too does the number of rejections. Journal editors far prefer the opportunity to select only the best papers for their journal vs. not having enough acceptable submissions to fulfill the page budget. Journals with high rejection rates usually have higher impact factors because they choose only top-quality papers, and better and more important papers tend to be cited heavily. It is important for reviewers to understand this dynamic to appreciate why their reviews are so important to both the authors and the journals.

SUMMARY AND CONCLUSIONS

I have tried to provide background and helpful advice on reviewing papers for scientific journals. I provided an overview of the peer review process, reasons for having peer review, why scholars would want to be peer reviewers and tips on how to be a good reviewer. I have done this primarily from the point of view of a journal editor, but have emphasized authors' points of view as well. I encouraged you to apply the Golden Rule and be the type of reviewer you would want to review your submissions to journals. If you take an author's point of view, it will greatly help you in being a good reviewer. Peer review is a very important part of the scientific process. Your work as reviewers is greatly appreciated and necessary. I hope this chapter helps you improve your reviewing skills.

ACKNOWLEDGEMENTS

I would like to thank the editors and other authors of chapters in this book who provided constructive reviews of this chapter that greatly improved its content and clarity.

REFERENCES AND FURTHER READING

Glen, J.W. (2003) Editorial processing of manuscripts and proofs. In H. Maisonneuve, P.H. Enkell, A.K.S. Polderman and R. Thapa (Eds.), Science Editor's Handbook, European Association of Science Editors.

Enckell, P.H. (2003) Guidelines on good refereeing practice. In H. Maisonneuve, P.H. Enkell, A.K.S. Polderman and R. Thapa (Eds.) Science Editor's Handbook, European Association of Science Editors.

Enckell, P.H. (2003) Dealing with referees - judges or colleagues? In H. Maisonneuve, P.H. Enkell, A.K.S. Polderman and R. Thapa (Eds.) Science Editor's Handbook, European Association of Science Editors.

Fletcher, R.H. and Fletcher, S.W.. (2003) The effectiveness of journal peer review. In F. Godlee and T. Jefferson (Eds.) Peer review in health sciences, 2nd edition. London: BMJ Books.

Girden, E.R. (2001) Evaluating Research Articles. 2nd Edition. Thousand Oaks: Sage Publications.

Godlee, F. and Jefferson, T. (eds) (2003) Peer review in health sciences, 2nd edition. London: BMJ Books.

Hames, I. Peer review and manuscript management in scientific journals: Guidelines for good practice. (2003) Malden, MA: Blackwell Publishing.

Jefferson, T., Alderson, P., Wagner, E. and Davidoff, F. (2002) Effects of editorial peer review. A systematic review. JAMA 2784-2786.

National Institutes of Health. (1996) Report of the Committee on Rating of Grant Applications. [available online at http://grants.nih.gov/grants/peer/rga.pdf, accessed on August 2, 2007]

Overbeke, J. and Wagner, E. (2003) The state of evidence: What we know and what we don't know about journal peer review. In F. Godlee and T. Jefferson (eds), Peer review in health sciences, 2nd edition. London: BMJ Books.

CHAPTER 11
DANTE'S INFERNO: SEVEN DEADLY SINS IN SCIENTIFIC PUBLISHING AND HOW TO AVOID THEM

THOMAS F. BABOR AND THOMAS MCGOVERN

Relinquish all hope, ye who enter here.

Dante Alighieri, *Inferno*, Canto III, 9

More than 700 years ago, Dante Alighieri (1265-1321) wrote an epic poem about a man's journey through the afterworlds of Hell, Purgatory and Heaven. In his *Divine Comedy*, he catalogued the vices and virtues of people who had passed into those spiritual domains, in part to provide a valuable insight to us, the living. Dante described hell as a very unhappy and inhospitable place that had different levels ranging from the blazing inferno of the eternally damned to a rather benign area, called the First Circle, which was reserved for worthy individuals who were born before the world was redeemed and therefore could not enter the gates of heaven.

Within this general metaphor, this chapter will take the reader on an educational journey through the various levels of scientific misconduct. Our purpose is not to scare the fear of God into the gentle hearts of our readers. Rather, like Dante's journey through the netherworld, it is important for us to see the mortal consequences of scientific misconduct so that we can learn how to avoid them. Box 11.1 shows the seven types of misconduct this chapter explores. In addition to describing these various 'sins' and the people who commit them, we also discuss their relative seriousness, the punishments that can result, and how to prevent these kinds of problems before they arise. In the chapter following this one, we discuss the same issues within a framework of ethical decision-making, using case studies to illustrate each topic.

The first issue is carelessness, exemplified by citation bias, understating the accomplishments or findings of others, and neglecting to reference findings that an informed reader would need to know to interpret the author's conclusions. In its most benign form, this problem consists of a failure to read and understand the articles one cites. A more serious offence is the distortion of others' work so that their ideas or findings support a preconceived point of view that the author is trying to advance. Carelessness can also be manifested in poor management or inaccurate presentation of data.

The second ethical issue is redundant publication, which occurs when two or more papers share any of the same data without full cross-referencing.

The third issue we consider is unfair or irresponsible authorship. According to standard Ethical Practice Guidelines published by the International Society of Addiction Journal Editors and similar guidelines of other organizations (e.g., Committee on Publication Ethics), all persons named as authors should have made a major contribution to the work, not just a token contribution.

BOX 11.1 THE CIRCLES OF HELL IN RELATION TO THE SINS AND PUNISHMENTS OF THOSE WHO ENGAGE IN PUBLISHING MISCONDUCT

CIRCLE	SIN	EXAMPLES	PUNISHMENTS
1	Carelessness	Citation bias, understatement, negligence	Request for correction, letter to editor
2	Redundant publication	Same tables or literature reported without noting prior source	Rejection of ms., copyright infringement
3	Unfair authorship credit	Failure to include eligible authors; honorary authors	Angry colleagues, complaints to editor or employer
4	Undeclared conflict of interest	Failure to cite funding source	Letter to editor, public apology
5	Human/animal subject violations	No ethical approval	Rejection of ms., notification of employer
6	Plagiarism	Reproducing others' work or ideas as one's own	Retraction of ms., notification of employer
7	Scientific fraud	Fabrication or falsification of data; misappropriation of others' ideas or plans given in confidence	Retraction of ms., notification of employer, publication ban

Failure to declare a conflict of interest is the fourth ethical issue considered in this chapter. A conflict of interest is a situation or relationship in which professional, personal, or financial considerations could be seen by a fair-minded person as potentially in conflict with the researcher's or author's independence of judgment.

The fifth ethical violation is the failure to conform to minimum standards of protection for animal subjects or human research participants. The latter includes confidentiality of patient records and other data, informed consent, and proper explanation of the risks of research participation. Abiding by standards set by national and institutional boards for the protection of animal or human subjects is an important aspect of research under this rubric.

Plagiarism is the sixth issue. Plagiarism ranges from the unreferenced use of others' published and unpublished ideas, including research grant applications, to submission under 'new' authorship of a complete paper.

The final level is scientific fraud. This form of misconduct consists of the deliberate fabrication of data or the alteration of findings to make a study more credible and acceptable for publication.

How prevalent are these various ethical problems among addiction scientists? The International Society of Addiction Journal Editors (ISAJE) conducted an informal survey of its members to learn about the kinds of ethical misbehaviour of most concern to journal editors (Stenius and Babor 2003). Duplicate publication in various forms and inappropriate citations were the most common problems encountered by journal editors in their routine processing of manuscripts. A substantial number of journals had experienced at least some of the more serious forms of scientific misconduct, such as plagiarism and failure to declare conflict of interest. Authorship problems were also noted quite often. Although most problems were considered infrequent occurrences by the editors, it is likely that these issues are often hidden from the eyes of busy editors and reviewers. For example, editors and reviewers are unlikely to detect scientific fraud in the normal editorial process because data fabrication can be easily hidden in lab records and computer files that are inaccessible during the review process. Skilled reviewers are more likely to detect plagiarism and citation bias, but there is a general suspicion that the cases of identified and provable misconduct are the tip of an iceberg that needs to be melted rather than remaining submerged.

In the following sections of this chapter, each of these ethical improprieties is discussed in terms of its relative importance, possible consequences, and strategies for avoidance. Box 11.2 provides definitions of the various types of ethical problems discussed in the chapter.

NEGLIGENT CARELESSNESS AND CITATION BIAS

The First Circle of Hell described in Box 11.1 is reserved for minor forms of negligent carelessness and citation bias that are likely to mislead readers and distort the value of scientific research. Perhaps the most benign and most prevalent form of ethical impropriety, negligent carelessness, is characterized by such deficiencies as a failure to adequately review the literature on a topic, lack of candour or completeness in describing one's research methods, or presentation of data that are based on faulty statistical analyses. A related problem occurs when an author cites articles taken from other reports or from published abstracts without having read the primary sources. A more serious form of carelessness in scientific writing is citation bias. One variety of this bias is the selective citation of only those articles that support a particular point of view, ignoring or understating the importance of articles that contradict that viewpoint. The intention to deceive others makes this practice especially reprehensible. Another form of citation bias is selective citation to enhance one's reputation, epitomized by self-citation. We discuss these issues in Chapter 7 in terms of various deviations from ideal citation practice. A case analysis of these practices in Chapter 12 further illustrates the ethical dimensions of such transgressions.

Box 11.2 DEFINITIONS OF TERMS REFERRING TO VARIOUS FORMS OF SCIENTIFIC MISCONDUCT

Citation bias	A form of carelessness that ranges from a rather benign failure to read the articles one is citing to the distortion of the meaning of others' work.
Copyright	The legal right granted to an author, publisher, or distributor to exclusive publication, production, sale, or distribution of a scientific work.
Divided publication	Information from a single research study is divided for publication in two or more papers. Also called "salami science."
Duplicate publication	Re-publication of the same information in two different places
Fabrication	Presenting data in a research report that have not been obtained in the manner or by the methods described in the report.
Fractionally divided publication	Reporting in a single paper only a fraction of the data that have been or will be reported in their entirety in another paper.
Misappropriation	Illicitly presenting or using in one's own name an original research idea, plan or finding disclosed in confidence.
Misrepresentation (falsification) of findings	Altering or presenting original findings in a way that distorts the result in a scientifically unjustified way, or by omitting results or data pertinent to conclusions.
Partial repetitive publication	Repeatedly publishing parts of the same information in modified form.
Plagiarism	To present someone else's manuscript, article, text, or idea as one's own.
Repetitive publication	Publishing the same information two or more times (e.g., in journal articles and book chapters).
Self-plagiarism	To copy and present one's own text or article without properly attributing its original source.
Unethical authorship	Authorship which violates the principle that all persons named as authors should have made a major contribution to the work reported and be prepared to take public responsibility for it.

CONSEQUENCES

If the effect of these practices is to mislead or misinform the reader, then they are considered a mild form of scientific misconduct, especially if they only occur at the drafting stage when they are often detected by observant colleagues or reviewers who are likely to request a more balanced literature review, or the correction of obvious mistakes. In some cases an editor may reject an otherwise acceptable manuscript if reviewers raise questions about the author's objectivity or intellectual sloppiness. The consequences could be more serious if carelessness or citation bias is detected only after the article is published. If readers of a published article detect a statistical mistake, a clear bias in the formulation of a research question or the selective reporting of the literature, they may write letters to the editor pointing out the problem. Editors in turn may ask for corrections to the text or the data analyses, which are subsequently published as a special note to readers. Beyond these embarrassing consequences, failure to cite relevant studies and bias in the interpretation of previous research are likely to create a negative impression of the author among his or her colleagues. Another negative consequence may be opprobrium and damage of reputation experienced by the institution with which the author is affiliated.

PREVENTION

As discussed in Chapters 5, 6 and 7, the best way to avoid these problems is to follow appropriate citation practices, conduct a thorough review of the literature, read all of the articles you cite, present research findings accurately, and interpret them objectively. Authors who collaborate on multi-authored papers have a special responsibility to read all drafts of a manuscript with extreme care to make sure that these problems are detected during the early stages of the publication process. Even when several authors divide responsibility for writing different sections of a research report, authors should always check each others' work.

REDUNDANT PUBLICATION

Authors wishing to reach the widest possible audience, or a variety of specific audiences, may seek to report a single definable body of research in more than one paper, in repeated reports of the same work, in fractional reports, or in reports in more than one language (Huth 1986). But there are also less noble motives for redundant publication, including the desire for multiple publications to enhance one's reputation.

Redundant publication occurs when two or more papers, without full cross-reference, share the same data (Committee on Publication Ethics 2001). According to the Editorial Policy Committee of the Council of Biology Editors, repetitive publication refers to "publication of essentially the same study more than once without clear notification of editors, reviewers, and other appropriate parties" (see Jerrells 2001). In general, journal editors expect authors to ensure that no significant part of the submitted material has been published previously and that the article is not concurrently being considered by another journal. Repetitive publication has become such a serious problem that many journals now require authors to state in writing whether the data have been previously reported in part or in whole.

As indicated in Box 11.2, a number of different terms have been used to describe this phenomenon. Although there are some important differences among prior, duplicate, repetitive, fragmented, and redundant publication, they are all part of a common problem. Redundant publication and its variants consume valuable resources that otherwise might be devoted to other authors who are publishing original data or ideas. Because of limited journal space, the publication of one person's paper means that another's paper will be rejected. If there are questions about the extent of the overlap between two articles, editors and reviewers need to take extra time to review several publications to determine the extent of redundancy and whether it violates any copyright agreements.

Regardless of whether the repetition occurs with data or ideas (e.g., repetitive review articles), the information from duplicated sources is sometimes inadvertently cited in a way that implies that the findings or conclusions are independent of each other, when in fact they are based on the same source. Without proper identification, meta-analyses and review papers may come to biased conclusions because the effect of a given finding is multiplied or distorted.

As Huth (1986) has noted, some types of repetitive publication are legitimate and should not be considered scientific misconduct. This is particularly the case in the publications associated with large datasets that involve multiple investigators across many sites. Often, the collaborating investigators have included measures related to a particular hypothesis or methodology, which could and should be reported in separate articles even though the article presents the same subjects, methods, procedures and even some of the same data as other articles. Such publications may be intended to highlight the relevance of particular clinical findings for a particular audience, especially if they have been first published in a technical journal that did not permit the reporting of particular findings or the discussion of clinical implications. Another acceptable variant is publication of the same article, often in its entirety, in two different languages. It is also acceptable to re-publish ideas, data, or review findings when journal editors or book editors request that a popular author write a topical review or commentary for their publication. As long as the author tells the editor about previously published material and cites all relevant reports in the commissioned paper, it is generally acceptable to re-publish or update such material.

A special case of redundant publication is 'self-plagiarism'. According to Griffin (1991), this occurs when an author re-uses text from a previously published paper in a way that fails to give proper acknowledgement to its source and its owner. By 'owner' is meant the person or organization that owns the copyright (see Box 11. 2 for definition), which is often the publisher of the previous version of the borrowed text, not the original author. This problem typically occurs when authors re-use text from a literature review or the Methods section of an article either without changing the wording or by quoting the original text. Unlike the re-use or re-publication of original data, self-plagiarism is something that is more the result of laziness than dishonesty. It can also be a form of self-aggrandizement.

CONSEQUENCES

If a duplicate publication constitutes a copyright infringement, it may result in a reprimand for the author, a retraction of the article, or an apology to the journal editors and the publishers involved. If editors are embarrassed by the need to publish a retraction, they may adopt policies and regulations that place an added burden on honest authors who follow the rules. And when instances of scientific misconduct like this are reported to the public, they diminish the reputation of scientists and their work. In general, an author is not allowed to re-use previously published material when the rights have been assigned to the publisher, which occurs in most instances of scientific journal publications. Reprinting more than one or two sentences verbatim without proper attribution may constitute a violation of copyright and could result in legal sanctions, although this rarely occurs in cases of minor copyright violations. Editors are unlikely to consider small amounts of 'borrowing' to be a major problem, but if an observant reviewer detects widespread self-plagiarism, the editor may reject the article. Nevertheless, the more that authors re-use text without proper quotation or attribution, the more they risk adverse consequences from editors and publishers, ranging from a reprimand to legal action for copyright violation.

PREVENTION

Authors of overlapping papers would be seriously remiss in failing to cite their previously published work (see Jerrells 2001 for a discussion of this problem). When there is any possibility of repetitive publication, authors must notify editors to explain the connection between the current paper and its predecessors. Ideally, the author should submit all related publications to the editor along with an explanation of the potential overlap and the reasons for the new report. Second, all versions of related papers must contain appropriate citations and complete references to the related papers so that readers and editors can evaluate the implications of the repetition and overlap. This includes citing illustrations or tables reprinted or adapted from other journals.

The publication of the same paper in two different languages is acceptable when the editors of both journals agree to it and when the second version cites the previous version as the primary publication.

Regarding self-plagiarism, set off short quotations from a previously published article in quotation marks and cite the original version. Permission must be requested from the publisher or other copyright holder when large sections are reproduced. When there is a need to repeat the information contained in a previously published literature review or a Methods section, the best solution is to change some of the wording in each sentence and to refer the reader to relevant sources for previously published material (e.g., 'As discussed in our previous report [Bloggins 1899]').

UNFAIR AUTHORSHIP

Authorship of a scientific report refers not only to the writing of a manuscript, but also to the origin of a writing project, any experimentation or other research connected with it, and the substantive kinds of work that led up to it.

According to the ISAJE Ethical Practice Guidelines and other codes (Committee on Publication Ethics 2001), all persons named as authors should have made a major contribution to the work reported and be prepared to take public responsibility for its contents (in proportion to the credit they claim on the author list). An editorial (Editor, 1982, p. 613) in the *Annals of Internal Medicine* defines relevant terms as follows:

> *Responsibility* means the ability and willingness to defend the content of the paper if it is challenged by readers. *Public* means that authors are willing to carry out this responsibility in a published defense, such as a signed letter to the editor; private defense in private correspondence would not reach the scientific public.
>
> *Content* means not simply packages of data but also the conceptual framework on which they are hung: the justification for a study or clinical observations; the basis for the study design; methods for collection of valid data: the analysis and interpretation of the data; and the logic that led to the conclusions.

There are a number of ways in which authorship decisions can result in ethical improprieties. First, some persons who have made significant contributions to an article may not receive sufficient credit, or may receive no credit at all. This occurs when an article is drafted without the knowledge or consent of someone who made a substantive contribution earlier in the process. It also occurs when a decision to list the order of contributions is not made fairly with the full agreement of the co-authors, as when a major contributor is listed after a minor contributor to enhance the ego or career of the minor contributor. Another instance of inappropriate credit occurs when a co-author, such as a science writer, is not listed because the research group might be embarrassed to admit that someone else wrote the paper, such as a science writer hired by a drug company to expedite the publication of favorable findings. This is called 'ghost' authorship because the author's identity is unknown to those who read the article.

A second type of authorship problem arises when some persons are listed as co-authors even though they made no substantive contribution to the article or the research. A common example is the practice of listing the head of a department or a research centre director, often at the end of the authors' list, a custom known as gratuitous, honorary or gift authorship. Again, in the light of this practice, one must question the ethical climate in research settings that allow such behaviour to occur. Ethical guidelines, appropriately crafted and implemented, might deter such transgressions.

Between these two extremes, there are a number of related infractions, such as the failure to give proper recognition to a person's contribution by listing him or her inappropriately low in the author list, or the tendency to award co-authorship for minor contributions based on personal or political considerations. A more complete discussion of authorship issues is provided in Chapters 4 and 8, which also describe procedures to minimize ethical and interpersonal problems related to authorship credits. Our purpose here is to discuss the seriousness and consequences of this type of misconduct, and to summarize the steps that can be taken to prevent its occurrence.

CONSEQUENCES

Authorship credits may be one of the most contentious issues in scientific publishing. At the level of collaborating research groups, the consequences range from hurt feelings to formal complaints made to a scientist's unit director or institutional authority. In between these extremes there are likely to be recriminations, perceptions of unfairness, and poisoned working relationships, which could damage the reputations of some of the parties involved. When instances of unfair authorship credit are detected, the editor's response could range from the rejection of a pending manuscript to the call for a correction to a published paper. But these matters rarely come to the attention of editors unless there is a case of scientific fraud, where co-authors might claim that they were not sufficiently involved in the writing of the paper to detect the fabrication in the first place.

PREVENTION

How can authors best deal with ethical issues related to authorship? As noted in Chapter 8 early agreement on the precise roles of the contributors and collaborators, and on matters of authorship and publication, is advised. The lead author should periodically review the status of authorship credits within a designated working group by having open discussions of substantive contributions with all prospective collaborators. In order to avoid disputes, distribute and discuss authorship guidelines with all potential collaborators on a manuscript. An open discussion, related to authorship, should be on the academic agenda of research centres. Involving an institutional ethics committee in drawing up institutional guidelines might also be helpful. Open and ongoing conversation about these issues, combined with institutional policies, is the best way to avoid problems.

UNDECLARED CONFLICT OF INTEREST

A conflict of interest is a situation or relationship in which professional, personal, or financial considerations could be seen by a fair-minded person as potentially in conflict with independence of judgment (ISAJE 1997). One way to determine whether a conflict of interest exists is to ask the question: If the situation or relationship were revealed to the editor or the reader only after the paper was published, would it make a reasonable person feel misled or deceived? Conflict of interest is not in itself wrongdoing. It is the failure to declare real or potential conflicts to an editor, one's co-authors, and the readers of a paper that constitutes scientific misconduct, to the extent that potential conflicts are very important in the evaluation of any piece of scientific work.

There are three levels of conflict of interest: real, apparent, and potential. A *real* conflict of interest means that the author, or the administrative unit with which the author has an employment relationship, has a financial or other interest that could unduly influence the author's position with respect to the subject matter being considered. An *apparent* conflict of interest exists when an interest would not necessarily influence the author but could prompt others to question the author's objectivity. A *potential* conflict of interest exists when there is an interest or relationship that would make a reasonable person uncertain or suspicious whether or not it should be reported.

Conflicts of interest can be financial, personal, political, or academic. Financial interests include employment, research funding, stock or share ownership, payment for lectures or travel, consultancies, and company support for staff (Committee on Publication Ethics 2001). These kinds of conflict are most often discussed in ethics codes and reports on research integrity because they are easier to document and quantify. In addition to financial and commercial conflicts of interest, a conflict may be personal, political, or academic. Personal conflicts might include a vendetta against another researcher who is disliked by the author of an article. Political conflicts exist when researchers distort their findings or interpretation to conform to 'politically correct' ideas or ideology. Academic conflicts include the attempt to validate 'pet' theories supporting one's own ideas. These kinds of conflict are difficult to detect, but they should nevertheless be considered by authors when evaluating their own work. Authors in the past have been provided with little guidance in evaluating and responding appropriately to issues of conflict of interest. The existence of compliance offices in research settings is helpful, but these institutions of themselves will not solve the problem. Researchers need appropriate training about the ethical dimensions involved as well as opportunities for ongoing dialogue and conversation, in order to develop informed individuals and groups (Institute of Medicine 2002).

As discussed in more detail in Chapter 13, the potential for conflict of interest in the addiction field is enhanced by any relationship or funding connected with the tobacco industry, the alcohol beverage industry, for-profit health care systems, private hospitals, the pharmaceutical industry, and 'social aspect organizations' that receive their primary support from these sources. For example, in the search for drugs that may be used to treat tobacco, alcohol, or drug dependence, scientists involved in research on a particular product may have financial ties with companies that have a business interest in that product. The alcohol and tobacco industries have also funded researchers to conduct policy studies or policy-related program evaluations. Sometimes the industry funds studies directly; at other times it funds studies indirectly through 'social aspect' organizations that receive their support from industry sources. In addition to research funding, industry ties can include paid consultancies, conference presentations, stockholding, advisory board membership, and patent holding.

Two major questions regarding the need for conflict of interest policies and precautions are whether industry funding affects the quality and eventual publication of research, and whether the effect is deleterious. Bias toward 'positive' results may exist even among articles where financial ties to industry are disclosed (Cho 1998). For example, pharmaceutical industry-supported drug studies are significantly more likely to report 'positive' findings (i.e., the manufacturer-associated drug better than placebo) than non-industry funded studies (Stelfox et al. 1998). In the addiction field, one analysis found that industry-supported studies were more likely to conclude that secondhand smoke has no health effects than non-industry funded studies (Lambe et al. 2002). Another risk is publication bias, in which industry-favourable studies are more likely to get published than unfavourable ones.

There are several possible mechanisms to explain how conflicts, especially those connected with industry ties, may lead to publication bias (see Cho 1998). One is suppression of publication, whereby negative findings are not published because either the author fears loss of funding from industry sponsors or the industry itself imposes restrictions on publication. Another mechanism is self-selection or industry selection of researchers who are more likely to get positive results.

CONSEQUENCES

One consequence of competing financial interests is the possible limitation of publication options. Although most journals do not ban publication of articles because of their authors' financial interests, some journals have now begun to prohibit authors of editorials and review articles from publishing if the author has a substantial financial interest in the product discussed in the editorial or review (Relman 1990). This policy does not apply to authors of scientific reports that present original data. Undeclared conflicts of interest, when detected, may have serious consequences, such as the rejection of a pending article, the retraction of a published article or the author's need to publish an apology. A more subtle effect of real or apparent conflict of interest is the perception by one's scientific colleagues that one's scientific work is biased because of a personal or financial interest.

PREVENTION

According to Loue (2000), the best way to avoid problems associated with potential conflict of interest is self-elimination from participation in potentially conflicting activities. Short-term consulting arrangements with the tobacco, alcohol, and pharmaceutical industries are often not worth the questions that must be faced about the scientist's objectivity. Arrangements with industry can be particularly problematic when the researcher is asked to sign a restrictive contract regarding the ownership of data, the sponsor's control of the data, and the investigator's right to publish it.

Many academic institutions have rules governing financial support for faculty activities. These rules describe when faculty must disclose particular interests, and when they must divest themselves of particular financial interests. Conflict of Interest Committees, when they operate as part of Ethical Review Committees, are a part of institutional compliance oversight, and hold promise in this respect.

Authors should pay close attention to the guidelines issued by these committees. As noted in Chapter 13, the scientific community has issued warnings about the advisability of accepting any funding from the tobacco and alcohol industries, and has suggested rigorous adherence to voluntary ethical codes when such funding is accepted. Even when these guidelines have been followed appropriately, however, each author should declare to the editor any real, potential or apparent conflict of interest with respect to his involvement in a particular publication. Each author should declare conflicts between (a) commercial entities and the participant personally; and (b) commercial entities and the administrative unit with which the participant has an employment relationship.

Authors should also declare sources of funding for a study, review, or other publication in a way that can be clearly understood by the reader. A footnote or an acknowledgement is the most appropriate mechanism. Describe funding sources in sufficient detail so that an average reader can recognize potential conflicts of interest. If a funding source is a social aspect organization with an ambiguous name such as 'The Alcohol and Health Fund', the reader should be informed that, for example, the organization is supported by a group of beer companies.

Disclosure alone will not necessarily eliminate publication bias. Researchers who are serious about avoiding even the appearance of conflict of interest are advised to dilute the conflicting relationship by getting funding from both industry and non-industry sources, and by refusing to sign industry agreements that do not guarantee the researcher's right to publish the results regardless of the study's outcome. Other management strategies include avoiding additional financial ties that are not absolutely necessary to the pursuit of the research, such as the acceptance of advisory board memberships, stock options, or consulting fees from companies sponsoring research (Cho et al. 2001).

HUMAN/ANIMAL SUBJECTS VIOLATIONS

Addiction research involving human and animal subjects has been conducted for over a century. During this period regulations governing human and animal experimentation have developed into a very complex set of procedures that are typically governed by appointed committees located at institutions involved in biomedical research. These procedures include ethical review of research protocols, safety monitoring of animals and human research participants, and informed consent requirements for human participants. These procedures were developed out of concern for the rights of research participants following a series of well-publicized medical experiments in which human subjects were exposed to harmful agents or had effective treatments withheld without their knowledge or consent (Loue 2000). It has now become customary, if not mandatory, to submit proposed research for independent review by an Ethical Research Committee to determine its ethical acceptability from the perspective of the local community and the researcher's institution (Institute of Medicine 2003). Such boards focus primarily on the protection of research participants by assuring that the study's procedures minimize risks of unwarranted harm to participants.

It is becoming increasingly recognized that scientific journals have an important role to play in the protection of human and animal research subjects. Journals are responsible for the dissemination of research findings. They "are obligated to publish research that meets high ethical standards […] for which the authors have attested to their compliance with regulatory ethical standards" (Institute of Medicine 2003, p. 205). A number of journals have implemented policies requiring authors to certify compliance with informed consent procedures, and the International Society of Addiction Journal Editors (1997) subscribes to these policies.

CONSEQUENCES

Failure to follow recommended or required journal procedures regarding protection of human and animal research subjects could have several important consequences. Although most journals do not ban publication of articles because they have not been submitted for ethical review, some journals now require authors to state whether their research conforms to the minimum standards outlined in the Helsinki Declaration. In particular, social and behavioural research such as survey studies and research involving archival records may not require stringent informed consent procedures. However, it would be an error to rely on this perception: surveys, on occasion, have resulted in significant harm to individuals and to institutions. It is safer to submit all research for institutional review, letting the committee decide whether the researcher is exempt or not. Failure to obtain ethical approvals or informed consent from research participants may lead an editor to question the purpose and value of the research, and could result in a decision not to send the manuscript out for review or, when the failure is detected during peer review, to decline the manuscript. Another consequence could be the notification of an official from the author's institution.

PREVENTION

It is always wise to mention both in the cover letter to the editor and in the text of a submitted manuscript that the researchers have followed appropriate ethical review procedures. If there are any questions regarding the applicability of human subjects requirements, these should be raised with the editor in the cover letter or in a telephone call or email message prior to submission of a manuscript. Often these questions can be resolved by consulting the journal's instructions to authors or website. The International Committee of Medical Journal Editors has provided the following guidance regarding ethical issues:

> When reporting experiments on human subjects, indicate whether the procedures followed were in accordance with the ethical standards of the responsible committee on human experimentation (institutional or regional) and with the Helsinki Declaration of 1975, as revised in 1983. Do not use patients' names, initials, or hospital numbers, especially in illustrative material. When reporting experiments on animals, indicate whether the institution's or a national research council's guide, or any national law on the care and use of laboratory animals was followed. (Source: www.icmje.org/index.html#top)

The Helsinki Declaration refers to the formal international standards developed to guide experimentation involving human participants. In particular, the 1975 and 1983 revisions emphasized the importance of voluntary informed consent to participate in research (Loue 2000).

PLAGIARISM

Plagiarism includes both the theft of intellectual property and the copying of unattributed textual material. Plagiarism ranges from the unreferenced use of others' published and unpublished ideas, including research grant applications, to submission under 'new' authorship of a complete paper, sometimes in a different language. It can also include copying of another's work verbatim or nearly verbatim in a way that misleads the ordinary reader about the author's own contribution. It may occur at any stage of planning, research, writing, or publication. It applies to both print and electronic versions of a publication.

The Office of Research Integrity (ORI), an office within the US Department of Health and Human Services that monitors investigation of research misconduct, considers plagiarism to include both the theft or misappropriation of intellectual property and the substantial unattributed textual copying of another's work, such as sentences, paragraphs or even entire manuscripts, in a way that misleads the ordinary reader regarding the contribution of the author.

CONSEQUENCES

The consequences of plagiarism can be serious, ranging from a reprimand from an editor to a formal hearing and loss of employment after an allegation is reported to the author's institutional officials. ORI generally does not pursue the limited use of identical or nearly-identical phrases that, for example, describe a commonly-used methodology or previous research because these are not considered to be substantially misleading to the reader or of great significance. Journal editors can be unrelenting and at times unforgiving if they detect instances of plagiarism. The typical approach is first to request a written explanation from the author soon after the plagiarism has been discovered. Most often these instances are discovered by knowledgeable and vigilant reviewers, or by readers who sometimes report that their own words, sentences, paragraphs or articles have been misappropriated. If the author's explanation is credible and the amount of copying is small, the consequences may be nothing more than a letter of reprimand and possibly the rejection of the manuscript. More extensive types of plagiarism may result not only in the rejection of the manuscript, but also in the publication of a correction if the material has already been published. More importantly, such matters may then be referred to the author's institutional employer, who typically will have responsibility for dealing with allegations of scientific misconduct. This is discussed in more detail in the next section. Although failure to attribute the original source of a sentence or paragraph may constitute a copyright infringement and could result in civil proceedings, such cases are rarely prosecuted.

PREVENTION

All sources should be disclosed through appropriate citation or quotation conventions, and if a large amount of other people's written or illustrative material is to be used, the author must seek permission to reprint the material (Committee on Publication Ethics 2001). Legal definitions may vary from country to country regarding plagiarism, copyright, and intellectual property rights.

The author should review these with the editor when there is any question. A more common problem that may result in an embarrassing revelation is the unintentional copying of small amounts of textual material or the borrowing of others' ideas or concepts without appropriate attribution. These cases are usually the result of negligence, sloppiness, or laziness, as when an author fails to use quotation marks or paraphrases someone else's ideas without stating the source. In these instances the best prevention method is the careful documentation of all source documents in the course of note-taking, and the development of writing habits that allow ample time to prepare a manuscript.

OTHER TYPES OF SCIENTIFIC FRAUD

According to the Finnish National Advisory Board on Research Ethics (2004), scientific fraud is manifested in the following forms:

- fabrication i.e., presenting data in a research report that have not been obtained in the manner or by the methods described in the report;
- misrepresentation (falsification) of findings, i.e., altering or presenting original findings in a way that distorts the result in a scientifically unjustified way, or by o mitting results or data pertinent to conclusions;
- plagiarism, i.e., to present someone else's manuscript, article, or text as one's own;
- misappropriation, i.e., illicitly presenting or using in one's own name an original research idea, plan or finding disclosed in confidence.

Fraud can occur in the course of proposing, conducting or reporting research. It is most often detected at the time of publication, primarily because reviewers, editors and readers of scientific articles are very critical and skeptical by nature and profession. In the course of this chapter, and in other parts of this book (see Chapters 4, 7, and 8), we have described several of the less serious instances of scientific misconduct, such as the selective interpretation of others' findings, inappropriate citation practices, unfair authorship practices, selective reporting of data, or use of inappropriate statistics. The problem with these and the more serious forms of misconduct (such as data fabrication) is the damage it does to the scientific enterprise, to the extent that it misleads other scientists and establishes a false record that may be misinterpreted by the public, policymakers, or clinicians. Definitions of scientific misconduct vary from country to country and sometimes involve the need to prove the intention of the author (Loue 2000). Box 11.3 provides an example of scientific misconduct from the field of addiction research.

Box 11.3 AN EXAMPLE OF SCIENTIFIC FRAUD FROM THE TOBACCO FIELD

In December 2003, the Court of Justice of the Canton of Geneva gave its sentence in an (in)famous case of scientific fraud. A Swedish professor at The University of Geneva and formerly of Gothenburg University had charged two tobacco activists with libel after they accused him of 'unprecendented scientific fraud' concerning the risks of passive smoking.

The court dismissed the case, stating that "Geneva has indeed been the platform of a scientific fraud without precedent in the sense that. Professor Ragnar Rylander has acted in his capacity of associate professor at the University, taking advantage of its influence and reputation and not hesitating to put science at the service of money, in disregard of the mission entrusted to this public institution." According to the court, for thirty years the professor had had a close but secret relationship with Philip Morris, which included substantial financial rewards. Thus he lied when he stated to The European Journal of Public Health that he had never had contact with Philip Morris. In his research on passive smoking and in several conferences on the topic he questioned the risks connected with passive smoking. According to the Court, the professor "did not hesitate to deceive the general public in order to show himself favourable to the tobacco company." In particular, the Court reported as apparently fraudulent a study on respiratory diseases in children in which he altered the database so that no link could be made between passive smoking and the frequency of respiratory infections.

Sources: Domstol i Geneve slår fast svenskt vetenskapsfusk (Court in Geneva gives sentence on Swedish scientific fraud). *Svenska Dagbladet*, 16.12.2003
www.prevention.ch/rypr151203.htm, accessed 11 June 2004.

CONSEQUENCES

Journal editors, funding agencies, and academic institutions take allegations of scientific misconduct seriously, especially those institutions that depend on government support for their research. Typically, an editor who receives information about possible misconduct or who suspects it during the course of a manuscript review has a limited number of options, starting with the notification of the author. Many scientific and academic institutions have procedures to deal with allegations of misconduct, so an editor can begin by passing the allegation and the author's response to an appropriate institutional official or review committee for further action if the allegation seems credible. Generally, the process begins with a preliminary investigation, followed by a more formal inquiry if the allegation has sufficient substance or importance. In such cases, the withdrawal or rejection of the manuscript, or the publication of a correction in the case of an already published paper, is the least of the author's worries.

PREVENTION

There can be no substitute for careful mentoring and training of scientists in the prevention of scientific misconduct. Most scientists have such high respect for the values of science that they would never deliberately fabricate data or mislead their colleagues about the data they have collected or its interpretation. Milder forms of scientific misconduct may result from ignorance, so that deliberate exposure to ethical training may help individual scientists avoid these kinds of problems.

Because scientists typically work in groups along with research support staff, the best way to prevent fraud is to carefully check the data as well as colleagues' work at every stage in the process of conducting a research project and preparing a scientific report.

CONCLUSION

At various times in its short history, addiction research has had its credibility damaged because of ethical breaches in its research and publication practices. Today the field is experiencing an even greater crisis in values, caused by increasing pressure to publish, conflicts of interest, and ethical committee restrictions on research (Babor, in press).

This situation has been exacerbated by the fact that researchers and organizational entities such as journals and professional societies do not have a consistent framework of ethical standards and ethical decision-making that can protect authors, the scientific community and the public from the ethical problems that arise in research and scientific writing. Even when ethical issues are considered professionally, they are more likely to be addressed in an abstract or prescriptive way ('Thou Shalt Not ') rather than as part of an ethical problem-solving process based on generally accepted ethical values. A practical, case-based approach with appropriate ethical analysis, designed to address the realities of research and publishing, follows in Chapters 12 and 13.

In most countries, the general public rates biomedical and social scientists highly in terms of their occupational prestige and credibility. When scientific misconduct is detected and publicized, scientists violate this trust and science loses public support. By following the preventive measures described in this chapter, researchers can avoid most of the major and minor ethical dilemmas associated with scientific misconduct. But the obligation of ethical conduct in reporting research in journal publications does not rest with the authors alone. The US Institute of Medicine (2002) report affirms what this chapter espouses in terms of the integrity of individual authors (researchers) by advocating "above all a commitment to intellectual honesty and personal responsibility for one's actions and to a range of practices which characterize the responsible conduct of research" (p. 5). This report also notes that individuals can only flourish in institutions that "establish and continuously monitor structures, processes, policies and procedures [that support] integrity in the context of research and use this knowledge in continuous quality improvement" (Institute of Medicine 2002, p. 5).

REFERENCES

Alighieri, D. *The Divine Comedy*. Translated by Laurence Binyon (1947) in *The Portable Dante*, New York: The Viking Press.

Babor, T.F. (in press) Alcohol research and the alcoholic beverage industry: Issues, concerns, and conflicts of interest. *Addiction.*

Cho, M.K. (1998) FUNDamental conflicts of interest. The shift toward industry funding biomedical research. *HMS Beagle Home*, Op-Ed., 24, 1-8.

Cho, M.K., Shohara, R., and Rennie, D. (2001) What is driving policies on faculty conflict of interest? Considerations for policy development. Conference Proceedings: Investigating Research Integrity.

Committee on Publication Ethics (2001) Guidelines on good publication practice. *BMJ International*, 85, 2-7. URL http://www.publicationethics.org.uk

Griffin G. C. (1991) Don't plagiarize - even yourself. *Post Graduate Medicine*, 89, 15-16.

Editor (1982) Authorship from the reader's side. *Annals of Internal Medicine*, 97, 613-614.

Huth E.J. (1986) Irresponsible authorship and wasteful publication. *Annals of Internal Medicine*, 104, 257-259

Institute of Medicine (2002) *Integrity of Scientific Research: Creating an Environment that Promotes Responsible Conduct.* Washington, DC: National Academy of Sciences Press.

Institute of Medicine (2003) *Responsible Research: A Systems Approach to Protecting Research Participants*. Washington, DC: National Academies Press.

International Society of Addiction Journal Editors (1997) The Farmington Consensus. *Addiction*, 92, 1617-1618.

Jerrells, T.R. (2001) Duplicative publication of data and other ethical issues in publishing of scientific findings. *Journal of Substance Abuse Treatment*, 20, 111-113.

Lambe, M., Hallhagne, E. and Boethius, G. (2002) Cyniskt spel inom tobaksindustrin. Tvångspublicerade interna dokument avslöjar mångåriga anströngningar att förneka eller tona ner tobakens negativa hälsoeffekter. [The cynical policies of the tobacco companies -- internal documents reveal deliberate cover-up of the health hazards of smoking]. *Läkartidningen*, 99: 2756-2762.

Loue, S. (2000) *Textbook of Research Ethics: Research and Practice*. New York: Kluwer.

National Advisory Board on Research Ethics (2004) Academy of Finland guidelines on research ethics. Helsinki, Finland: Ministry of Education, www.aka.fi/modules

Relman, A.S. (1990) New 'Information for Authors' - and readers. *New England Journal of Medicine*, 321, 56.

Stelfox, H.T., Chua, G., O'Rourke, K. and Detsky, A.S. (1998) Conflict of interest in the debate over calcium-channel antagonists. *New England Journal of Medicine*, 338, 101-106.

Stenius, K. and Babor, T.F. (2003) Ethical problems and ethical guidelines of addiction journals: A report to the ISAJE membership. International Society of Addiction Journal Editors. Unpublished manuscript.

CHAPTER 12
THE ROAD TO PARADISE: MORAL REASONING IN ADDICTION PUBLISHING
THOMAS MCGOVERN, THOMAS F. BABOR, AND KERSTIN STENIUS

With the gesture of a guide, whose goal's in sight,
She spoke: 'We from the greatest body move,
Emerging in the heaven that is pure light;
Light of the understanding, full of love,
Love of the true good, full of joy within,
Joy that transcends all the heart conceiveth of.

Dante Alighieri, *Paradiso*, Canto XXIX, 37-42

INTRODUCTION

Reflection and conversation are at the heart of ethical dialogue in any setting. The road to the unethical publication pitfalls described in the previous chapter is paved with good intentions. Perhaps 'good conversation' is equally a culprit, as discussion about ethical issues in research does not seem to have influenced actual behaviour. L.R. Kass (2002), a seasoned veteran in the field of bioethics, complained that 'in bioethics at the present, the action is mostly talk' (p. 57). In our search for the best solution to ethical problems, we have lost sight of the original goal of ethics - to improve the quality of our behaviour. How then can we provide meaningful direction for researchers wishing to avoid the seven deadly sins catalogued in the previous chapter's circles of hell, and at the same time devise a virtuous path leading to responsible research?

Let us abandon ethics as 'good conversation', an approach advocated by many respected authorities (Brody 1990; Glaser 1994), and concentrate exclusively on practical recommendations to guide the behaviour of authors and researchers. The Greeks, in their wisdom, saw virtue, the quality of 'being good' in any human endeavour, as the condition of being poised between the two extremes of any given situation. In proposing an approach to ethical issues in addiction research and publishing, we embrace the advice of the Greeks, which accounts for both talk and action in fashioning practical responses to moral questions.

We begin with some reflection about ethics as the human endeavour in addiction research. This approach to ethics is characterized by twin goals: 'to be good' and 'to do good'. Being good is at the heart of 'virtue' or 'character' ethics and espouses qualities such as integrity, honesty, and compassion for others. Doing good is the basis for principle-based ethics, such as **autonomy**, **beneficence**, and **justice** (see Box 12.1 for definitions of bolded ethical terms).

We combine both goals in the ethical discussion in this chapter, and bring them to bear on two basic questions that are interwoven in every research enterprise: 1) can we do it? (the technical or research question) and 2) should we do it? (the ethical or moral question). Both questions, individually and collectively, are challenging: they hold us to equally rigorous scientific and ethical standards in all of our research and publishing undertakings.

BOX 12.1 KEY ETHICAL PRINCIPLES USED IN MORAL REASONING AND DECISION-MAKING

Autonomy	Respect people's choices and do not obstruct their actions unless those actions are harmful to others
Beneficence	Do good: provide competent and compassionate care and maximize benefits to individuals, institutions, society
Nonmaleficence	Do no harm: minimize risks to individuals, institutions, society
Justice	Give each person his or her due
Fairness	Avoid discrimination and exploitation
Stewardship	Use resources efficiently and justly

THE ETHICAL CHALLENGE

Scientific issues in the addiction field, as elsewhere, embrace three ethical realms: the individual, the institution, and society (Glaser 1994). In affording respect to each of these realms, researchers honour what Kass (2002) describes as "the rich broth of our social, civil, cultural, and spiritual life together and of the ways in which it seasons us without our knowledge" (p. 65). The well-being of the individual, of institutions, and of society as a whole is at stake in assessing the ethical issues that arise in addiction research. Consider the following scenario as an invitation to apply our discussion up to this point to the realities of a possible research publication situation:

> *A university research team wishes to examine drug use in a poor, disadvantaged minority neighbourhood with an identifiable ethnic population. The intent of the study is to test a new treatment for addiction that holds great promise for society as a whole. The political climate in which the research is conducted is one that is willing to provide research support for biological and social research, but is not prepared to address the deeper societal issues underlying drug problems. In addition, the community in which the research is to be conducted sees drug use as both a matter of choice and best controlled through stringent and oppressive legal measures. Furthermore, the larger community views the minority drug-using group*

with suspicion and distrust. The individuals who will constitute the research population are disadvantaged, have little education, and are a vulnerable population that can be easily exploited in a research endeavour.

Can such research be conducted in a manner that meets appropriate scientific standards? The answer is yes: many measures can be taken to assure its appropriateness. For instance, researchers can offer guarantees that ensure respect for the dignity of the research participants. Researchers can also safeguard the vulnerability of the individuals involved, together with the community as a whole, by meeting the standards of ethical review committees and other governmental and institutional regulations on research. At first sight, the ethical and scientific standards for responsible research seem able to be met at the individual level.

But what of the larger community and societal implications of this research? How will the individuals involved in the research be treated by the larger community if the study shows a high prevalence of drug dependence in the population? Conceivably, an increase in discrimination and further oppression might occur (McGovern 1998), a result researchers would want to avoid. Another consideration centres on who shall benefit from the favourable outcomes of the research: the individuals in the poor neighbourhood or the more privileged members of society? Balancing individual, institutional, and societal concerns can lead to a better understanding of the risks and benefits of research in such situations. Whether or not such research should be undertaken determines whether or not it is published.

A helpful perspective on research and publishing as a whole, as well as the case under consideration, can be found by applying the theories and principles associated with 'doing good'. In analyzing the proposed scenario, a utilitarian approach might seek to maximize the good and minimize the harm. In its most simplistic application, utilitarianism is based on the maxim that the end justifies the means. One could argue from this perspective that the benefit accruing to the majority of the population outweighs the harm to the individual research participants. A duty-driven or deontological approach would counter by arguing that humans can never be used as a means to an end, that their basic dignity must be valued as an end in itself. Two very different responses to the legitimacy of the research and of its subsequent publication thus result from invoking the utilitarian and the deontological positions. One must be always vigilant of research and publications that are justified on the basis of utility or expediency. Grave harm can be inflicted on minority populations or on persons unable to adequately protect their basic dignity (Elwood 1994). Such a caveat needs to be heeded by authors and editors alike.

In following the road to ethical paradise in research and in publication, then, it's helpful to remember a number of principles derived from ethical theory. **Autonomy**, or respect for persons, obliges the researcher in our scenario and those who oversee research to respect the dignity of those involved in the research project. This is guaranteed by safeguarding privacy, confidentiality, and informed consent - with special attention given to assure that research participants fully understand the risks and benefits involved in the study. Likewise, the principle of **nonmaleficence**, i.e., doing no harm to individuals, to communities, and to society as whole, is of the utmost importance. Conducting research in a competent and compassionate fashion is embodied in the principle of **beneficence**. Though often criticized as the basis for a paternalistic approach, this principle is indispensable in addressing the needs of vulnerable individuals and vulnerable communities, as in the scenario under consideration.

The ethical principle of **justice** guarantees persons their due and guards against discrimination. We would invoke this principle to ensure that we do not expose the research population to undue risks for the benefit of another population. **Fairness**, as a guiding principle, is difficult to invoke in a society over-zealous in its defense of individualism and autonomy, without equal attention to the common good (cf Ross et al. 1993, pp. 17-28, for discussion of these principles). Finally, **stewardship** demands that investigators use resources responsibly and efficiently.

TOWARDS A PROBLEM-SOLVING APPROACH

The first step in the development of an effective problem-solving approach to ethical dilemmas in addiction publishing is to create a code of professional practice for use by research organizations and scientific journals. Such a code now exists in the form of the ethical practice guidelines developed by the International Society of Addiction Journal Editors (ISAJE Ethics Group 2002). The ISAJE guidelines articulate values and define the boundaries of appropriate and inappropriate conduct in addiction research (see http://www.parint.org/isajewebsite/ethics.htm). As such, they provide a moral compass authors can use to guide ethical decision-making.

However, the most enlightened and practical direction might be found in the comprehensive analysis of actual situations, especially if they can be considered paradigm cases. This approach finds expression in casuistry, with its ancient roots in moral philosophy and in theology, which provides a consistent focus on individual moral behaviour (Jonsen and Toulmin 1988). It values broad consensus, the development of maxims based on practical wisdom, and the acceptance of probable certitude as the ultimate outcome. Casuistry is attractive because it most closely resembles how we approach moral issues in day-to-day living. Brody (1990) argues that if we examine any ethical situation in research or publishing from every possible angle we will be able to arrive at a consensus and in doing so cover all the various ethical approaches, including theory and principles.

Another necessary step toward ethical decision-making is to learn how to apply these codes in a practical way. To this end, the main part of this chapter is devoted to the analysis of a set of case studies. These cases are presented in the form of short vignettes that describe a situation or problem, followed by an analysis of the ethical principles involved and the appropriate course of action to be taken by the author. The vignettes have a touch of humour in their presentation, intended as a relief from the doom and gloom of traditional moral analysis.

We have also organized the critical incidents depicted in the vignettes according to the following topics (i.e., the seven 'sins' of the previous chapter):

1. Citation bias: a selective reporting of the literature
2. Redundant publication: when two or more papers share any of the same data or text without full cross-reference
3. Unethical authorship: all persons named as authors should have made a major contribution to a publication and be prepared to take public responsibility for its contents.
4. Undeclared conflict of interest
5. Failure to conform to minimal standards of protection for animal or human subjects
6. Plagiarism: unreferenced use of others' published and unpublished ideas
7. Scientific fraud

The analyses provide guides to action, rather than definitive decisions, by deriving conclusions about the most appropriate course of action from sound (and for the most part universal) ethical principles such as autonomy, beneficence, justice, honesty, conscientious refusal, stewardship and non-maleficence.

A SYNTHETIC MODEL FOR THE ANALYSIS OF ETHICAL DILEMMAS

In their book, *Critical Incidents: Ethical Issues in the Prevention and Treatment of Addiction*, White and Popovits (2001) describe a synthetic model for ethical decision-making that borrows from the major traditions and ethical principles described above. The goal is not to provide definitive answers to difficult ethical choices, but rather to stimulate thinking about ethical complexity and to suggest options for an ethical course of action. The model involves the application of three questions:

I. *Whose interests are involved and who can be harmed?* Stating this question in another way, who are the potential winners and losers? In the situations described in this chapter, the main parties likely to be involved are the authors of a particular journal article, the editor of the journal, the author's co-workers, the institution with which the author is affiliated, the professional community of addiction researchers, and society at large. By reviewing the interests and vulnerabilities of these different stakeholders, it becomes possible to identify areas of conflicting interest, where the benefits to one party must be balanced against the harm that could be done to another party or institution.

II. *What universal or culturally-specific values apply to this situation and what course of action is suggested by these values?* According to White and Popovits (2001), this question requires one to explore how widely-held ethical values (defined in Box 12.1) can be applied to guide the best course of action in a particular situation. The identification of values that may be in conflict (e.g., honesty versus loyalty) is an important part of this process, leading to a resolution of the conflict by choosing the higher value. White and Popovits indicate that "the higher value is often determined by the degree of good to be achieved or the degree of harm to be avoided [as] identified through the first question" (p. 27).

III. *What standards of law, professional propriety, organizational policy, or historical practice apply to this situation?* The third step in this process involves the review of established standards of professional conduct, which prescribe or proscribe certain actions for the situation in question. These standards include legal mandates (e.g., copyright laws), professional practice standards, human subjects requirements, and institutional policies.

BOX 12.2 CHECKLIST FOR ANALYSIS OF CRITICAL INCIDENTS

Incident/situation____________________

1. Whose interests are involved; who can be harmed, how serious is the potential harm? Which interests, if any, are in conflict?

	significant	moderate	minimal/none
Your own interests			
Co-workers			
Research participants			
Your institution			
Professional field or science			
Society			

2. Application of universal values. Check all that apply to your case.

_____ Autonomy (freedom over one's own destiny)
_____ Beneficence (do good; help others)
_____ Nonmaleficence (don't hurt anyone)
_____ Justice (be fair; distribute by merit)
_____ Obedience (obey legal and ethically permissible directives)
_____ Conscientious refusal (disobey illegal or unethical directives)
_____ Gratitude (pass good along to others)
_____ Competence (be knowledgeable and skilled)
_____ Stewardship (use resources wisely)
_____ Honesty and candor (tell the truth)
_____ Fidelity (keep your promises)
_____ Loyalty (don't abandon)
_____ Diligence (work hard)
_____ Discretion (respect confidence and privacy)
_____ Self-improvement (be the best that you can be)
_____ Restitution (make amends to persons injured)
_____ Self-interest (protect yourself)
_____ Other culture-specific values

3. What laws, standards, policies, practice guidelines, historical practices should guide us in this situation?

Adapted from White and Popovits (2001)

CASE STUDIES

In this section we present seven case studies, each dealing with an important ethical dilemma. Following each case are a series of discussion questions that draw attention to the moral reasoning issues covered. After considering these questions, the reader should follow the outline shown in Box 12.2, which provide further guidance about how to resolve a particular dilemma. Then compare your responses to the ethical analysis that follows each case, which are conducted according to the moral reasoning procedures proposed by White and Popovits (2001).

CASE 1. SELECTIVE REPORTING OF THE LITERATURE

Mr. C. Lective is a graduate student in clinical psychology at Orgone University who has just finished his doctoral dissertation under the direction of his mentor, the prominent clinical psychologist Prof. Ann Dorphin. The dissertation topic was based on Professor Dorphin's Theory of Addiction Reflection, which proposes that drug users' brainwaves give off an aura of escaping endogenous opiates that can be captured by perceptive therapists and re-cycled to form a therapeutic alliance. After several promising quasi-experimental studies and case reports of Addiction Reflection therapy, all published by Prof. Dorphin or her students, two independent randomized trials produced negative results. A review paper was then published questioning the validity of the theory as well as the unorthodox research methods used at Orgone University. Consistent with previous studies at Orgone U, Mr. Lective's dissertation has produced positive but unimpressive results in support of the theory. Prof. Dorphin strongly suggests that the results be published, and collaborates in the drafting of a paper that recommends that Addiction Reflection therapy be adopted widely in routine clinical practice. The paper is submitted to a small psychotherapy journal. After receiving the reviews, the editor of the journal writes the following letter to Mr. Lective:

"I have now received two reviews of your manuscript. The first reviewer liked the paper and has few recommendations for revision. The second reviewer, however, notes that your literature review fails to describe recent studies of Addiction Reflection therapy, including a highly critical review paper, and thereby presents an inaccurate and misleading characterization of the current status of the theory. Although your study does not seem to contain any fatal flaws, I have decided not to accept the paper because of the reviewer's criticism that the background, rationale, hypotheses and discussion are all in need of major revision, and the level of scholarship reflected in the paper's introduction suggests that the authors are either unfamiliar with recent research on the topic, or are being unusually biased in their reporting of the background to their study."

DISCUSSION QUESTIONS

1. What could Mr. Lective and Prof. Dorphin have done to avoid this situation?
2. Who is responsible for the selective reporting of the literature, the first author (Mr. Lective), the second author (Prof. Ann Dorphin), or both?
3. Whose interests are involved and what ethical principles apply to this case?

ETHICAL ANALYSIS

The responsibility for providing a complete account of the literature and research pertaining to Addiction Reflection therapy rests with both authors, with Ann Dorphin shouldering most of the responsibility because of her supervisory position. Selective reporting of the literature to support a particular point of view is a significant ethical infraction. It clearly deviates from accepted standards of citation, as described in Chapter 7. Using the White-Popovits grid (see Box 12.2) for the analysis of critical incidents as a guide, this ethical violation has significant moral implications for the authors, their institution, the addiction field, and society as a whole. The reprimand that the authors received from the editor, together with the rejection of the manuscript and the accompanying professional embarrassment, are minor inconveniences compared to the greater harm that might have resulted from the publication of their work. Consider how their faulty research might have harmed the well-being of clients being treated by service providers who, in good faith, followed the researchers' clinical recommendations.

The authors' actions, probably motivated by self-interest, violated the ethical principles of non-maleficence and justice. There is a clear mandate to 'do no harm' enshrined in the principle of non-maleficence. Lective and Dorphin's lack of honesty in espousal of self- interest has the potential to endanger the well-being of all clients and institutions involved with the new therapy. In addition, the principle of justice (fairness) becomes relevant when one considers the fruitless expenditure of scarce resources on a futile mode of treatment. In addition, Prof. Dorphin is clearly in a position to violate the student's autonomy (self-determination) by bringing undue pressure on him to publish his research in a manner supportive of her original theory. This form of coercion, which is clearly unethical, is often ignored in research situations, with consequences for everyone involved when this is uncovered. Much of the harm, real and potential, involved in this situation could have been avoided by following the established standards of citation practice i.e., to present all sides of the related literature.

CASE 2. REDUNDANT PUBLICATION

A junior faculty member, Dr. Salame Science, is approaching tenure review at a large university that places great emphasis on the number of first-authored publications as the main criterion for promotion. Dr. Science, who has been working with three other investigators on a large collaborative survey study, suggests that the investigators report their findings separately for each of 16 drugs, thereby giving each of the investigators four first-authored publications. Dr. Science develops a template in which the literature review, methods, and statistical analyses are virtually the same for each article, with only the name of the drug being changed for the 16 articles. When one of the papers dealing with a new rave drug is submitted to a journal for review, the authors fail to advise the editor of the other 15 papers under review at different journals, and do not cite any of these papers in their report. Moreover, the co-authors all sign an ethical statement required by the journal indicating that the paper has not been published in whole or in part by another journal, and is not under consideration by another journal.

DISCUSSION QUESTIONS

1. What should Dr. Science and her co-investigators have done with the reporting of the survey findings?
2. What, if anything, should they have told the editor at the time they submitted the manuscript?
3. Whose interests are involved and what ethical principles apply to this case?

ETHICAL ANALYSIS

As noted in Chapter 11 the Second Circle of Hell houses those guilty of promoting their own self-interest in the practice of redundant publication, in violation of accepted ethical norms. Salame Science and her three collaborators find themselves in this unholy situation by submitting material that is (partially) under consideration by another journal, and by using verbatim material without quotation marks or attribution. By signing the journal's ethical statement, they have blatantly lied about the existence of the other papers and their relationship to the rave drug study.

Thus, however inadvertent it initially appears, the deception involved in failing to disclose the relationship between the papers has serious ethical implications. Referencing again the White-Popovits Analysis grid (see Box 12.2), several types of harm can result at professional, clinical, and societal levels. First, if all 16 articles were in fact published (as opposed to one or two comprehensive articles) the authors would deny as many as 15 competing and perhaps equally worthy authors of the opportunity to publish in the same journals, because many journals have limited space and must reject a high proportion of submitted papers. Second, the task of reviewing and processing these redundant papers creates unnecessary work for reviewers and editors, most of whom volunteer their time as a service to the peer review system. Whether the possible harm rises to the level of 'significant' in the White-Popovits grid is debatable; it is certainly 'moderate,' in terms of harm inflicted by any standard of ethical analysis. Clearly, the authors' actions have violated the standards of honesty, candour, fidelity, and diligence. The decision of the authors to lie in their ethical declaration attacks the basic trust that undergirds the scientific enterprise and has the capacity to inflict the type of 'irreparable damage to scientific investigators, editors and the community' described in Chapter 11.

By following established standards for citing the interrelationships involved in their collaborative studies, and by responding honestly to the statement required by journal editors and publishers, the authors could have avoided both the ethical and legal censure and the opprobrium resulting from their deception and dishonesty.

CASE 3. AUTHORSHIP CREDITS

Mary Doogood is a post-doctoral fellow at the prestigious National Addiction Research Centre (NARC). She is conducting research on prescription drug addiction under the direction of her mentor, Dr. Arthur Stringalong. After a preliminary analysis of the findings, Dr. Stringalong (who helped design the study, secure grant funding, and analyze the data) suggests that they prepare an article for submission to the Journal of Irreproducible Results.

When Dr. Doogood finishes the first draft, Dr. Stringalong insists on two additions to the list of authors: 1) the scientific director of NARC, who had nothing to do with the study or the writing of the manuscript and 2) the research assistant who conducted the interviews, entered the data, and did a literature search, but who otherwise had little involvement in the study design, data analyses, interpretation of findings and drafting of the manuscript. Dr. Stringalong tells Mary that with the NARC director as last author, the paper would have a better chance of being accepted by the Journal of Irreproducible Results. *He also suggests that the research assistant, Ms. Day Tamanager, deserves to be listed as a reward for her hard work; a publication credit will help her application for admission to graduate school.*

DISCUSSION QUESTIONS

1. Whose interests are involved and what ethical principles apply to this case?
2. What should Mary do about the suggestion to add the name of the scientific director of NARC?
3. What should Mary do about the suggestion to add the name of the research assistant?

ETHICAL ANALYSIS

One could argue that this situation has significant ethical implications for Drs. Doogood and Stringalong on an individual basis, and moderate implications for the scientific director and the research assistant. Stringalong violates Mary Doogood's autonomy as first author by insisting on the addition of the extra names, although he would not violate her autonomy if he merely suggested it. Stringalong's insistence is all the more egregious because of the implications of the duress deriving from his position of authority. There are also issues of 'doing no harm' and of fairness, understood as distribution of credit according to merit. Tamanger, the research assistant, may have some claim to co-authorship from a fairness perspective, but does not really meet the criteria for authorship described in Chapter 8 of this book. Of course, Doogood could include both in the acknowledgment section without violation of the rule of appropriate attribution of authorship credit. Should the names be included as co-authors, an argument could be made that the profession, the field, and society could be moderately damaged.

Stringalong might counter, from a utilitarian viewpoint, that using the scientific director's name to assure the publication of the data would work towards the betterment of individuals and society, and thereby outweigh the harm involved by including the additional author. He might likewise remind us that names are regularly added to lists of authors without being seen as a major ethical violation.

The counter-argument points to the damage, certainly moderate and possibly significant, inflicted on the field by the violations of honesty, equity, fidelity, and loyalty involved in this practice of gift authorship. It is clearly contrary to the practice guidelines endorsed by journal editors over the past several decades. In summary, the issues raised in this case involve ethical violations at the individual, institutional, and societal levels and therefore cannot be justified.

CASE 4. UNDECLARED CONFLICT OF INTEREST

Dr. Boyam I. Greedy was asked by the editor of the Journal of Neuropsychopharmacoepidemiology (NPPE)*, Dr. Tom Naïve, to submit a review paper on the subject of anti-dipsotropic medications. Naïve based his invitation on Dr. Greedy's expertise in the pharmacological treatment of craving and his widely cited articles on a new anti-craving drug called Payola. Dr. Greedy prepared the review and submitted it to the journal editor. In the article Dr. Greedy cited both published and unpublished reports to support his contentions that:*

- *anti-craving drugs like Payola reduce drug craving and substance abuse,*
- *a large multi-center clinical trial of Payola is currently underway by the manufacturer, Chemical Therapeutics, Inc., and*
- *methods to deliver Payola via patch technology have been developed.*

Because the Journal of NPPE *has no formal policy, Dr. Greedy was not asked to declare any real or apparent conflicts of interest. Additionally, in the acknowledgements section of the article, Dr. Greedy included pertinent information about the people who helped him prepare the article. But neither his communications with the editor nor the acknowledgements section revealed the following information:*

- *Dr. Greedy holds US Patent 6,375,999 on 'Methods and Devices for Transdermal Delivery of Payola'.*
- *Dr. Greedy is a member of the Scientific Advisory Board of Chemical Therapeutics, Inc., and as such received an option to purchase 7,000 shares of stock at 5 cents per share. When the projected initial public offering of shares by Chemical Therapeutics occurs in the near future at the corporation's estimated share price of $25.00 per share, Dr. Greedy's equity will be valued at more than $250,000.*
- *Dr. Greedy received substantial consulting payments from Chemical Therapeutics, including first class airfare to numerous international meetings, where he spoke about his research on Payola.*

DISCUSSION QUESTIONS

1. What ethical issues could arise in this convergence between Dr. Greedy's role as a scientist writing a review paper and his connections with the drug company, Chemical Therapeutics, Inc.?
2. To what extent does Dr. Greedy stand to gain financially by gratuitously promoting his patented Payola patch?
3. To what extent does Dr. Greedy stand to gain financially from the interest that his positive assessment of Payola might generate for Chemical Therapeutics in advance of a public stock offering?

4. What are the real or apparent conflicts of interest in this case?
5. What are Dr. Greedy's ethical obligations in this case?

ETHICAL ANALYSIS

Dr. Greedy has many personal, professional, and financial interests embedded in the promotion of Payola. His ability to influence a wider public and to advance the acceptance of the new drug is closely tied to the publication of his review article. A real conflict of interest exists and a host of ethical concerns arise at the individual, institutional, and societal levels.

At the outset, it is important to establish the stakeholders, i.e., those who are likely to benefit or lose from the publication of a review article that fails to acknowledge the author's financial stake in Payola's development. First, the author stands to profit in many ways from the publication of the review piece, although the extent of this benefit depends partly on the prestige of the journal and its influence on readers. Second, patients experiencing addiction stand to gain if knowledge of the efficacy of the new medication becomes widespread knowledge following the article's publication.

In his defence, Dr. Greedy might say that the promotion of the new product was the province of the advertising arm of Chemical Therapeutics Inc., and that neither he nor the company would benefit unduly from the publication of the review article itself. He might even add that his ownership of the patent and his financial ties to the company were matters of public record and these activities are perfectly legal and ethical (accepted even in academic circles) in his role an entrepreneur-scientist. He made his decision to publish his findings solely out of respect for the editor, Dr. Naïve. If the journal had a disclosure policy about conflict of interest, he would have had the option of either complying with it or declining the invitation to publish his data.

Another important set of stakeholders in this case includes the journal itself, its editor, and the publisher. An objective bystander might question the professional and ethical judgment of the editor, Dr. Naïve, in inviting Dr. Greedy to submit an article without first consulting the editorial board. Here Dr. Naïve has failed in his fiduciary responsibilities to the author, the publisher, the journal, and its readers. Even if Dr. Greedy's review were fair, balanced, and critical, deserving of the broadest possible dissemination, the integrity of both the journal and the field are nonetheless called into question by Naïve's lack of responsibility. The absence of a conflict of interest disclosure policy excuses neither the editor nor the author. In a like vein, neither Dr. Greedy nor Dr. Naïve should claim that the possible good resulting from the publication of the review article outweighs the harm done. One could further argue that if this practice of non-disclosure became widely accepted, irreparable harm could result for patients, the publishing field, and society as a whole.

This case gives us pause when we acknowledge a certain reluctance on the part of the entire scientific community - in its individual, academic, and research components - to provide full disclosure. The relationship among research, industry, and publishing outlets is a necessary one, but ethical standards are needed to manage conflicts between self-interest and concern for the common good.

CASE 5. HUMAN SUBJECTS REQUIREMENTS

Dr. X. Ploit, a clinical psychologist working at the Department of Parole, hears about a dataset consisting of clinical records, demographic information, and rearrest data for parolees (i.e., convicted criminals who are released to the community under close supervision) who were exposed to a new substance abuse treatment programme. Since the programme could not accommodate all parolees, only people being released from prison on alternate weeks were assigned to the programme. The others received no treatment. When Dr. Ploit learns of this 'natural experiment', he concludes that the data could comprise a very valuable contribution to the literature, as the parolees were in effect randomly assigned to treatment and control conditions, and were not pre-selected for participation in a research project. Because of his lack of ethical training, Dr. Ploit is unaware of the need to obtain Ethical Review Board (ERB) approval to access these kinds of records for research purposes, even though he has legitimate access to the same records because of his clinical responsibilities. Thus, he obtains the names of the selected paroled prisoners, looks up their remand records, and conducts a statistical analysis. The analysis reveals that the parolees who were exposed to treatment were significantly less likely to return to prison for parole violations associated with alcohol and drug use. Dr. Ploit writes up the results and submits them to the Journal of Drug Criminalization.

When he submits the paper, Dr. Ploit is asked to sign a form stating that the study had received all necessary human subjects approvals by an Ethical Review Board. Although Dr. Ploit feels conflicted about signing the statement, he decides to lie about his failure to seek ethical approval, reasoning that 1) the results do not identify individual prisoners and 2) the ERB would probably have given him permission to access the data anyway. Dr. Ploit also hesitates to seek post-hoc permission from the ERB at this point, as they might now deny permission. He reasons that the value of the findings for society and the prisoners far outweighs his minor ethical transgression.

DISCUSSION QUESTIONS

1. Why did the editor require Dr. X. Ploit to submit documentation that he had met ethical review requirements for the study?
2. What is the function of institutional and editorial requirements regarding the treatment of human participants?
3. Do compliance standards in themselves assure ethical behaviour in research?

ETHICAL ANALYSIS

In this case, it is appropriate to emphasize the vulnerability of persons with addictions in all aspects of their well-being, including treatment and research, and the intensification of such vulnerability in particular environments such as correctional facilities. Such concerns are central to Dr. Ploit's research, which describes the response of parolees to an innovative treatment programme. Even though the way in which participants were originally assigned to the new treatment arose out of limited resources, ethical review is very important to make sure that coercion was not a factor. These questions arise in the presence or absence of a research protocol.

The question of ethical approval, requested by the editor as a condition for accepting this piece for review, is an important one. Ethical review gives some assurance that the research itself meets basic ethical standards and also includes the expectation to provide oversight of the ongoing research in terms of participant well-being in a research environment. The Ethical Review Board, if it had been involved in the discussion of this research, could have decided that the research enjoyed exempt status under the rubric of quality assurance and chart review. On the other hand, it may have required full compliance with all the requirements of a regular research protocol. In addressing a journal's ethical concerns about compliance with ethical review committees or other supervisory bodies, the nature of Dr. Ploit's work changes when it becomes research. The editorial board could reasonably restrict Dr. Ploit's research to data gathered subsequent to approval.

Compliance with regulatory bodies generally satisfies legal requirements in research undertakings and guarantees that basic ethical standards are in place. The regulatory research bodies share with journal editors a concern for the promotion of good and the avoidance of harm at the individual, institutional, and societal levels. The author has a fiduciary relationship with the ERB and with the editor, and all parties are mutually dependent on each other acting in good faith and in compliance with a commonly accepted ethical framework that promotes the common good. Compliance standards in and of themselves guarantee minimum protection for stakeholders in research undertakings; ethical standards often espouse a higher degree of care

CASE 6. PLAGIARISM

Hans Besserwisser and Gretchen Schnell are new doctoral students working on a project at the University of Freudberg that explores the impact of the therapist-patient relationship in psychoanalytic treatment for female abusers of prescribed psychotropics. Reading the background literature, they find a very good article by Professor Eve N. Id in one of the big US-based psychoanalytic journals. In the article, Dr. Id explores how the angle of the analyst's sofa can influence the level of subconsciousness that the patient is able to reach in therapy. The article establishes the so-called Divanaltitude theory.

The two ambitious students decide to submit an article to the Bayerische Zeitschrift für Psychoanalytische Alkoholstudien *to demonstrate that they are on the cutting edge of current research. Their article, written in German, presents the Divanaltitude theory along with some findings from a small, local survey that the students conducted to learn what alcohol and drug therapists think about the design of sofas in therapeutic settings. Besserwisser and Schnell inform the editor that they consider their text to be an overview and not a piece of original research.*

The editor, who is not familiar with the Divanaltitude theory, sends the text to a referee. The referee's critique comes back after two weeks. She has discovered that the introduction is a direct translation of Professor Id's abstract. Several subtitles and the structure of the first part of the article are identical to Dr. Id's. The fact that the authors have one reference to Dr. Id's article in the second paragraph of the text is obviously not enough; the referee considers this to be a case of plagiarism.

The editor subsequently sends a letter to the young authors stating that he cannot accept the article for publication since large sections of the text are identical to an already published article. He states that their submission breaches internationally accepted ethical rules of publishing and demands an explanation. The editor also informs the authors that he will send a copy of his letter to the head of their department at Freudberg.

DISCUSSION QUESTIONS

1. How could the students have avoided the reprimand of the journal editor and the possible censure of their chair and university?
2. What harm, real or potential, could result from the students' action?
3. Could the students claim that they were unfamiliar with the ethical rules of publishing? If they were unfamiliar, whose obligation was it to inform them?

ETHICAL ANALYSIS

The students' plagiarism has important implications, with the possibility of harm for the students themselves, the original author, the research institution, the addiction field, and for society as a whole. The students, according to the White-Popovits grid, exposed themselves to the risk of possible dismissal from their doctoral programme as punishment for their violation of accepted ethical norms. It is conceivable, however, that they acted out of ignorance, and that they had not received appropriate ethics training from their professors or their institution. Had the individual professors and the institution been remiss in providing appropriate direction for the students, then the institution and its representatives would be as culpable as the students.

The actions of the students obviously involved a form of theft where Dr. Id's work is concerned, but any damage to her reputation will be moderate or minimal according to the White-Popovits scale. Their transgressions also present the possibility of injuring the professional field and society as a whole, especially if such actions were to become commonplace in the publishing field. According to the White-Popovits scheme of universal values, the students violated the values of justice, honesty, and diligence in their failure to acknowledge the work of the original author. They acted out of self-interest, with lack of regard for established ethical and professional guidelines. They might be accused of violating the original researcher's autonomy by denying her the opportunity to control her own work through appropriate citations. If the students failed to receive appropriate ethical formation and direction from their institute, then the administrators and professors at the institute would be in violation of the principles of beneficence and non-maleficence. Institutions have a moral responsibility to provide an environment in which integrity and honesty are an essential part of their research undertaking (Institute of Medicine 2002). Stewardship also enters into the equation because, from a societal perspective, institutions have a social responsibility to use resources wisely.

CASE 7: SCIENTIFIC FRAUD - 'DATA TRIMMING'

Dr. Frank N. Stein is a junior faculty member in the Department of Anatomical Protuberances at a large Transylvanian medical school. His latest research project deals with the effects of brain transplants on addiction careers. Preliminary analysis of the data on the first 10 transplants shows an interesting trend, but the p value is just shy of statistical significance. Dr. Stein's statistician, Igor Numbers, suggests they conduct a few more transplants to increase statistical power and then add an equal number of cases to the control group (without the benefit of random assignment). Igor also suggests they conduct a one- tailed test to get a more favourable alpha level, and drop some of the covariates to increase the degrees of freedom. After Stein and Numbers have made all these protocol changes, they submit their paper for publication as a true random assignment study with significant differences between groups. One of the reviewers questions the use of a one- tailed test, suggesting that the authors include more covariates in their analyses, and asks the editor to obtain more detailed information from the authors (Stein and Numbers) about the way they assembled their samples. Dr. Stein's institution has granted appropriate approval for the research. In addition, the research enjoys societal approval through funding that provides appropriate resources for good scientific work.

DISCUSSION QUESTIONS

1. Was it ethical for Dr. Stein to use the one-tailed test?
2. How should Stein respond to the editor?

ETHICAL ANALYSIS

The stakeholders are the recipients, the scientists, the medical school, and society as a whole. The good espoused by Dr. Frank N. Stein's research is the enhancement of the addiction field through the advancement of knowledge about the effects of brain transplants. Whether or not to continue this research depends on outcome studies, largely dependent on the findings of Stein and Numbers, who are convinced that the changes in their statistical analysis are minor and ethical. They feel that the continuation of their work will confer immense benefits on all involved and especially people with addictive disorders. Their decision to use the new statistical analyses, together with their justification of this approach in their response to the review process, shows they believe the end justifies the means. After all, this is new cutting edge enquiry where data trimming on a minor scale may be considered no more than a minor peccadillo.

The researchers, despite their idealism and good intentions, are blind to the implications of honesty, stewardship, and fairness in their decisions. Their dishonesty impinges on the well-being and safety of the recipients of brain transplants. In addition, they are not good stewards of the funds that supported this research. Furthermore, their unethical use of funds constitutes disservice to the other, unfunded scientists whose requests for funding are based on honest and responsible findings.

Our tongue-in-cheek response to this fanciful scenario uncovers many ethical pitfalls resulting from what might appear *prima facie* as minor adjustments in one's statistical approach. Rigorous honesty must inform the research itself, and authors must be candid with editors about methods and outcomes. The relationship between the two parties is a fiduciary one, and the engendered trust touches the basic integrity of scientific publishing. Using the White- Popovits grid, one could award this case a perfect score of 'significant' on all the interests and vulnerability items.

CONCLUSION

The intent of this chapter was to illustrate an ethical framework that provides practical guidance for researchers in publishing responsible and trustworthy research. Central to this understanding is a high degree of trust, as demonstrated in the case analyses. A fiduciary relationship is at the heart of the assurance whereby researchers address the well-being of individuals, institutions, and of the overall common good.

In a climate of self-interest, often nurtured by a high regard for an exaggerated form of individualism (which is inimical to the common good), it is difficult to develop a consistent appreciation of the place of trust in research undertakings, as elsewhere in society (Institute of Medicine 2002). Societal safeguards need to be in place, as envisaged by ethical review committees and other regulatory agencies, to ensure that the trust that individuals, institutions, and society afford to research is well placed and respected. Research communities and regulatory agencies need to establish the highest level of collaboration as a first step in creating and maintaining a climate of trust.

Regulatory agencies in and of themselves cannot ensure ethical behaviour in research or publishing, both of which have trust as their foundation. Other forces are in play such as virtue and character considerations. Individuals, institutions and publishing enterprises should idealy encompass qualities such as integrity, fairness and trust in their undertakings. But evaluating the presence or absence of virtue in larger bodies is not easy. It is difficult to determine if an institution is virtuous based on an analysis of the goodness of the institution where the research occurs.

Many centuries ago, Plato wrestled with this problem in his dialogue with Socrates as recounted in his work, Meno: "Can you tell me Socrates, is virtue something that can be taught? Or does it come by practice? Or is it neither teaching nor practice that gives it to a man, but natural aptitude or something else?" (translation by Thompson 1980). In fashioning a character-based ethic to guide the behaviour of researchers and authors, traditional wisdom might prompt one to respond 'all of the above' in answer to Plato's questions.

The "something else" to which Plato alludes is intriguing and invites comment as a concluding thought for this chapter. Perhaps Plato was hinting, for our present day edification, that the fullest ethical analysis of persisting contemporary issues in research and publication, along the lines of the case studies in this chapter, is that 'something else'. Ongoing conversation about actual issues is the best assurance that an ethical climate will inform research ethics and promote responsible publishing behaviour.

REFERENCES

Alighieri, D. *The Divine Comedy*. Translated by Laurence Binyon (1947) in The Portable Dante, New York: The Viking Press.

Brody, H. (1990) Applied Ethics: Don't Change the Subject. In: Hoffmaster, B., Freedman, B. and Raser, F., eds. *Clinical Ethics*: Theory and Practice. Clifton, NJ: Human Press, pp. 183-200.

Elwood, W. (1994) *Rhetoric in the War on Drugs*: *The Triumph and Tragedy of Public Relations*. Westport, CT: Praeger.

Glaser, J.W. (1994) *Three Realms of Ethics: Individual, Institutional, Societal*. Kansas City, MO: Sheed and Ward.

Institute of Medicine (2002) *Integrity in Scientific Research: Creating an Environment That Promotes Responsible Conduct*. Washington, D.C: National Academy of Sciences Press.

ISAJE Ethics Group (2002) Ethical practice guidelines in addiction publishing for authors, journal editors and other partners. London, UK: International Society of Addiction Journal Editors (unpublished document, see http://www.parint.org/isajewebsite/ethics.htm).

Jonsen, A.R. and Toulmin, S. (1988) *The Abuse of Casuistry: A History of Moral Reasoning*. Berkeley, CA: University of California Press.

Kass, L.R. (2002) *Life, Liberty and the Defense of Dignity: The Challenge of Bioethics*. San Francisco, CA: Encounter Books.

McGovern, T.F. (1998) Vulnerability: reflection on its ethical implications for the protection of participants in SAMSHA programs. *Ethics and Behaviour* 8(4), 293-304.

Plato. *Meno*. Edited by Thompson, E.S. (1980) New York: Garland Publishers.

Ross, J.W., Glaser J.W., Rasinski-Gregory, D., McIver Gibson, J. and Bayley, C. (1993) *Health Care Ethics Committees: The Next Generation*. Chicago, IL: America Hospital Publishing, Inc.

White, W.L. and Popovits, R.M. (2001) *Critical Incidents: Ethical Issues in the Prevention and Treatment of Addiction* (2nd edn). Bloomington, IL, Lighthouse Institute.

CHAPTER 13
RELATIONSHIPS WITH THE ALCOHOLIC BEVERAGE INDUSTRY, PHARMACEUTICAL COMPANIES, AND OTHER FUNDING AGENCIES: HOLY GRAIL OR POISONED CHALICE?

PETER MILLER, THOMAS BABOR, THOMAS MCGOVERN, ISIDORE OBOT, AND GERHARD BÜHRINGER

The ethical dimensions of the relationships between researchers, research organizations, journal editors and the various industries that profit from addictive substances and behaviours are complicated and extensive. They embrace the individual, institutional and societal dimensions of ethical reflection. In a way this chapter is a case study on a grand scale that calls for profound ethical analysis. The forces and interests involved are of necessity interwoven and researchers are dependent on many funding sources as a mainstay for their research. These will be covered in detail as the chapter unfolds. At the heart of the ethical conversation is an issue of trust for individuals and institutions. Ultimately, there are no simple guidelines to help an investigator decide which funding sources to accept or reject. However, it is vital that researchers go through an ethical assessment to consider the issues involved. In this chapter we will explore the ways in which different interest groups have influenced the research process before demonstrating the use of the PERIL analysis (Adams, 2007), an ethical decision-making framework developed specifically for this issue.

A high proportion of an active researcher's workload is spent applying for grant income. Successful receipt of grant monies is seen as an independent measure of a scientist's worth to the field. But the successful awarding of research money can occasionally be a "poisoned chalice" because of the problems engendered by an association with a funding agency. Such problems include having commercial or other vested interests set the research agenda, determine the way in which research is conducted, or define when and where research is published. Contracts that might seem reasonable when the cash is being waved under one's nose may prevent entire studies from being published or, worse, result in selective publication that does not portray the actual findings accurately. These types of experiences can devastate individual researchers, both personally and professionally. From the outset we want to emphasise that individual researchers cannot deal with these issues alone, but need support from senior colleagues, their institutions, professional associations and academic journals.

A GROWING CONCERN

> *In a climate of self-interest, often nurtured by a high regard for an exaggerated form of individualism (which is inimical to the common good), it is difficult to develop a consistent appreciation of the place of trust in research undertakings, as elsewhere in society.*
>
> (McGovern et al., 2004: 122)

Concerns about the integrity of the evidence base of addiction science have been raised in a number of forums recently (e.g. Adams, 2007; Hall, 2006a; Miller et al., 2006). Many of the authors expressing these concerns have reminded us that while safeguards such as ethical review committees and other regulatory agencies are in place, ensuring the integrity of the evidence is an ongoing task that requires an awareness of new players (e.g. the gambling industry) seeking to influence the evidence base, as well as new technologies for doing so (Hall, 2006a), such as paid contributions to edited books that look scholarly but often have a hidden political agenda .

Miller et al. (2006) highlighted the role that major funding bodies (such as pharmaceutical companies and government departments) can have in influencing research findings and the information dissemination process. This was considered important from two angles: 1) keeping true to the ideal of science and 2) adhering to the ethical principle of beneficence (see Chapter 12). Maintaining the ideal of science was seen as essential for the field, not only in terms of sustaining public trust (as mentioned above), but also in terms of ensuring that the field moves towards the most effective interventions available. Adhering to the ideal of beneficence (the obligation to maximise possible benefits and minimise possible harms) was viewed as equally important when considering whether research (which may be censored, be partially reported or go unpublished) could truly be said to be in the best interests of the research participants.

The recent debate within academic journals and subsequent commentaries has added substantially to our knowledge of how funding bodies influence research both directly and indirectly (Adams, 2007; Ashcroft, 2006; Babor, 2006; Hall, 2006a, 2006b; Hough & Turnbull, 2006; Khoshnood, 2006; Lenton & Midford, 2006). The observations collected from various authorities and presented in Box 13.1 highlight some of the main issues and point to the fact that influences on the research process go far beyond industry-related funding bodies alone.

Box 13.1 OBSERVATIONS ABOUT RESEARCH FUNDING FROM DIFFERENT COMMENTATORS

"Because …research may adversely affect the reputations of governments and government departments, "project management" has become an increasingly central part of contractual arrangements between researchers and funders" (Hall, 2006b: 240).

"[I]n the current funding climate, universities and research centres have incentives not to adhere rigorously to these norms" (Ashcroft, 2006: 238).

"In recent years almost all [Australian] state and federal funded drug education research has been commissioned according to funder specifications, rather than being investigator driven" (Lenton & Midford, 2006: 244).

"Certainly, too, government departments set research agendas - and specify research methodologies to suit their own interests, rather than to contribute in a disinterested way to the body of knowledge that relates to policy issues. Government departments do not intentionally commission research that will embarrass their ministers" (Hough & Turnbull, 2006: 242).

"Senior academic researchers should be prepared to 'out' funding bodies for bad behaviour. Researchers with seniority and the protection afforded by tenure should be prepared to protect junior researchers and advocate for an unencumbered right to publish research results" (Hall, 2006b: 240).

TYPES OF ADVERSE INFLUENCE

Miller et al (2006) identified five major avenues through which funding bodies can regulate research in an adverse way: 1) direct censorship (where material is edited or dissemination is interfered with), 2) limiting access to data (either affecting some point or to be used as coercion for favourable interpretation), 3) ongoing funding insecurity (attaching conditions to subsequent funding if previous findings have been awkward or unwelcome), 4) using under-qualified or easily influenced researchers (which allows funders to control the quality of investigation being carried out, even before the research has commenced), and 5) setting research agendas or *dilution* (whereby decisions are based on the political, financial or ideological interests of the funder). For example, pharmaceutical companies oversubscribe to studies that examine the efficacy of pharmacotherapeutic solutions to drug-related problems, which could make the evidence base appear to be overly favourable for such an intervention (Wagner & Steinzor, 2007: 5). Other authors (e.g. Gruning et al., 2006: 26; Kassirer, 2004: 168) have provided similar, although slightly different, descriptions of the ways in which interest groups have influenced health policy and scientific research (see Box 13.2).

Box 13.2 THE TOBACCO INDUSTRY IN GERMANY

Gruning and colleagues (2006) identified five ways in which the tobacco industry in Germany distorted science:

Suppression, through actions such as closing the German Industry Research Institute (which it funded) when its head published results unfavourable to the industry, and having subsequent scientists in its employ guarantee that unfavourable results would not be published.

Dilution, through selective funding of research and the recruitment of scientists who had doubts about the adverse health effects of smoking or whose previous work had found no links, as well as funding research projects designed to find no association between smoking and disease (e.g.,Wander & Malone, 2006).

Distraction, by selecting and supporting a large number of "confounder studies," which are research projects aimed to distract attention from smoking by investigating other potential causes of smoking related diseases.

Concealment, using "third party" scientists whose connection to the industry was hidden to increase the credibility and impact of the studies published.

Manipulation, the vetting of articles and presentations by the industry before publication or presentation.

Source: Gruning et al., 2006: 26.

THE TOBACCO INDUSTRY

The best known example of the way a funding body can act to undermine research integrity and muddy the waters surrounding a topic of interest is the concerted campaign by the tobacco industry first to deny the links between smoking and lung cancer and then more recently to support programmes which attribute responsibility to the individual smoker rather than the tobacco companies. Investigations into tobacco companies continue to identify new ways in which the industry seeks to encourage smoking and at the same time divest itself of responsibility for the subsequent health costs (Drope et al., 2004; Iida & Proctor, 2004; King, 2006; Muggli et al., 2004; Ong & Glantz, 2000). There are numerous examples of how tobacco companies have acted to undermine or adulterate health initiatives. The tobacco industry has been found to influence research using every one of the techniques discussed earlier (e.g. Hirshhorn et al., 2001; King, 2006). According to one authority, "perhaps research grants coming from tobacco companies should carry their own Surgeon General's warning. Caution: Tobacco industry sponsorship may be hazardous to the public's health" (Parascandola, 2005: 549).

THE ALCOHOL INDUSTRY

Using terms of justification like "corporate social responsibility" and "partnerships with the public health community," the alcohol beverage industry (mainly large producers, trade associations and "social aspects" organizations) funds a variety of "scientific" activities that involve or overlap with the work of independent scientists using techniques that range from efforts to influence public perceptions of research to the direct commissioning of research that is consistent with their public relations priorities.

There are at least three organizations funded predominantly by alcohol industry sources for the primary purpose of conducting scientific research on alcohol: the European Research Advisory Board (ERAB), the Alcoholic Beverage Medical Research Foundation (ABMRF) and the Institut de Recherches Scientifiques sur les Boissons (IREB). Although some consider the operations of these organizations as a model of the way industry should contribute to alcohol science, questions have been raised about the way they operate and their influence on the scientific process (Babor, in press).

For example, IREB commissions its own studies in addition to funding investigator-initiated projects, thereby increasing the possibility that industry-favorable topics are promoted. It has also been suggested that a scientist's objectivity might be compromised by receipt of the honoraria and travel funds involved, and the opportunities to fraternize with industry executives at international meetings. Each of these organizations also funds research on industry-favorable topics like the health benefits of moderate drinking, which then are used as a part of the marketing strategies by the wine and beer industries, or as reasons why regulation and taxation should not be imposed on the alcohol industry.

In addition to indirect support of research through third party organizations, there have been several instances in which individual alcohol producers or industry-supported "social aspects/public relations" organizations (SAPROs) provide direct support to university based scientists engaged in alcohol research. The most notable examples include the Ernest Gallo Clinic and Research Center established by the Gallo Winery at the University of California to study basic neuroscience and the effects of alcohol on the brain, Anheuser-Busch's support of social norms research at seven U.S. universities, and a research center on youth binge drinking funded by Diageo Ireland, part of Diageo PLC, the world's largest producer and distributor of alcohol (Babor et al., 1996; Babor, 2006; Babor, in press).

Little is known about the internal marketing research conducted by the alcohol industry and contract research organizations because the information is not shared with the public, the scientific community, or public health professionals. In the case of tobacco, previously secret internal industry documents have revealed that independent analysis of research on sensory perception was used to inform product design for targeted segments of the cigarette market, including young adults (e.g. Carpenter et al., 2005), and there is evidence that the alcohol industry does similar research (Babor, in press). Contract research requires the services of social and behavioral scientists, so it may pose ethical problems to the extent that such research could facilitate the marketing of products (such as alcopops) that are misused by vulnerable populations.

These kinds of funding initiatives not only have the potential for conflict of interest, but they may also affect the objectivity of independent scientists and the integrity of science. At best, the scientific activities supported by the alcohol industry provide financial support and small consulting fees for basic and behavioral scientists engaged in alcohol research; at worst, they confuse public discussion of health issues and policy options, raise questions about the objectivity of industry-supported alcohol scientists, and provide industry with a convenient way to demonstrate "corporate responsibility" in its attempts to avoid taxation and regulation (see Box 13.3 for further examples of industry activities).

Box 13.3 THE RESEARCH PEDIGREE OF THE INTERNATIONAL CENTER FOR ALCOHOL POLICIES (ICAP)

ICAP is an industry-funded public relations "social aspect" organization located in Washington, D.C., USA. It defines its task as "changing the debate about alcohol's place in the world by shifting the discussion from the commodity to the behaviour," away from "the traditional focus of policy discussions [which] has been on the regulation of beverage alcohol" (Room, 2005: 1803). Despite ICAP's facade of science and objectivity and its claims to being a go-between that can bring together the different constituencies in the world of alcohol policy, ICAP's work has been identified as an ideological instrument on behalf of a set of political actors with deeply vested interests that "bastardises" the scientific process (Foxcroft, 2005). There is also evidence that ICAP-supported research is of poor quality and is biased in favour of industry positions supporting alcohol education over more effective alcohol policies (Babor and Xuan, 2004). ICAP also pays scientists to edit and write chapters for commissioned books that have been criticized for their bias toward industry-favourable positions on alcohol policy (Stimson, et al., 2006; Caetano, 2008).

THE PHARMACEUTICAL INDUSTRY

The pharmaceutical industry has become more interested in the discovery and evaluation of medications that can be used for the treatment of addiction, including opiate substitution therapies and nicotine replacement therapies. As such, pharmaceutical companies represent a different type of research funder from those who sell dangerous consumables, such as the tobacco industry. The pharmaceutical industry commissions and funds legitimate research that has genuine benefit for consumers. This has certainly been the case with pharmaceutical therapies for illicit drug use (such as buprenorphine for heroin dependence). However, pharmaceutical companies are as profit-driven as the tobacco and alcohol industries and have demonstrated a willingness to engage in such activities as *suppression*, through delayed or non-publication of null or negative findings, and *dilution*, through the selective funding of certain types of research (Kassirer, 2005). There is also evidence that some industry-supported research is biased (Kassirer, 2005; Singer, 2008; Brennan et al., 2006). In an interesting case study that combines pharmaceutical companies and tobacco, Etter, Burri and Stapleton (2007) assessed whether the source of funding affected the results of trials of nicotine replacement therapy (NRT) for smoking cessation. They found that compared with independent trials, industry-supported trials were more likely to produce statistically significant results and larger odds ratios.

In general, it has been found that researchers who report a financial conflict of interest are more likely to present positive findings (Friedman & Richter, 2004). Such behaviour has not been documented within the addictions field, although drugs used by many addicted patients for other complaints such as depression and anxiety have been the subject of controversial research practices.

Within the addictions field, it is likely that the most common way that pharmaceutical companies have distorted the evidence base is by creating a publication bias. For instance, pharmaceutical companies can oversubscribe to studies that examine the efficacy of pharmacotherapeutic solutions to drug-related problems, which will result in the evidence base appearing to be overly favourable to such an intervention.

THE GAMBLING INDUSTRY

Problem gambling has been strongly linked to a range of personal and social problems (Gupta & Derevensky, 1998). Previous research from North America highlights how young weekly gamblers' involvement with gambling outstrips their participation in smoking, drinking, and taking other drugs (Gupta & Derevensky, 1998; Shaffer & Kidman, 2003). The opportunities for addiction scientists to receive funding from gambling industry sources have increased significantly over the last decade, raising a number of ethical and organisational risks not unlike those associated with accepting such funding from other dangerous consumption industries (Adams, 2007).

As in the case of the tobacco and alcohol industries, relationships with SAPROs have been used to mitigate potential negative associations and to give the impression either that the activity leads to public good or that they have at least attempted to rectify potential harm (Adams & Rossen, 2006). In countries such as Australia and New Zealand, a government or quasi-governmental agency has been created to manage voluntary funds in a way that appears independent of the source. Adams and Rossen point out that the major problem with such arrangements "is the perception that donor organisations should still retain a significant say in how the money is used" (2006: 11). This culture leads to uncritical acceptance of gambling industry perspectives and misrepresents the industry's willingness to trade profits for public health. This has meant in the past that industry officials were "consistently instrumental in ensuring that activities that might threaten the consumption of gambling were unlikely to receive significant funding (this particularly applied to research, health advocacy, and public health initiatives)" (Adams & Rossen, 2006: 12). This may explain why there have been few studies of the role of the gambling industry in the promotion of gambling behaviour and pathological gambling.

It has been proposed that government-mandated contributions provide an alternative option to support research and provide a way to mollify criticism. In this arrangement governments enact legislation that requires gambling providers to allocate a portion of their net income to projects, including research, with a community purpose. The major difficulty with this arrangement is the risk of increasing financial dependency leading scientists to avoid criticising gambling interests (Adams & Rossen, 2006). Likewise, the responsibility of governments to regulate gambling and prevent gambling problems may be compromised by the possibility that governments have themselves become “addicted” to the tax revenues derived from gambling.

GOVERNMENT AGENCIES

Albert Einstein (1934) once said that the "pursuit of scientific truth, detached from the practical interests of everyday life, ought to be treated as sacred by every government, and it is in the highest interests of all that honest servants of truth should be left in peace." Einstein's plea, directed at the fascist government of Mussolini, has been honoured by most government funding agencies, but there are several cases in which it rings sadly true in the current funding environment. In a similar situation to pharmaceutical companies, national and international governmental bodies fund many valuable research studies. However, as seen in earlier examples, research has sometimes been used to achieve political or financial goals such as supporting current policies or undermining less popular alternative strategies. Miller et al. (2006) identified two examples in which government funders acted to distort research findings in Australia and the UK, particularly around more controversial activities such as needle and syringe programmes (NSPs). Small and Drucker (2006) also point to the difficulty in obtaining funding for research into the effectiveness of NSPs, and the way in which the US National Institute of Drug Abuse (NIDA) does not support research on some forms of harm reduction. They report senior scientists' beliefs that while evidence supports the efficacy of NSPs, the US government will not fund research into their effectiveness, or indeed the more important topic of how to improve their effectiveness on what actually constitutes models of best practice (Pollak, 2007).

OTHER FUNDING AGENCIES

Increasingly, charitable organizations such as the Robert Wood Johnson Foundation in the US, the Joseph Rowntree Foundation in the UK and the Millennium Trust in Australia have taken on agenda-setting roles that include funding research. While most do not have profit imperatives akin to those seen in the tobacco, alcohol and pharmaceutical industries, some nonetheless have their own agendas and only a worthy few employ transparent peer review. For example, the Wates Foundation in the UK only funds research that supports abstinence-only approaches. Furthermore, nepotism and personal conflicts of interest can come into play when trustees back projects supported by their friends or projects in which they are personally involved. This lack of peer review and external accountability means that such organisations may end up skewing the evidence base by only supporting research into certain types of intervention. While some of this might be balanced by different foundations having different interests, the reality is that these funders have the potential to at times favor ideologically and politically simple and popular interventions. For example, while a small number of trusts, such as the Soros Foundation, have funded research into harm reduction and drug policy reform, there are many more foundations that will only fund abstinence-based programmes or programmes aimed at abstinence, such as education programmes. While there are many reasons for this, most revolve around trustees not being knowledgeable about the available evidence and theory. In addition, many trustees and directors are politically aware individuals who are in the public spotlight. They may be reluctant to become associated with politically sensitive topics. All of this means that researchers should be aware of the possible consequences of applying for funding from such organisations because even limited research might contribute to the overall publication bias in the field.

OTHER INTEREST GROUPS

Funding bodies are not the only groups to control research findings. For instance, Hall (2006b) identified the possibility of drug user groups and socially conservative members of ethics committees prioritising their own interests at the expense of the integrity of the research. Members of ethics committees hold very powerful positions when it comes to rejecting, delaying or modifying research proposals. While most declare financial conflicts of interest, ideological positions are different and, indeed, many would not identify strongly held beliefs as being a conflict of interest. For example, individual members of ethics committees who are strongly attached to abstinence-only programmes may block or delay research into controlled drinking interventions in the belief that they cannot be morally justifiable.

There is also substantial room for conflict of interest inherent in the current peer review framework (Hall, 2006a). With increasing competition over scarce resources, individuals may thwart the publication of research papers that counter their own theories or the findings of their major competitors for funding. While some journals have begun to publish ethical statements for editors, similar statements for reviewers of articles and funding applications may soon be required. Similarly, we should not forget that most researchers have their own pet theories, which can result in skewed research findings, particularly when those theories align with the interests of others such as professional societies, governments or industry bodies. As noted in Chapter 11, these kinds of conflict are difficult to detect, but they should nevertheless be considered by authors when evaluating their own work.

Other social groups that might seek to influence research include professional associations, fellowship groups, religious organizations and even service providers. Professional associations (such as medical societies) have traditionally sought to maintain or increase their influence regarding any number of areas of knowledge and practice (Willis, 1989). Each discipline produces its own literature base. The size and complexity of this literature base helps to determine differential power structures within treatment settings. In the alcohol and drug sector, medicine (with the support of the pharmaceutical industry) dominates the literature base, resulting in the medical model (and pharmacotherapies) having the strongest evidence base. In a different type of influence, some fellowship groups may influence research findings through non-participation (e.g., Wilton and DeVerteuil, 2006).

Service providers are also not disinterested parties. Almost all (with a few notable exceptions) derive their income (and some of their raison d'etre) from treating addiction. This has substantial implications for the politics of treatment and the vested interests many people bring to the research enterprise. The political and economic weight of mantras such as *treatment works* bear little relation to the complex evidence base and far more to the pragmatic needs of governments and service providers. While many service providers use the discourse of charitable objectives, they are invested both financially and existentially in the perceived success of the treatment they provide. This raises substantial ethical issues when conducting research in treatment settings, especially if the evaluation is funded by the service provider or its funding body. Ethical considerations such as the true reporting of findings (even when negative), full editorial control of research projects, and the assurance of adequate dissemination should be negotiated before research commences. Such issues require that researchers, reviewers and journal editors within the field apply a strong critical gaze to research and encourage an ethos of independence, even when such independence may not be economically prudent.

FUNDING ISSUES IN THE DEVELOPING WORLD

All of the examples discussed thus far describe the situation in the developed world. However, the issues facing researchers in the developing world are likely to be even more complicated and are much less likely to be documented. Like their counterparts in the more developed parts of the world, researchers in developing countries face many challenges in their work. In both environments, success is tied to the availability of resources and the overall intellectual climate (Adair, 1995). Significant achievements as a scholar in a university or research institute require the ability to attract funding for research and also productivity in publishing research findings, preferably in journals of high repute. Though the expectations from employers and the public might be the same, both activities are not always easy to execute by scholars in poor countries where there are virtually no local resources for research.

When asked about the major problems encountered in their work, researchers and service providers affiliated with drug demand reduction organizations in Nigeria not surprisingly identified lack of funding as the leading challenge (Obot, 2004). Indeed it is a rare country in Africa and other low income parts of the world where one can find consistent and near-sufficient outlay for scientific research on any topic, including addiction and other public health issues. This is especially the case for researchers in countries that constitute the "bottom billion" (Collier, 2007) or countries often described as least developed. In addition, competing for scarce resources with colleagues in resource-rich countries is often an impossible challenge in their prevailing circumstances. For the enterprising researcher, therefore, the response to this dearth of local funding opportunities is to conduct self-sponsored research (with all the limitations that this entails) or seek support from less competitive external sources. This situation provides a good opportunity for organizations with ideological positions to propagate their interests and for others with economic interests to gain a foothold through financial support for research and training in these countries.

This is a potential source of growing danger for research in many developing countries and one that has not received sufficient attention. While there has been active discussion about unfair distribution of benefits of international research, especially coming from concerns about the ethical dimensions of clinical trials in developing countries (e.g., Bhutta, 2002), the exploitation that is implicit in some sources of funding for research in developing countries deserves greater scrutiny. Exploitation is more likely to occur in situations where there is little understanding of conflict of interest, low economic capacity, limited infrastructure, and lack of ethical oversight, all of which are conditions that characterize most low income countries.

In the field of alcohol research, developing countries are experiencing a growing interest by representatives of the alcoholic beverage industry masquerading as "social aspects" organizations and seeking partnerships with researchers and policy makers. Usually the amount of money involved is a fraction of what would be spent for similar efforts in western countries but it goes a long way for the scholar to whom such support is a lifeline, enabling research and the publication of a book with an international imprint. In Africa, for example, the International Center for Alcohol Policy (ICAP, see Box 13.3 above) has provided support for data collection, write-up and publication of work with the potential of influencing local alcohol policy (see, for example, Haworth & Simpson, 2004). For the funding organization, association with (usually) a high profile academic or policy expert in a developing country validates their professed selfless motives. This can be a particularly pernicious strategy because, unlike in western countries where there are many voices, the developing country scholar who has been co-opted by the alcohol, tobacco or pharmaceutical industry might be the same scholar on whom government depends for advice when needed.

Research is not the only mechanism used to gain entry into a country, and economic gain is not always the only motive. Conferences and workshops touting issues like "best practices" have become quite a popular way to make friends and influence scholars and policy makers, usually at the same time. Outside the addiction field, the most well-known current example of funding for service delivery with ideological strings attached is PEPFAR, the President's Emergency Plan for AIDS Relief, launched by President Bush in 2003 to combat HIV/AIDS in selected focus countries. PEPFAR supports programmes that promote abstinence and not condom use for young people. The focus of funded work is service delivery but some research is involved. Because PEPFAR is a major source of funding for HIV/AIDS work in countries in dire need, recipients are oblivious to the ideological implications of helping sustain public health interventions with little or no evidence of effectiveness (Epstein, 2007; *Lancet*, 2006).

It is not always lack of financial resources that drives the accommodation to untested imported theories and practices. Sometimes it is lack of knowledge, or even naïveté. A researcher in a developing country might find it difficult to suspect the motives of a funding agency that is acceptable to that country's government, and one that is supported or led by internationally recognized academics or professionals. In order to guard against establishing or sustaining relationships with funding agencies that might lead to bad science or bad policy, it is important for researchers in developing countries to be more skeptical of easy money by questioning its source and the motives of its providers. That is easier to do today than it might have been ten years ago because most of the time all the information that is needed to decide whether to take the money or not can be found on the Internet.

CONFLICT OF INTEREST: WHAT IT IS, WHY IT IS IMPORTANT

As suggested by the examples reviewed above, funding sources can influence scientific integrity in a variety of ways, ranging from subtle bias in the way research findings are presented to outright distortion of the research agenda or the scientific literature. One way to approach the ethical implications of many of the issues raised in this chapter is through the concept of conflict of interest. Conflicts of interest can be financial, personal, ideological, political and academic. A conflict of interest does not in itself constitute wrongdoing; rather, it acknowledges that the researcher has an interest which may be put above the integrity of the research being conducted. It is only the failure to declare real or potential conflicts to an editor, one's co-authors, and the readers of a paper that constitutes scientific misconduct. Potential conflicts are very important when it comes to the ability of the reader to assess the validity of any piece of scientific work. As noted above and in Chapter 11, conflict of interest may take many forms. For example, recently the issue of ideological bias has been raised as a possible conflict in medical research. A series of articles and responses about prayer as medicine has raised substantial concerns about the interface between faith and science (Clarke, 2007; Jantos & Kiat, 2007). It has been suggested that "for the benefit of a secular readership, in articles concerning religion and medicine in the Journal, the Editor should require the authors' religious position to be stated under 'competing interests'" (Clarke, 2007: 422).

HOW TO AVOID CONFLICTS OF INTEREST AND OTHER THREATS TO SCIENTIFIC INTEGRITY AND ACADEMIC FREEDOM

Just as there are many forms of conflict of interest, so too are there many different ways to avoid or reduce undue influence, although many commentators believe that none of the possible options is entirely satisfactory or risk-free (Adams and Rossen, 2006). By far the most commonly proposed way to avoid or ameliorate conflict of interest is through communication with one's peers, particularly when done alongside ethical awareness exercises (e.g. White and Popovits, 2001). Adams (2007) recommends that individuals, organisations and others involved with interested parties engage in processes that raise ethical consciousness in conjunction with transparent regulatory frameworks that ensure accountability and independence from organisations, government and professional associations. This kind of communication and awareness-raising has begun to occur at a number of levels.

Recently, the institutions responsible for the production and dissemination of research (i.e., journals, professional societies and academic institutions) have taken some important initiatives.

<u>Academic journals</u> have increasingly begun to enact COI strategies including: a) requiring author statements that declare funding source, which are then published with the article; b) a positive statement that all authors had complete control over the research process; c) reviewer and editor statements similar to those of authors; and d) prior registration with the ICMJE-approved clinical trials register as a pre-requisite for publication. Journal editors have also begun to look at strategies for assessing publication bias within their journals and at a more general level. Some journals have used their editorial pages to name and shame parties that behave inappropriately (e.g. Edwards et al., 2005).

Professional associations have begun to draw up guidelines regarding the behaviour of acceptable funding bodies, conflicts of interest, and related issues. For example, the Federation of American Societies for Experimental Biology (FASEB, 2007) has issued a call to the scientific community to adopt more consistent policies and practices for disclosing and managing financial relationships between academia and industry in biomedical research. The FASEB Toolkit (see http://opa.faseb.org/pages/Advocacy/coi/Toolkit.htm) consists of a set of model guidelines that speak specifically to institutions that develop and enforce policies for their investigators, editors who develop disclosure policies for authors, and scientific and professional societies that have a role in promoting professional ethics. Similarly, the RESPECT Code of Practice (Dench et al., 2004) is a voluntary code of practice regarding the conduct of socio-economic research. The proposed guidelines are a synthesis of several professional and ethical codes of practice designed to protect researchers from unprofessional or unethical demands.

Institutions such as universities and research centres have developed policies around acceptable funding bodies and some scrutinise research contracts for possible conflicts of interest. For example, a growing number of universities (e.g., Kings College London) have refused to accept funding from the tobacco industry, and some research centres have developed their own internal policies (see Box 13.4). There is also scope for institutional ethics review boards to assess the appropriateness of funder-researcher relationships. Such responses would support individual researchers in the decision-making process and provide more reliable and consistent approaches to this complex issue (Babor and McGovern, 2007; Miller et al., 2006).

Box 13.4 ONE RESEARCH INSTITUTION'S GUIDELINES ON ACCEPTABLE RESEARCH FUNDING

Dealing with possible conflicts of interest related to the financing of our research projects

The proportion of industry research funding within the financial budget of the institute has been very low since the foundation of the IFT in 1973. But caution is needed as this support is provided by organizations and companies which produce or distribute psychoactive substances (e.g. alcohol or pharmaceutical industry) or are active in the gambling business (including private lottery companies licensed or owned by the German States), and because of the internationally known incidents of scientific misconduct.

The IFT does not reject funding of research by commercial institutions in principle, but is aware of the particular responsibility in this area. In times of short or even declining public research funding and direct demands of the public to cooperate with industry and to expand commercial third-party funds for research, it is hardly possible to abandon such sources of funding in principle. The institute has in this context the following rules:

- Research requests (i. e., to conduct a study on a given research question) will only be accepted if (1) the question is formulated globally and is undirected (e.g., the extent of drug abuse in the population) and not biased (e.g., the study is expected to demonstrate that a certain behaviour bears no risk for the population), (2) the research question is scientifically relevant, and (3) the free and unrestricted further design of the study is guaranteed by the contract.
- A further precondition for accepting funding by industry sources is the guaranteed independent formulation of the research objectives, hypotheses and the study methodology, and the unrestricted statistical analysis, interpretation and publication of results. The funds have to be granted to the IFT as unrestricted educational grants or donations.
- Currently, we do not accept funding of research projects by the tobacco industry (reasons: evidence of long lasting one-sided and unacceptable manipulation of scientists and scientific results).
- A single funding source must not contribute to more than 10 % of the annual budget, and all industry funds should not exceed 20 %. It is notable that these limits have never been reached: The current contribution is about 2 %, and it has never exceeded 5 % in the past.
- All results will be published.
- Lectures given in the context of industry organisations are accessible via the website of the IFT.

Funding in the "grey area" between public and commercial organisations

Examples are charitable organizations, (non-profit) health insurance companies, industry associations. In most cases, these organizations are accountable to the public or the commercial sector. The IFT applies in each case the same rules as for commercial organisations.

Source: The German IFT (Institut für Therapieforschung) website - www.ift.de

However, resolving these issues remains in large part the responsibility of individual authors, many of whom have a limited ability to understand or act upon the complex ethical, political, clinical and scientific issues surrounding the initiatives coming from a particular funding source. Fortunately, most addiction scientists have chosen to eliminate themselves from participation in activities with obvious conflicts of interest, such as consulting arrangements with the tobacco and alcohol industries and restrictions from funding sources that prevent them from retaining ownership of data and the investigator's right to publish it (Babor & McGovern, 2004). Nevertheless, what is needed is a more systemic set of procedures that allow individuals to conduct a risk analysis of different funding opportunities.

DECISION-MAKING APPROACHES

Several approaches have been suggested to guide decision-making by independent scientists regarding collaboration with the alcohol beverage industry and other dangerous consumption industries (Babor, in press). Decisions regarding collaboration with bodies that may seek to influence research can range from a "hands-off" position to full collaboration. Adopting a "hands-off" position, in which members of the scientific community and their organizational sponsors refuse to engage in communication or collaboration with industry representatives, is based on the assumption that commercial interests are incompatible with the values and aims of public health in general and with health-related scientific research in particular. Some have argued that the main effect of industry's recent cooperation with scientists and public health professionals has been to improve their corporate image with the public and with government policymakers, rather than to promote science (Babor et al., 1996; Gmel et al., 2003; McCreanor et al., 2000; Munro, 2004).

The other end of the spectrum is to engage in dialogue with industry representatives, accept industry funding for research, and participate as "partners" in industry-funded scientific activities such as the publication of books (e.g. Stimson et al., 2006).

A third approach is based on the growing number of case studies, ethical reviews and documentary information now available with respect to industries that have an important stake in products that affect public health (Brennan et al., 2006; Hirshhorn et al., 2001; Rampton & Stauber, 2002; Rundall, 1998). This approach avoids categorical recommendations to either allow or discourage relationships between science and industry in favor of a more nuanced set of guidelines that outlines conditions of cooperation between science and industry (Adams, 2007).

PERIL

Peter Adams' (2007) PERIL framework (Purpose, Extent, Relevant harm, Identifiers, Link) provides a structured means of evaluating individual situations from an ethical perspective. Depending on circumstances, each of the five PERIL subcontinuums is influenced in varying ways by the different domains of risk.

Purpose refers to the degree to which purposes are divergent between funder and recipient. For example, if the primary purpose of the recipient is the advancement of public good, receiving funds from dangerous consumption industries such as tobacco, alcohol and gambling will probably conflict with this purpose. Similarly, the risk is mitigated partially if the funder has a clear public good role. For example, the provincial government of Ontario runs a state monopoly on liquor distribution, the profits from which they invest in a broad range of research (Adams, 2007).

Extent is the degree to which the recipient relies on this source of funding. As the proportion of income increases, it becomes more difficult to separate from expectations associated with the source. For example, a young investigator may find an award from an industry-sponsored organization is the sole source of salary support, which could create pressure to obtain industry-favorable results to ensure the continuation of funding.

Relevant harm is the degree of harm associated with this form of consumption. The level of harm generated by different forms of consumption varies. Lower potency products, such as lottery tickets or low-alcohol beer, are on the whole less likely to lead to problems than more potent products, such as electronic gambling machines or extreme alcohol content beers.

Funders are unlikely to contribute anonymously because for them the point of the exercise is often to be *identified*, to form a visible association with public good activities for the purposes of positive branding. This in turn can be used for political or commercial purposes. The extent of visible association can be reduced by moving away from high profile advertisements (such as media releases of findings) to more discrete acknowledgements on plaques or at the end of publications. Through reputational risk, this strategy indirectly discourages engaging in industry-supported research.

The more direct the *link* between funder and researcher, the stronger the influence and the more visible the association. For example, direct funding by a tobacco company involves more exposure than receiving the funding via an independent intermediary agency, such as a foundation or government funding body. As long as there are no major conflicts of interest for the intermediary agency, the separation reduces the likelihood that recipients will feel obligations, even coercion, for their activities to comply with the interests of the donor. The overall extent of moral jeopardy ranges from very high levels, as indicated by high ratings on all five subcontinuums, to very low levels, as indicated by consistently low ratings. Decisions regarding future industry relationships are made accordingly. Boxes 13.5 and 13.6 provide two case studies to illustrate how a PERIL analysis can be applied to specific funding opportunities.

Box 13.5 PERIL ANALYSIS OF A FUNDING OPPORTUNITY FROM PHILLIP MORRIS

A university-based School of Medicine distributes an email announcing to all faculty and staff the availability of a new research funding opportunity. The announcement reads: "Please see the link below for an available funding opportunity from the Philip Morris External Research Foundation (http://resadm.uchc.edu/orsp/funding/opps/2007 RFA.pdf)." The website invites scientists to submit funding proposals to Philip Morris' independent, peer reviewed, external research programme, which is willing to support research on the disease mechanisms and health endpoints of tobacco smoking and smoke exposure. The programme's Scientific Advisory Board Members are listed on one of the pages of the Request for Applications (RFA), an impressive looking group of academics, including department chairs, distinguished professors, and even the President of the Hungarian Academy of Sciences. This announcement raises a number of questions about the moral hazards of industry sponsorship of scientific research.

Assume you are a tobacco researcher at a large academic medical center whose dissertation was recently completed on a topic related to the announcement. Should you apply for the funds? A PERIL analysis along the lines recommended in Adams' paper would require some independent research and a review of the literature on tobacco industry tactics.

PERIL analysis

Is the *purpose* of your academic institution (e.g., "excellent medical care through research and education") consistent with the stated purpose of Phillip Morris (i.e., to sell cigarettes to adults, without taking any responsibility for the millions of adolescents who become addicted before they can legally purchase tobacco products)? If your institution is in any way devoted to health, the answer is that the purposes are incompatible. In addition, some have pointed to the anti-scientific record of Phillip Morris. The reason Phillip Morris' research foundation is now called "external" is that the company was ordered to disband a prior organization that was found by a US court of law to be biased in the way it awarded grants to scientists.

What about the *extent* of the funding? Is it sufficient to compromise the independence of an academic medical center with a large portfolio of research grants and contracts? Probably not, but for individual investigators it could create a dependence on tobacco money when other sources of funding become more scarce.

Is there *relevant harm* associated with Phillip Morris's continued marketing of tobacco products? The evidence is incontrovertible.

Will the recipient of the funds be *identified* with the funder so that Phillip Morris might benefit from its support of university-based scientists? And could funded scientists eventually be exposed to reputational risk if their names were associated with Phillip Morris? The answer is a possible yes to both questions.

Finally, is the nature of the *link* between recipient and donor direct or indirect? In this case it is indirect, so it may not involve a major conflict of interest, and there are no limitations on publication imposed by the funder.

In summary, the analysis indicates that there are incompatible institutional interests, a potential for developing dependence on an industry funding source, relevant harms to the public if tobacco sales continue as more research is conducted, a potential for future reputational risk, and a possible political benefit for Phillip Morris.

Box 13.6 PERIL ANALYSIS OF A FUNDING OPPORTUNITY LIMITED BY CONDITIONS IMPOSED BY A COLLABORATING ORGANIZATION.

A residential rehabilitation charity approaches you to collaborate in an application to fund doctoral research into the long-term effectiveness of its project. The charity reports that it has been involved in research previously and has found it beneficial. The methodology is discussed and agreed. The application is designed to go to a government funding body which provides match funding for collaborations between community organisations and universities. The charity expresses concern about the confidentiality of its service users and requests that "We would, however, want the research findings to be kept confidential except in so far as they are needed to fulfill the requirements for the degree." Subsequent investigation shows that while the charity refers to a strong research pedigree, findings have only been published in non peer-reviewed trade magazines or internal reports.

PERIL analysis

Is the *purpose* of your academic institution (e.g., excellent medical care through research and education) consistent with the stated purpose of the charity? At first glance it would appear that the charity has the laudable goal of assessing its effectiveness though independent research. However, its desire to control dissemination (presumably in case of unfavourable findings) and its previous track record of publishing only in non peer-reviewed journals would suggest that its goal might not be excellence.

What about the *extent* of the funding? In this example this is unlikely to be a major factor as the amount involved would be comparatively small.

Is there *relevant harm*? There is a chance of some harm in this case if the findings are unfavourable and the charity chooses not to disseminate the report. In this situation, the charity is clearly providing ineffective treatment and using resources that might be better used elsewhere. In addition, it may be skewing the knowledge-base through omission of negative findings.

There is also a significant issue that the researchers and university will be *identified* with the evaluation. It is within the interest of the charity to point to the fact that the research was independently conducted.

Finally, is the nature of the *link* between recipient and donor direct or indirect? In this case it is indirect, so it may not involve a major conflict of interest, and there are no limitations on publication imposed by the funder. In this case, it would be possible for the researchers or the university to insist that the charity remove its right to control release of the data. If that were done, the PERIL analysis would suggest that the funding is worth pursuing.

SUMMARY

Every individual, discipline, and funding organization brings its own agenda to the research process. The practical and ethical conundrums associated with research funding are becoming increasingly complex in a context in which research plays a greater role in the regulation and marketing of potentially addictive products. The examples reviewed in this chapter suggest that addiction scientists should be vigilant about the funding they accept from any source, particularly when there are restrictions on the design, interpretation and publication of the resulting data. In particular, researchers should be very wary about accepting research funding directly from various dangerous consumption industries, their trade associations, and public relations organizations. Consulting arrangements wherein scientists are paid by parties with a clear conflict of interest to critique the work of other scientists can constitute a serious financial conflict of interest that is unlikely to benefit either science or the investigator. Acceptance of fees for writing book chapters, preparing background reports, attending industry-organized conferences and writing letters to the editor should be prefaced by careful consideration of the following questions:

1. To what extent is the scientific activity designed to promote the commercial interests of a particular industry?
2. Will the funding source be acknowledged?

Funding obtained from "independent" research organizations that are supported exclusively by a particular dangerous consumption industry may be consistent with scientific and public health aims if the grant review process is independent, transparent and peer reviewed, and the funding source does not impose rigid limits on the types of research to be conducted. But addiction scientists need to be careful that their objectivity and independence are not compromised by fraternizing with industry executives as well as paid travel to meeting sites and consulting fees. Investigators in particular need to be attentive to the possibility that industry funding in many health areas is being contested on both ethical and scientific grounds (Foxcroft, 2005; King, 2006; Babor, in press; Brennan et al., 2006). Finally, researchers should examine all funding sources using PERIL analysis, which allows the individual scientist and his or her institution to review relevant information about the motives of the funding source and the uses of the research that will be conducted.

REFERENCES

Adair, J. G. (1995). The research environment in developing countries: contributing to the national development of discipline. *International Journal of Psychology*, 30(6), 643-662.

Adams, P. J. (2007). Assessing whether to receive funding support from tobacco, alcohol, gambling and other dangerous consumption industries. *Addiction,* 102(7), 1027-1033.

Adams, P. J., & Rossen, F. (2006). Reducing the moral jeopardy associated with receiving funds from the proceeds of gambling. *Journal of Gambling Issues*(17), 1-21.

Ashcroft, R. E. (2006). Getting what you pay for?: The ethics of selective publication. *International Journal of Drug Policy*, 17(3), 238-239.

Babor, T. (in press). Alcohol research and the alcoholic beverage industry: Issues, concerns, and conflicts of interest. *Addiction*.

Babor, T. F. (2006). Diageo, University College Dublin and the integrity of alcohol science: it's time to draw the line between public health and public relations. *Addiction*, 101(10), 1375-1377.

Babor, T. F., Edwards, G., & Stockwell, T. (1996). Science and the drinks industry: cause for concern. *Addiction*, 91, 5-9.

Babor, T.F. & Xuan, Z. Alcohol policy research and the grey literature. N*ordic Studies on Alcohol and Drugs 2004*; 125-37.

Babor, T. F., & McGovern, T. F. (2007). Minimizing Moral Jeopardy: Perils of the Slippery Slope. *Addiction*, 102(7), 1037-1038.

Bhutta, A. (2002). Ethics in international health research: a perspective from the developing world. *Bulletin of the World Health Organization,* 80(2), 114-120.

Brennan, T. A., Rothman, D. J., Blank, L., Blumenthal, D., Chimonas, S. C., Cohen, J. J., et al. (2006). Health industry practices that create conflicts of interest: a policy proposal for academic medical centers. *JAMA*, 295(4), 429-433.

Caetano, R. (2008). About smoke and mirrors: the alcohol industry and the promotion of science. *Addiction* 103 (2), 175-178.

Carpenter, C. M., Wayne, G. F., & Connolly, G. N. (2005). Designing cigarettes for women: new findings from the tobacco industry documents. *Addiction*, 100(6), 837-851.

Clarke, J. (2007). Religion as a competing interest. *MJA*, 187 (7), 421-422.

Collier, P. (2007). *The bottom billion: why the poorest countries are failing and what can be done about it.* New York: Oxford University Press.

Dench, S., Iphofen, R., Huws, U. (2004). Code of ethics for socio-economic research. Institute for Employment Studies, Brighton UK. Available online: http://www.respect project.org/code/index.php.

Drope, J., Bialous, S. A., & Glantz, S. A. (2004). Tobacco industry efforts to present ventilation as an alternative to smoke-free environments in North America. *Tob Control*, 13 Suppl 1, i41-47.

Edwards, G., West, R., Babor, T. F., Hall, W., & Marsden, J. (2005). The integrity of the science base: a test case. *Addiction*, 100(5), 581-584.

Einstein, A. (1934). The World As I See It. *Forum and Century: Living Philosophies,* 84, 193-194.

Epstein, H. (2007). *The invisible cure: Africa, the West, and the fight against AIDS.* New York: Farrar, Straus and Giroux.

Etter, J.-F., Burri, M., & Stapleton, J. (2007). The impact of pharmaceutical company funding on results of randomized trials of nicotine replacement therapy for smoking cessation: a meta-analysis*. *Addiction*, 102(5), 815-822.

Foxcroft, D. (2005). International Center for Alcohol Policies (ICAP)'s latest report on alcohol education: a flawed peer review process. *Addiction*, 100(8), 1066-1068.

Friedman, L. S., & Richter, E. D. (2004). Relationship between conflicts of interest and research results. *J Gen Intern Med*, 19(1), 51-56.

Gmel, G., Heeb, J. L., & Rehm, J. (2003). Research and the alcohol industry [letter to the editor]. *Addiction*, 98, 1773-1774.

Gruning, T., Gilmore, A. B., & McKee, M. (2006). Tobacco industry influence on science and scientists in Germany. *Am J Public Health*, 96(1), 20-32.

Gupta, R., & Derevensky, J. L. (1998). Adolescent Gambling Behavior: A Prevalence Study and Examination of the Correlates Associated with Problem Gambling. *J Gambl Stud*, 14(4), 319-345.

Hall, W. (2006a). Ensuring that addiction science is deserving of public trust. *Addiction*, 101(9), 1223-1224.

Hall, W. (2006b). Minimising research censorship by government funders. *International Journal of Drug Policy*, 17(3), 240-241.

Haworth, A., & Simpson, R. (Eds.). (2004). *Moonshine markets: issues in unrecorded alcohol beverage production and consumption*. Florence, KY: Brunner-Routledge.

Hirshhorn, N., Aguinaga-Bialous, S., & Shatenstein, S. (2001). Philip Morris' new scientific initiative: an analysis. *Tob Control*, 10, 247-252.

Hough, M., & Turnbull, P. (2006). Over-regulation or legitimate control? *International Journal of Drug Policy*, 17(3), 242-243.

Iida, K., & Proctor, R. N. (2004). Learning from Philip Morris: Japan Tobacco's strategies regarding evidence of tobacco health harms as revealed in internal documents from the American tobacco industry. *Lancet,* 363(9423), 1820-1824.

Jantos, M., & Kiat, H. (2007). Prayer as medicine: how much have we learned? *MJA 186* (10 Suppl), S51-S53.

Kassirer, J. P. (2005). *On the take: How medicine's complicity with big business can endanger your health*. New York: Oxford University Press.

Khoshnood, K. (2006). The regulation of research by funding bodies: A wake-up call. *International Journal of Drug Policy*, 17(3), 246-247.

King, J. (2006). Accepting tobacco industry money for research: has anything changed now that harm reduction is on the agenda? *Addiction*, 101(8), 1067-1069.

Lancet. (2006). HIV prevention policy needs and urgent cure. *Lancet*, 367 (9518), 1213.

Lenton, S., & Midford, R. (2006). Research regulation by omission and by publication. *International Journal of Drug Policy*, 17(3), 244-245.

McCreanor, T., Casswell, S., & Hill, L. (2000). ICAP and the perils of partnership. *Addiction*, 95(2), 179-185.

McGovern, T., Babor, T. F., & Stenius, K. (2004). The Road to Paradise: Moral Reasoning in Addiction Publishing. In T. F. Babor, K. Stenius & S. Savva (Eds.), *Publishing Addiction Science: A Guide for the Perplexed* (First ed., pp. 103-120). Rockville, MD: International Society of Addiction Journal Editors and World Health Organisation. Available online: http://www.parint.org/isajewebsite/isajebook/isajewebbook.htm.

Miller, P. G., Moore, D., & Strang, J. (2006). The regulation of research by funding bodies: An emerging ethical issue for the alcohol and other drug sector. *International Journal of Drug Policy*, 17(1), 12-16.

Muggli, M. E., LeGresley, E. M., & Hurt, R. D. (2004). Big tobacco is watching: British American Tobacco's surveillance and information concealment at the Guildford depository. *Lancet,* 363(9423), 1812-1819.

Munro, G. (2004). An addiction agency's collaboration with the drinks industry: Moo Joose as a case study. *Addiction*, 99(11), 1370-1374.

Obot, I. S. (2004). Responding to drug problems in Nigeria: the role of civil society organizations. *Substance Use and Misuse*, 39(8), 1289-1301.

Ong, E. K., & Glantz, S. A. (2000). Tobacco industry efforts subverting International Agency for Research on Cancer's second-hand smoke study. *Lancet*, 355(9211), 1253-1259.

Parascandola, M. (2005). Science, industry, and tobacco harm reduction: a case study of tobacco industry scientists' involvement in the National Cancer Institute's Smoking and Health Program, 1964-1980. *Public Health Rep*, 120(3), 338-349.

Pollak, H. (2007). *How Should Harm Reduction Interventions be Evaluated*? Paper presented at the International Society for the Study of Drug Policy, Oslo.

Rampton, S., & Stauber, J. (2002). Research funding, conflicts of interest, and the meta-methodology of public relations. *Public Health Rep*, 117(4), 331-339.

Room, R. (2005). Drinking patterns as an ideology. *Addiction*, 100(12), 1803-1804.

Rundall, P. (1998). Should industry sponsor research? How much research in infant feeding comes from unethical marketing? *BMJ*, 317(7154), 338-339.

Shaffer, H. J., & Kidman, R. (2003). Shifting perspectives on gambling and addiction. *J Gambl Stud*, 19(1), 1-6.

Singer, M. (2008). *Drugging the poor: legal and illegal drugs and social inequality.* Long Grove, Il.: Waveland Press.

Small, D., & Drucker, E. (2006). Policy makers ignoring science and scientists ignoring policy: the medical ethical challenges of heroin treatment. *Harm Reduction Journal*, 3(1), 16.

Stimson, G., Grant, M., Choquet, M., & Garrison, P. (2006). *Drinking in Context: Patterns, Interventions, and Partnerships*. Washington DC: Routledge.

Wagner, W., & Steinzor, R. (2007). Introduction: Principled science. In W. Wagner & R. Steinzor (Eds.), *Rescuing Science from Politics: Regulation and the Distortion of Scientific Research* (pp. 1-21). New York: Cambridge University Press.

Wander, N., & Malone, R. E. (2006). Making Big Tobacco Give In: You Lose, They Win. *Am J Public Health*, 96(11), 2048-2054.

White, W. L., & Popovits, R. M. (2001). *Critical Incidents: Ethical Issues in the Prevention and Treatment of Addiction* (2nd ed.). Bloomington, IL: Chestnut Health Systems.

Willis, E. (1989). *Medical Dominance: the Division of Labour in Australian Health Care* (Rev. ed.). Sydney: Allen & Unwin.

Wilton, R., & DeVerteuil, G. (2006). Spaces of sobriety/sites of power: Examining social model alcohol recovery programs as therapeutic landscapes. *Social Science & Medicine*, 63(3), 649-661.

CHAPTER 14
ADDICTION PUBLISHING AND THE MEANING OF (SCIENTIFIC) LIFE
THOMAS F. BABOR AND KERSTIN STENIUS

The global scientific enterprise of addiction studies that has developed during the past half century would be impossible without the infrastructure of the publishing industry. At the core of this infrastructure lies the peer-reviewed scientific article and the expanding network of journals that publish such articles. Throughout the book we have focused on publishing scientific papers in peer-reviewed journals because this is a key part of the meaning of scientific life. Publishing allows the scientist to take a position and operate in a forum representing the free exchange of ideas and findings. In this final chapter we will explore this theme in greater detail in relation to addiction science, which for many highly trained researchers throughout the world is becoming a career commitment that is not only personally rewarding, but also beneficial to society.

In brief, our argument is as follows. Science is meaningless until it is communicated. Publication communicates scientific findings, and it is also the hallmark of a productive scientific career. Scientific integrity is another core feature of a successful career, and it must be nurtured by individuals, groups, and institutions, including scientific journals. Finally, to the extent that science constitutes a universal language and method, there is a special need for addiction careers in low and middle income countries.

THE MEANING OF SCIENCE

A seminal article by Ilkka Niiniluoto (2002), professor of philosophy at Helsinki University, traces the history of science through the various milestones in the search for knowledge from the time of the ancient Greeks to the present time.

The legacy of Aristotle, according to Niiniluoto, lies above all in the organised description of how we come to know the world and its generally accepted laws ('why' knowledge). A second phase in the history of science came with Galileo's search for regularities in changes in the world ('how' knowledge).

Compared to these steps the third one is more complicated. A much later change in the development of science began at the end of the 19th century when Charles Pierce introduced the notion of fallibility, which claimed that human beings constantly make mistakes in their search for knowledge and that all claims about the real world should be questioned. "This is true also of research, even if the scientific method of the research community, at least in the long run, is the most reliable way to produce and motivate conceptions of the world" (Niiniluoto 2002 p. 32, authors' translation).

Niiniluoto talks about science as a self-correcting process. The modern scientific community has its own quality assessment system (e.g., the peer review process), scientific claims are public, and all parties in the scientific community have the right to discuss, criticise, or refute those claims. According to Niiniluoto, contemporary science is characterized by objectivity (gaining as true a picture of the object studied as possible), a critical attitude (research should be public and open for critical discussion in the research community), autonomy (the scientific community operates independently of religious, political, economic, personal, and social influences), and progressivity (science creatively seeks new solutions and builds on old ones).

Arguing further that science is a social institution, he refers to Merton's (1973) four imperatives for the ethos of science: 1) universalism (the truth of claims shall be judged on impersonal grounds irrespective of the race, nationality, class, or personal characteristics of the person who presents them), 2) communism (scientific findings result from social cooperation and should be common property), 3) disinterestedness (scientists present and analyse scientific knowledge without considering the career or prestige of the researcher), and 4) organized skepticism (scientists assess scientific results on the bases of empirical and theoretical criteria).

Niiniluoto says that Merton's principles have been criticized as deficient, insufficient, and inconsistent with the everyday life of research in the contemporary world. Big Science, increasing competition for personal repute, and the inequitable concentration of resources have eroded the ethos of science, as has the use of science in war and commercial production, which has produced a form of applied science that is businesslike and breaches the principles of communism and universalism. Niiniluoto argues, though, that this activity is not really *scientia* and should be viewed as something other than academic research.

In addiction research, the increasing competition for research positions and financial resources can foster temptation to neglect ethical rules as well as the ethos of science. Career considerations can orient one's research to what is popular or fundable, rather than toward what is interesting or important. The growth in private research funding may lead to secrecy instead of the open exchange of new ideas and research results, and to new priorities that favour business interests rather than the public good.

If we accept Niiniluoto's assertions, we can understand why good publication practices, of the type described in this book, are crucial for science and the search for meaning in scientific life. Good publication practices represent the principles that should guide the quest for truth and at the same time demonstrate how to become a respected member of the scientific community. If science is to be used properly in the search for meaning as well as the basis for the betterment of humankind, then there needs to be open access to the enormous reservoir of scientific knowledge in the world. That knowledge not only needs to be readily available, it must also be recorded in a way that is understandable, useable, and certifiably scrutinized for of error and bias. This is the role of journals and the responsibility of their authors. As noted by Lafollette (1992), a journal serves as the arbitrator of the authenticity and legitimacy of knowledge. It provides an historical record of a particular area of knowledge, and confers implicit certification on authors for the originality of their work.

CAREERS IN ADDICTION SCIENCE

Publishing with scientific integrity is for many the *sine qua non* of a productive scientific career in addiction science. The remarkable growth of addiction science worldwide (Babor 1993, 2002) coincides with the development of a variety of career options for those interested in basic, clinical, or social research. Research societies, sub-specialties within professional organizations, and research centres have proliferated in many parts of the world, as has the availability of addiction specialty journals (see Chapter 2). There is growing evidence that a career in addiction science has become a viable and rewarding way to spend one's professional life (Edwards ed. 1991, 2002). As noted in Chapter 2, journals and the process of scientific publication serve the interests of career advancement and provide a vehicle for scholarly achievement. Indeed, the easiest way to understand a scientist's career is to review the publications proudly listed in his or her curriculum vitae. When one looks at the seminal thinkers and scientists in the field, it is the published works that constitute the main record of their professional lives as well as their achievements. Boxes 14.1-14.3 provide examples of how productive and influential addiction researchers reflect upon qualitative and quantitative aspects of their research and scientific communications.

Box 14.1 GENEVIEVE KNUPFER

Genevieve Knupfer received her professional training in sociology (Brussels; Wellesley, Mass.; Columbia, NY) and in medicine (Rochester, NY). She worked with the Alcohol Research Group at the University of California, Berkeley, and was an advisor to the World Health Organization's alcoholism programme for many years. When asked about her general approach to research, she responded with a description of a paper she had published:

Too often the conclusions of a research publication, no matter how tentative, are what is remembered. Too seldom are the basic data really spelled out. To my mind, that is what we need to look at, not at the lot of arithmetical means, multiple regressions and correlation coefficients. I suspect, for example, that the term 'statistically significant' means to many people 'significant' in the more general sense. My recent paper on 'Drinking for Health' (Knupfer 1987) was an attempt to expose some of these fallacies.

Biographical and interview data from Edwards, ed. (1991, pp. 155-162).
Quotation from Edwards, ed. (1991, p. 160).

Box 14.2 CHARLES S. LIEBER

Charles Lieber was born in 1931 in Antwerp, Belgium. He was a refugee in Switzerland during the Second World War. He qualified in medicine from Antwerp in 1955. Most of his professional life has been spent in the USA with senior research appointments at the Harvard Medical School, Cornell Medical College, and Mount Sinai Medical School. His prolific published work has centered on biological aspects of alcohol abuse, including the mechanisms underlying the development of alcoholic cirrhosis of the liver. Here he describes one of the discoveries that changed the course of biological research on alcohol:

There seemed to be an adaptive system which helps us survive in modern society because it is relatively non-specific and detoxifies foreign compounds even when the body has never been exposed to them before. When we observed a similar morphological response after alcohol, I postulated that alcohol may therefore also be a substrate for this system. This hypothesis led to the discovery of the microsomal ethanol oxidizing system (MEOS) as a new pathway of ethanol metabolism.

Biographical and interview data from Edwards, ed. (2002, pp. 11-28).
Quotation from Edwards, ed. (2002, p. 19).

Box 14.3 MARTHA SANCHEZ-CRAIG

Martha Sanchez-Craig, PhD, joined the Addiction Research Foundation (ARF), Toronto, Canada, as director of a halfway house for homeless alcoholics. In 1977 she moved to the Clinical Institute of the ARF as a Senior Scientist where her main line of research was in the area of brief interventions for alcohol and drug-related problems. Despite her extensive publication career, she cautions about the 'publish or perish' mentality:

... one of the senior people, who was conducting experiments with small numbers of non-human subjects, said 'I don't have much regard for any scientist who doesn't publish at least six papers a year in peer-reviewed journals'. I was very worried about that. I met colleagues who would get depressed or seriously worried if they couldn't publish a paper every month. I began to think that there are a lot of people here who like to do science that looks good and only a few who like to do good science...

But discovery fascinates me, the kind of discovery that jumps out at you from the data. I spent countless hours with data print-outs, looking for patterns. I didn't want to rely on what the statistical experts would come up with as a result of multivariate analyses and so forth. I wanted to see patterns with my own eyes.

Biographical and interview data from Edwards, ed. (2002, pp. 115-125).
Quotation from Edwards, ed. (2002, p. 124).

INDIVIDUAL RESPONSIBILITY

Research can be a solitary endeavour, involving late nights spent in your study or laboratory, preparations to defend a thesis or question someone else's dissertation, standing alone on a podium to present a scientific paper. These are all individual responsibilities experienced in the course of a professional career. In many cases it is impossible, at least without considerable effort, for an outsider to know whether a researcher has conducted his research ethically. All researchers are thus responsible for guarding the integrity of the public trust in research.

But research is also a highly social enterprise, which introduces its own ethical concerns. Much scientific research is now conducted via teams of investigators and support staff that share responsibility for the completion of a project and the publication of a scientific report. In this context, individual responsibility sometimes becomes diluted and ambiguous in relation to ethical matters. The research world is also very hierarchical. Younger researchers are in certain ways like apprentices, being trained by their masters, economically dependent upon them for positions and promotions. These differential power relations can further dilute ethical responsibility.

In spite of these threats to research integrity, addiction scientists must adhere to the ideal of the *polis* of the ancient Greeks, where every free man (we will have to ignore the gender discrimination of the time) was an equal, with similar responsibilities to decide matters of importance and civil rights to support those responsibilities. Similarly, every researcher must accept his or her personal responsibility for creating a more transparent and ethical addiction research community, which includes young investigators and senior researchers alike, as well as editors of journals and peer reviewers. Everyone, for example, has a responsibility to use citations in a fair and informative way, to ensure the proper assignment of authorship credits, and to adhere to ethical rules. When all researchers view themselves as equals in the republic of science, they will create the best foundation for creative discussions, which in turn will lead to progress in research.

CREATING GOOD INSTITUTIONS

In many instances, exhortations to individual responsibility are not enough to guarantee scientific integrity. Good institutions must support creative research milieus with sound ethical principles. Informal structures, such as open communication within departments (not only about research but also about ethical problems), reading and commenting each other's work, democratic decision-making, and cooperation and teamwork on multidisciplinary projects, all emanate from participatory norms and strong leadership. In Boxes 14.4-14.7, productive and influential addiction researchers reflect upon the social and institutional aspects of their research and scientific communications.

Also helpful to scientific integrity are more formal structures, such as policies for the ethical conduct of research and procedures for the determination of authorship credits. Addiction scientists have a special responsibility to support these institutional structures rather than seeing them as inconveniences and hindrances.

In recent years addiction journals have emerged from their relatively obscure and modest origins to take a leadership role in the prevention of scientific misconduct. The ethical principles for authors included in this book represent the consensus of editors who are members of the International Society of Addiction Journal Editors. Integrity in scientific publishing can only be enhanced by education, vigilance, clear policies, and institutional norms that put science first.

Box 14.4 MUSTAPHA SOUEIF

Mustapha I. Soueif, PhD, was born in 1924. He completed his graduate studies in psychology at University of Cairo, Egypt. In addition to teaching psychology at the University of Cairo, he also worked for the World Health Organization. Here he describes the challenges of publishing in different languages and the conflicts between having a national commitment and an international vision:

It is a long time now that I have been living with this double identity; on the one hand I feel a world-citizen, on the other I belong to Egypt. This complex 'consciousness' or oscillating began in the late fifties when I was carrying out my first piece of clinical research in Egypt (at Abbassia Psychiatric Hospital) while keeping an eye on getting it published abroad. This was the paper on 'Testing for organicity in Egyptian psychiatric patients'. It was accepted for publication in Acta Psychologica (in Amsterdam). That was the first step towards establishing my reference group, defined in this case as a group of international scientists who would judge the worth of my research on its objective merits. My international identity, however, was definitely promoted through my contact with the WHO in Geneva. In 1966 I was approached by the WHO people to prepare a paper for publication in the UN Bulletin on Narcotics reporting on our work on 'Hashish Consumption in Egypt' which has been under way since 1957. This I did, and the paper was published in 1967. In 1970 I was invited to participate in a 'scientific group' meeting to be held at WHO headquarters. The recognition my work received there was deeply gratifying.

Biographical and interview data from Edwards, ed. (1991, pp. 427-444).
Quotation from Edwards, ed. (1991, p. 436).

Box 14.5 JOY MOSER

Joy Moser (1921-2001) studied languages before receiving a Masters degree in Public Health. She worked for the World Health Organization in Geneva (1950-1981), first as an editor, then as scientific assistant, and finally as Senior Scientist in the Mental Health Programme. Her extensive work at the WHO reflects the important role of mission-oriented commissioned papers and expert committee reports in the development of hypotheses, theories, and applied research that eventually are published in peer-reviewed journals. In the following quotation, she talks about how the WHO facilitated the seminal work of Griffith Edwards and colleagues (1977) in the development of the alcohol dependence syndrome concept and the introduction of a broader alcohol problems perspective to the international policy making process:

Between 1973 and 1975 a steering group prepared and discussed extensive reviews of the state of knowledge on these matters. All this material was synthesized by Dr. Edwards and the complete documentation was submitted to a wider group of investigators from various parts of the world. This group's final report was published together with several of the working papers ...

One result of this project was that the term 'alcohol dependence syndrome' described in the report was accepted for the ninth revision of the ICD. Moreover this project seems to have promoted considerably increased recognition that it is not enough to focus on treatment of the person with this syndrome (the 'alcoholic'). Many other disabilities related to alcohol consumption are likely to be of greater public health significance because they are so prevalent and have such an impact on society. Actually the term 'alcohol-related problems' soon came into very general use. At the same time, interest was growing in the need to develop more effective ways of preventing or limiting the impact of alcohol-related problems.

Biographical and interview data from Edwards, ed. (1991, pp. 3-23).
Quotation from Edwards, ed. (1991, pp. 12-13).

Box 14.6 KETTIL BRUUN

Kettil Edmund Bruun (1924-1985) received his doctoral training in sociology from the University of Helsinki. His alcohol research was most identified with his work at the Finnish Foundation for Alcohol Studies, where he served as a Scientist Director (1955-80). He received the Jellinek Prize in 1971. He is perhaps best known for his influential book, *Alcohol Control Policies in Public Health Perspective*, published in 1975 under the auspices of the World Health Organization. Known in some circles as the 'purple book' from the color of its cover in the English language edition, it attained an unusual prominence in the literature because of its fundamental argument that changes in the overall consumption of alcoholic beverages have a bearing on the health of the people in any society. Because alcohol control measures can be used to limit consumption, control of alcohol availability becomes a public health issue. In the following quotation, Bruun describes with characteristic modesty the process that gave rise to the book:

The background was that I had to rethink my ideas of alcohol control in the light of the Finnish experience in 1968/69 when controls had been suddenly relaxed with dramatic increase in consumption and harmful effects. My own liberal views on alcohol policies had received a blow. Then I was confronted in the European Office with international issues. I thought that I had to reconsider my position and that probably the best way to do it was to try to have a group which could develop a perspective beyond the specific situation in Finland. The situation was fortunate because many of the relevant questions had by then been focused for research. The group which emerged from my invitation did a marvelous job.

Biographical and interview data from Edwards, ed. (1991, pp. 365-375).
Quotations from Room (1986) Kettil Bruun, 1924-1985: an appreciation. *The Drinking and Drug Practices Surveyor*, 21, pp. 1, 42-49; and Edwards, ed. (1991, pp. 371-372).

Box 14.7 ALBERT TUYNS

Albert Tuyns was born in 1922 in Belgium. He received his MD from the University of Brussels in 1948, and was awarded an MPH from Johns Hopkins School of Public Health in 1962. He worked for 15 years as an epidemiologist with the International Agency for Research on Cancer (1967-1982). He was a recipient of the Jellinek Award in 1982. His published work with Georges Pequinot provided the first systematic link between alcohol and cancer, and the interactions with tobacco smoking. These findings had enormous implications for public health and health policy. Here he describes some of his professional writings on the subject:

It is one of my favorite theses that the aetiology of cancer is probably multi-factorial; the association of alcohol and tobacco is - I believe - the clearest demonstration of this. I tried to express this in an editorial (Tuyns 1991) in the British Journal of Cancer. (p. 318)

Alcohol and cancer? ....a large group of workers produced that monograph (International Agency for Research on Cancer 1988), people coming from various parts of the world. From the epidemiological standpoint we had no major difficulties, and I remember that we described the correlation between cancer of the breast and drinking. (p. 319)

You look at your past life and you say I have been working for 20, 25, 30 years, what did I do really? What has come out of it, beneficial or not? I did my job to the best of my capacities, that's all. I am grateful to society, to my parents, professors, friends, who gave me a chance to produce good work; in return I contributed some valid pieces of knowledge and other work which was not so valuable. I feel that I have been useful, that I have respected my contract, as we say in French. (p. 320)

Biographical and interview data from Edwards, ed. (2002, pp. 313-321).
Quotations from Edwards, ed. (2002).

AWARENESS OF GLOBAL INEQUALITY

Addiction is a global concern, and the concepts of universalism and autonomy suggest that knowledge gained from research should be shared throughout the world. Unfortunately, resources for both research and scientific communications are limited in many parts of the world, and research conducted in the more resourced countries often follows parochial interests. Moreover, the dominance of English as the *de facto* language of science comes at a price for the majority of the world where other languages predominate.

Addiction researchers in the English-speaking and the more developed countries have a special obligation to conduct and present their research, whenever possible, in a way that benefits the rest of humankind. The peer review process should be open to scientists from all languages and nationalities, as should the editorial boards of the journals serving as the gatekeepers for scientific truth. Language and culture should not limit publication in addiction science. This is not only a question of fairness, but it also speaks to the cross-cultural generalizability of scientific findings and the need to discover universal truths.

CONCLUSION: THE MEANING OF SCIENTIFIC LIFE

In Chapter 1 we referred to the medieval philosopher Maimonides and his *Guide for the Perplexed.* This was perhaps not a very modest analogy. We do not want to suggest that this book - or any book for that matter - can remove all confusion and provide a researcher with the guidance needed to have a successful career in addiction science. Even with faithful application of the information contained within these chapters, the route of the informed researcher does not lead to a Paradise where all problems that arise can be easily solved. Rather, we hope the information in this book will lead its readers to the *agora* of science, a community square or common ground where open and democratic discussions can take place between equals about the difficult problems all researchers, novices and career professionals alike, encounter in their everyday work.

Having explored the meaning of scientific life to this point, the editors will not be so presumptuous as to venture into the meaning of nonscientific life, except to say that, like science, meaning in life is probably found as much in the quest for truth as in its actual discovery.

REFERENCES

Babor, T.F. (2002) In their own words: conversations about the evolution of a specialist field. In Edwards, G., ed. *Addiction: Evolution of a Specialist Field.* Oxford, UK: Blackwell Science, pp. 383-389.

Babor, T.F. (1993) Megatrends and dead ends: alcohol research in global perspective. *Alcohol Health and Research World*, 17, 177-186.

Bruun, K., Edwards, G. and Lumio, M. et al. (1975) *Alcohol Control Policies in Public Health Perspective*. Helsinki: Finnish Foundation for Alcohol Studies, Vol. 25.

Edwards, G., ed. (2002) *Addiction: Evolution of a Specialist Field.* Oxford, UK: Blackwell Science.

Edwards, G., ed. (1991) *Addictions: Personal Influences and Scientific Movements*. New Brunswick (USA) and London UK: Transaction Publishers.

Edwards, G., Gross, M.M., Keller, M., Moser J. and Room, R. (1977) *Alcohol-Related Disabilities*. Geneva: WHO Offset Publication, No. 32.

International Agency for Research on Cancer (IARC) (1988) *Alcohol drinking*. Monographs on the Evaluation of the Carcinogenic Risks to Humans, Lyons, France: IARC, Vol. 44.

Knupfer, G. (1987) Drinking for health: the daily light drinker fiction. *British Journal of Addiction*, 82, 547-555.

Lafollette, M.C. (1992) *Stealing into Print. Fraud, Plagiarism, and Misconduct in Scientific Publishing*. Berkeley, CA: University of California Press.

Merton, R. (1973) *The Sociology of Science. Theoretical and Empirical Investigations.* Chicago: University of Chicago Press.

Niiniluoto, I. (2002) Tieteen Tunnuspiirteet [The characteristics of science] in: Karjalainen, S., Launis, V., Pelkonen, R. and Pietarinen, J. eds. *Tutkijan Eettiset Valinnat* [The ethical choices of the researcher], pp. 30-41. Tampere: Gaudeamus.

Room, R. (1986) Kettil Bruun, 1924-1985: an appreciation. *The Drinking and Drug Practices Surveyor*, 21, pp. 1, 42-49.

Tuyns, A. (1991) Alcohol and cancer. an instructive association. *British Journal of Cancer*, 64, 415-416.